ARISTOTLE'S
SYLLOGISTIC

ARISTOTLE'S SYLLOGISTIC

FROM THE STANDPOINT OF MODERN FORMAL LOGIC

BY

JAN LUKASIEWICZ

SECOND EDITION
ENLARGED

OXFORD
AT THE CLARENDON PRESS

Oxford University Press, Great Clarendon Street, Oxford OX2 6DP
Oxford New York
Athens Auckland Bangkok Bogota Buenos Aires Calcutta
Cape Town Chennai Dar es Salaam Delhi Florence Hong Kong Istanbul
Karachi Kuala Lumpur Madrid Melbourne Mexico City Mumbai
Nairobi Paris São Paolo Singapore Taipei Tokyo Toronto Warsaw
and associated companies in
Berlin Ibadan

Oxford is a registered trade mark of Oxford University Press

Published in the United States by
Oxford University Press Inc., New York

© Oxford University Press 1951
Special edition for Sandpiper Books Ltd., 1998

British Library Cataloguing in Publication Data
Data available

ISBN 0-19-824144-5

1 3 5 7 9 10 8 6 4 2

Printed in Great Britain
on acid-free paper by
Bookcraft (Bath) Ltd.,
Midsomer Norton

PREFACE TO
THE SECOND EDITION

THE first edition of this book did not contain an exposition of Aristotle's modal syllogistic. I was not able to examine Aristotle's ideas of necessity and possibility from the standpoint of the known systems of modal logic, as none of them was in my opinion correct. In order to master this difficult subject I had to construct for myself a system of modal logic. The first outlines of this I developed in connexion with Aristotle's ideas in my lectures delivered in the Royal Irish Academy during 1951 and in the Queen's University of Belfast in 1952. The complete system I published in *The Journal of Computing Systems*, 1953. My system of modal logic is different from any other such system, and from its standpoint I was able to explain the difficulties and correct the errors of the Aristotelian modal syllogistic.

My book on *Aristotle's Syllogistic* has met with a favourable reception to my knowledge in more than thirty articles and reviews published over the world in English, French, German, Hebrew, Italian, and Spanish. I have ever since been anxious for an opportunity to discuss some of the critical remarks of my reviewers, but in the present issue it has been possible only to add the chapters on modal logic (as the text of the first edition was already printed). I am most grateful to the Clarendon Press for the chance to do so.

J. Ł.

DUBLIN
30 *June* 1955

PUBLISHER'S NOTE

PROFESSOR Jan Łukasiewicz died in Dublin on the 13th of February, 1956, and thus could not see his book through the Press. This was done by his former pupil, Dr. Czesław Lejewski, who read the proofs of the added chapters and extended the index.

PREFACE TO
THE FIRST EDITION

In June 1939 I read a paper at the Polish Academy of Sciences in Cracow on Aristotle's syllogistic. A summary of this paper was printed in the same year, but could not be published because of the war. It appeared after the war, but was dated '1939'. During the summer of 1939 I prepared, in Polish, a more detailed monograph on the same subject, and I had already received the proofs of its first part when in September the printer's office was completely destroyed by bombing and everything was lost. At the same time my whole library together with my manuscripts was bombed and burnt. It was impossible to continue the work during the war.

Not till ten years later did I get a fresh opportunity to take up my investigations into Aristotle's syllogistic, this time in Dublin, where since 1946 I have been lecturing on mathematical logic at the Royal Irish Academy. At the invitation of University College, Dublin, I gave ten lectures on Aristotle's syllogistic in 1949, and the present work is the result of those lectures.

This work is confined to the non-modal or 'assertoric' syllogisms, since the theory of these is the most important part of the Aristotelian logic. A systematic exposition of this theory is contained in chapters 1, 2, and 4–7 of Book I of the *Prior Analytics*. These chapters in Th. Waitz's edition—now more than a century old—are the main source of my exposition. I regret that I could not use the new text of the *Prior Analytics* edited with an introduction and a commentary by Sir David Ross and published in 1949, since the historical part of my work was already finished when this edition appeared. I could only correct my quotations from Aristotle by the text of Sir David Ross. In the English version of the Greek texts of the *Analytics* I adhered as far as possible to the Oxford translation of Aristotle's works. Besides the text of the *Prior Analytics* I took into consideration the ancient commentators, especially Alexander. I may mention here that I owe to an anonymous ancient commentator the solution of historical problems connected with the alleged invention of the fourth syllogistical figure by Galen.

The present work consists of an historical part, Chapters I–III, and a systematic part, Chapters IV and V. In the historical part I have tried to expound the Aristotelian doctrines following the texts as closely as possible, but everywhere I have been anxious to explain them from the standpoint of modern formal logic. In my opinion there does not exist today a trustworthy exposition of the Aristotelian syllogistic. Until now all expositions have been written not by logicians but by philosophers or philologists who either, like Prantl, could not know or, like Maier, did not know modern formal logic. All these expositions are in my opinion wrong. I could not find, for instance, a single author who realized that there is a fundamental difference between the Aristotelian and the traditional syllogism. It seems to me therefore that my own exposition is entirely new. In the systematic part I have tried to explain some theories of modern formal logic necessary to an understanding of Aristotle's syllogistic, and have tried to complete this syllogistic on the lines laid down by Aristotle himself. I was again anxious to be as clear as possible, so that my exposition could be understood by scholars not trained in symbolic or mathematical thinking. I hope therefore that this part of my work may be used as an introduction to modern formal logic. The most important new results in this part I consider to be the proof of decision, given by my pupil J. Słupecki, and the idea of rejection introduced by Aristotle and applied by myself to the theory of deduction.

I am sincerely grateful to the Royal Irish Academy, which, by giving me a position in Dublin, has enabled me to write this book, and to University College, Dublin, for its kind invitation to deliver lectures on Aristotle's logic. I am grateful to the Professors of University College, Dublin, Father A. Gwynn, S.J., and Monsignor J. Shine, who were kind enough to lend me the necessary books. I owe a debt to Sir David Ross, who read my typescript and made some suggestions I was glad to accept. My special thanks are due to the late Father A. Little, S.J., who, although already dangerously ill, willingly corrected the English of the first chapter, to Victor Meally in Dublin, and in particular to David Rees of Bangor, who read and corrected the English of the whole work. I am also deeply indebted to the officials of the Clarendon Press for their zeal and courtesy in preparing my typescript for printing. The section on Galen is dedicated to my friend Professor Heinrich Scholz of Münster, Westphalia, who was of great assistance to myself and to my wife during the war, and especially during our stay in Münster in 1944. The whole work I dedicate to my beloved wife, Regina Łukasiewicz *née* Barwińska, who has sacrificed herself that I might live and work. Without her incessant care during the war, and without her continual encouragement and help in the loneliness of our exile after it, I could never have brought the book to an end.

J. Ł.

DUBLIN
7 *May* 1950

CONTENTS

CHAPTER I

ELEMENTS OF THE SYSTEM

CHAPTER II

THESES OF THE SYSTEM

CHAPTER III

THE SYSTEM

CONTENTS

CHAPTER IV

ARISTOTLE'S SYSTEM IN SYMBOLIC FORM

CHAPTER V

THE PROBLEM OF DECISION

CHAPTER VI

ARISTOTLE'S MODAL LOGIC OF PROPOSITIONS

CHAPTER VII

THE SYSTEM OF MODAL LOGIC

CHAPTER VIII

ARISTOTLE'S MODAL SYLLOGISTIC

ERRATA

Page 84, line 35: for *h* read *b*

Page 90, last line: exchange *a* and *c*

Page 120, line 29: for *100 × *61. *c/b* read *61 × *100. *b/c*

Page 129, line 24: for *Icd* read *NIcd*

ANCIENT TEXTS AND
COMMENTARIES

Aristoteles Graece, ex recensione Immanuelis Bekkeri, vol. i, Berolini, 1831.

Aristotelis Organon Graece, ed. Th. Waitz, vol. i, Lipsiae, 1844; vol. ii, Lipsiae, 1846.

Aristotle's Prior and Posterior Analytics. A Revised Text with Introduction and Commentary by W. D. Ross, Oxford, 1949.

Alexandri in Aristotelis Analyticorum Priorum Librum I Commentarium, ed. M. Wallies, Berolini, 1883.

Ammonii in Aristotelis Analyticorum Priorum Librum I Commentarium, ed. M. Wallies, Berolini, 1899.

Ioannis Philoponi in Aristotelis Analytica Priora Commentaria, ed. M. Wallies, Berolini, 1905.

The texts of Aristotle are quoted according to Bekker's edition. Example: *An. pr.* i. 4, 25^b37 means: *Analytica priora*, Book I, chapter 4, page 25, column b, line 37. The texts of the commentators are quoted according to the above editions of the Academy of Berlin. Example: *Alexander* 100. 11 means: page 100, line 11.

CHAPTER I

ELEMENTS OF THE SYSTEM

§ 1. *The true form of the Aristotelian syllogism*

IN three recently published philosophical works the following is given as an example of the Aristotelian syllogism :[1]

> (1) All men are mortal,
> Socrates is a man,
> therefore
> Socrates is mortal.

This example seems to be very old. With a slight modification— 'animal' instead of 'mortal'—it is quoted already by Sextus Empiricus as a 'Peripatetic' syllogism.[2] But a Peripatetic syllogism need not be an Aristotelian one. As a matter of fact the example given above differs in two logically important points from the Aristotelian syllogism.

First, the premiss 'Socrates is a man' is a singular proposition, as its subject 'Socrates' is a singular term. Now Aristotle does not introduce singular terms or premisses into his system. The following syllogism would therefore be more Aristotelian:

> (2) All men are mortal,
> All Greeks are men,
> therefore
> All Greeks are mortal.[3]

This syllogism, however, is still not Aristotelian. It is an inference, where from two premisses accepted as true, 'All men are mortal' and 'All Greeks are men', is drawn the conclusion 'All Greeks are mortal'. The characteristic sign of an inference is the word

---

[1] See Ernst Kapp, *Greek Foundations of Traditional Logic*, New York (1942), p. 11 ; Frederick Copleston, S.J., *A History of Philosophy*, vol. i: *Greece and Rome* (1946), p. 277 ; Bertrand Russell, *History of Western Philosophy*, London (1946), p. 218.

[2] Sextus Empiricus, *Hyp. Pyrrh.* ii. 164 Σωκράτης ἄνθρωπος, πᾶς ἄνθρωπος ζῷον, Σωκράτης ἄρα ζῷον. A few lines earlier Sextus says that he will speak about the so-called categorical syllogisms, περὶ τῶν κατηγορικῶν καλουμένων συλλογισμῶν, used chiefly by the Peripatetics, οἷς χρῶνται μάλιστα οἱ ἀπὸ τοῦ Περιπάτου. See also ibid. ii. 196, where the same syllogism is cited with the premisses transposed.

[3] B. Russell, op. cit., p. 219, gives form (2) immediately after form (1), adding in brackets the remark: 'Aristotle does not distinguish between these two forms; this, as we shall see later, is a mistake.' Russell is right when he says that these two forms must be distinguished, but his criticism should not be applied to Aristotle.

'therefore' (ἄρα). Now, and this is the second difference, no syllogism is formulated by Aristotle primarily as an inference, but they are all implications having the conjunction of the premisses as the antecedent and the conclusion as the consequent. A true example of an Aristotelian syllogism would be, therefore, the following implication:

(3)   If all men are mortal
        and all Greeks are men,
        then all Greeks are mortal.

This implication is but a modern example of an Aristotelian syllogism and does not exist in the works of Aristotle. It would be better, of course, to have as an example a syllogism given by Aristotle himself. Unfortunately no syllogism with concrete terms is to be found in the *Prior Analytics*. But there are some passages in the *Posterior Analytics* from which a few examples of such syllogisms may be drawn. The simplest of them is this:

(4)   If all broad-leaved plants are deciduous
        and all vines are broad-leaved plants,
        then all vines are deciduous.[1]

All these syllogisms, whether Aristotelian or not, are only examples of some logical forms, but do not belong to logic, because they contain terms not belonging to logic, such as 'man' or 'vine'. Logic is not a science about men or plants, it is simply applicable to these objects just as to any others. In order to get a syllogism within the sphere of pure logic, we must remove from the syllogism what may be called its matter, preserving only its form. This was done by Aristotle, who introduced letters instead of concrete subjects and predicates. Putting in (4) the letter A for 'deciduous', the letter B for 'broad-leaved plant', the letter C for 'vine', and using, as Aristotle does, all these terms in the singular, we get the following syllogistic form:

(5)   If all B is A
        and all C is B,
        then all C is A.

---

[1] *An. post.* ii. 16, 98ᵇ5–10 ἔστω γὰρ τὸ φυλλορροεῖν ἐφ᾽ οὗ A, τὸ δὲ πλατύφυλλον ἐφ᾽ οὗ B, ἄμπελος δὲ ἐφ᾽ οὗ Γ. εἰ δὴ τῷ B ὑπάρχει τὸ A (πᾶν γὰρ πλατύφυλλον φυλλορροεῖ), τῷ δὲ Γ ὑπάρχει τὸ B (πᾶσα γὰρ ἄμπελος πλατύφυλλος), τῷ Γ ὑπάρχει τὸ A, καὶ πᾶσα ἄμπελος φυλλορροεῖ. From this somewhat carelessly written passage—after τῷ B, τῷ δὲ Γ, and τῷ Γ, παντί ought to be inserted—we get the following syllogism in concrete terms: εἰ πᾶν πλατύφυλλον φυλλορροεῖ καὶ πᾶσα ἄμπελος πλατύφυλλος, πᾶσα ἄμπελος φυλλορροεῖ.

This syllogism is one of the logical theorems invented by Aristotle, but even it differs in style from the genuine Aristotelian syllogism. In formulating syllogisms with the help of letters, Aristotle always puts the predicate in the first place and the subject in the second. He never says 'All B is A', but uses instead the expression 'A is predicated of all B' or more often 'A belongs to all B'.[1] Let us apply the first of these expressions to form (5); we get an exact translation of the most important Aristotelian syllogism, later called 'Barbara':

> (6) If A is predicated of all B
> and B is predicated of all C,
> then A is predicated of all C.[2]

Starting with the unauthentic example (1) we have reached thus by a step-by-step transition the genuine Aristotelian syllogism (6). Let us now explain these steps and establish them on a textual basis.

§ 2. Premisses and terms

Every Aristotelian syllogism consists of three propositions called premisses. A premiss ($\pi\rho\acute{o}\tau\alpha\sigma\iota\varsigma$) is a sentence affirming or denying something of something.[3] In this sense the conclusion is also a $\pi\rho\acute{o}\tau\alpha\sigma\iota\varsigma$, because it states something about something.[4] The two elements involved in a premiss are its subject and predicate. Aristotle calls them 'terms', defining a term ($\acute{o}\rho o\varsigma$) as that into which the premiss is resolved.[5] The original meaning of the Greek $\acute{o}\rho o\varsigma$, as well as of the Latin *terminus*, is 'limit' or 'boundary'. The terms of a premiss, its subject and predicate, are the limits of the premiss, its beginning and end. This is the very meaning of the word $\acute{o}\rho o\varsigma$, and we should be careful not to identify this logical word with such psychological or metaphysical words as 'idea', 'notion', 'concept', or *Begriff* in German.[6]

---

[1] $\tau\grave{o}$ A $\kappa\alpha\tau\eta\gamma o\rho\epsilon\hat{\iota}\tau\alpha\iota$ $\kappa\alpha\tau\grave{\alpha}$ $\pi\alpha\nu\tau\grave{o}\varsigma$ $\tauο\hat{v}$ B or $\tau\grave{o}$ A $\acute{v}\pi\acute{\alpha}\rho\chi\epsilon\iota$ $\pi\alpha\nu\tau\grave{\iota}$ $\tau\hat{\omega}$ B. See also p. 14, n.

[2] *An. pr.* i. 4, 25^{b}37 $\epsilon\grave{\iota}$ $\gamma\grave{\alpha}\rho$ $\tau\grave{o}$ A $\kappa\alpha\tau\grave{\alpha}$ $\pi\alpha\nu\tau\grave{o}\varsigma$ $\tauο\hat{v}$ B $\kappa\alpha\grave{\iota}$ $\tau\grave{o}$ B $\kappa\alpha\tau\grave{\alpha}$ $\pi\alpha\nu\tau\grave{o}\varsigma$ $\tauο\hat{v}$ Γ, $\dot{\alpha}\nu\acute{\alpha}\gamma\kappa\eta$ $\tau\grave{o}$ A $\kappa\alpha\tau\grave{\alpha}$ $\pi\alpha\nu\tau\grave{o}\varsigma$ $\tauο\hat{v}$ Γ $\kappa\alpha\tau\eta\gamma o\rho\epsilon\hat{\iota}\sigma\theta\alpha\iota$. The word $\dot{\alpha}\nu\acute{\alpha}\gamma\kappa\eta$ omitted in the translation will be explained later.

[3] Ibid. i, 24^{a}16 $\pi\rho\acute{o}\tau\alpha\sigma\iota\varsigma$ $\mu\grave{\epsilon}\nu$ $o\mathring{v}\nu$ $\dot{\epsilon}\sigma\tau\grave{\iota}$ $\lambda\acute{o}\gamma o\varsigma$ $\kappa\alpha\tau\alpha\phi\alpha\tau\iota\kappa\grave{o}\varsigma$ $\mathring{\eta}$ $\dot{\alpha}\pi o\phi\alpha\tau\iota\kappa\grave{o}\varsigma$ $\tau\iota\nu\grave{o}\varsigma$ $\kappa\alpha\tau\acute{\alpha}$ $\tau\iota\nu o\varsigma$.

[4] Ibid. ii. 1, 53^{a}8 $\tau\grave{o}$ $\delta\grave{\epsilon}$ $\sigma\upsilon\mu\pi\acute{\epsilon}\rho\alpha\sigma\mu\alpha$ $\tau\grave{\iota}$ $\kappa\alpha\tau\acute{\alpha}$ $\tau\iota\nu\acute{o}\varsigma$ $\dot{\epsilon}\sigma\tau\iota\nu$.

[5] Ibid. i. 1, 24^{b}16 $\acute{o}\rho o\nu$ $\delta\grave{\epsilon}$ $\kappa\alpha\lambda\hat{\omega}$ $\epsilon\grave{\iota}\varsigma$ $\grave{o}\nu$ $\delta\iota\alpha\lambda\acute{v}\epsilon\tau\alpha\iota$ $\mathring{\eta}$ $\pi\rho\acute{o}\tau\alpha\sigma\iota\varsigma$, $o\grave{\iota}o\nu$ $\tau\acute{o}$ $\tau\epsilon$ $\kappa\alpha\tau\eta\gamma o\rho o\acute{v}\mu\epsilon\nu o\nu$ $\kappa\alpha\grave{\iota}$ $\tau\grave{o}$ $\kappa\alpha\theta$' $o\mathring{v}$ $\kappa\alpha\tau\eta\gamma o\rho\epsilon\hat{\iota}\tau\alpha\iota$.

[6] Aristotle also uses the word $\acute{o}\rho o\varsigma$ in the sense of $\acute{o}\rho\iota\sigma\mu\acute{o}\varsigma$, i.e. 'definition'.

Every premiss is either universal, particular, or indefinite. 'All' and 'no' added to the subject are the signs of universality, 'some' and 'some not' or 'not all' are the signs of particularity. A premiss without a sign of quantity, i.e. of universality or particularity, is called indefinite, e.g. 'Pleasure is not good'.[1]

Nothing is said in the *Prior Analytics* about the terms. A definition of the universal and the singular terms is given only in the *De Interpretatione*, where a term is called universal if it is of such a nature as to be predicated of many subjects, e.g. 'man'; a term which does not have this property is called singular, e.g. 'Callias'.[2] Aristotle forgets that a non-universal term need not be singular, for it may be empty, like the term 'goat-stag' cited by himself a few chapters before.[3]

In building up his logic Aristotle did not take notice either of singular or of empty terms. In the first chapters of the *Prior Analytics*, containing the systematic exposition of his syllogistic, only universal terms are mentioned. Alexander justly remarks that the very definition of the premiss given by Aristotle has application to universal terms alone and is not suitable to individual or singular.[4] It is evident that the terms of universal and particular premisses must be universal. Aristotle certainly would not accept as meaningful expressions like 'All Calliases are men' or 'Some Calliases are men', if there were only one Callias. The same must be said about the terms of indefinite premisses: they, too, are universal. This follows both from the name Aristotle has chosen for them and from the examples he gives. A man who is

I willingly agree with E. Kapp, who says (op. cit., p. 29) that these two different meanings of the word ὅρος 'are entirely independent of one another and were never mixed up by Aristotle himself. But unfortunately no less a scholar than Carl Prantl . . . based his picture of Aristotle's logic on this homonymy . . . he identified the empty syllogistic *horos* ("term") with the metaphysical correlate of *horos* in the sense of definition ("Begriff" in Prantl's German). The result was a disastrous confusion.'

[1] *An. pr.* i. 1, 24ª17 (continuation of the text quoted in p. 3, n. 3) οὗτος δὲ ἢ καθόλου ἢ ἐν μέρει ἢ ἀδιόριστος. λέγω δὲ καθόλου μὲν τὸ παντὶ ἢ μηδενὶ ὑπάρχειν, ἐν μέρει δὲ τὸ τινὶ ἢ μὴ τινὶ ἢ μὴ παντὶ ὑπάρχειν, ἀδιόριστον δὲ τὸ ὑπάρχειν ἢ μὴ ὑπάρχειν ἄνευ τοῦ καθόλου ἢ κατὰ μέρος, οἷον τὸ τῶν ἐναντίων εἶναι τὴν αὐτὴν ἐπιστήμην ἢ τὸ τὴν ἡδονὴν μὴ εἶναι ἀγαθόν.

[2] *De int.* 7, 17ª39 λέγω δὲ καθόλου μὲν ὃ ἐπὶ πλειόνων πέφυκε κατηγορεῖσθαι, καθ' ἕκαστον δὲ ὃ μή, οἷον ἄνθρωπος μὲν τῶν καθόλου, Καλλίας δὲ τῶν καθ' ἕκαστον.

[3] Ibid. 1, 16ª16 τραγέλαφος.

[4] Alexander 100. 11 κατὰ γὰρ αἰσθητοῦ καὶ ἑνὸς κατ' ἀριθμὸν οὐκέθ' ἁρμόζει τὸ κατὰ παντός· οὐδὲ ὁ διορισμὸς ὅλως· ὁ γὰρ διορισμὸς τῶν προτάσεων ἐπὶ τῶν καθόλου χώραν ἔχει· τὰ δὲ ἄτομα οὐ καθόλου. Cf. ibid. 65. 26.

undecided whether it is true to say 'No pleasure is good' or only 'Some pleasure is not good', may say without defining the quantity of the subject: 'Pleasure is not good.' But in this last sentence 'pleasure' is still a universal term as it was in the two previous sentences. Throughout the whole systematic exposition of his syllogistic Aristotle in practice treats indefinite premisses like particulars without explicitly stating their equivalence.[1] This was done only by Alexander.[2]

Indefinite premisses are of no importance in the Aristotelian system of logic. No logical thesis, whether a law of conversion or a syllogism, is formulated by Aristotle with this kind of premiss. It was but right that they should be dropped by later logicians, who retained only four kinds of premiss, well known to every student of traditional logic, viz. the universal affirmative, the universal negative, the particular affirmative, and the particular negative. In this fourfold division there is no place left for singular premisses.[3]

§ 3. Why singular terms were omitted by Aristotle

There is an interesting chapter in the *Prior Analytics* where Aristotle divides all things into three classes. Some, he says, are such that they cannot be predicated truly of anything at all, like Cleon and Callias and the individual and sensible, but other things may be predicated of them, e.g. man or animal. Some other things, and these are the second class, are themselves predicated of others but nothing prior is predicated of them. For this class of things no example is given, but it is clear that Aristotle means what is most universal, like being, τὸ ὄν. To the third class belong those things that may be predicated of others and others of them, e.g. man of Callias and animal of man, and as a rule, concludes Aristotle, arguments and inquiries are concerned with this class of things.[4]

---

[1] See, for example, *An. pr.* i. 4, 26ᵇ29 ὁ γὰρ αὐτὸς ἔσται συλλογισμὸς ἀδιορίστου τε καὶ ἐν μέρει ληφθέντος, or 7, 29ᵃ27 δῆλον δὲ καὶ ὅτι τὸ ἀδιόριστον ἀντὶ τοῦ κατηγορικοῦ τοῦ ἐν μέρει τιθέμενον τὸν αὐτὸν ποιήσει συλλογισμὸν ἐν ἅπασι τοῖς σχήμασιν.

[2] Alexander 30. 29 περὶ δὲ τῶν ἀδιορίστων (scil. τῆς τῶν ἀδιορίστων ἀντιστροφῆς) οὐ λέγει, ὅτι μηδὲ χρήσιμοι πρὸς συλλογισμούς εἰσιν αὗται, καὶ ὅτι ἴσον ταῖς ἐπὶ μέρους δύνανται.

[3] Arguments on behalf of the thesis that singular propositions may be regarded as forming a sub-class of universals—see, for example, J. N. Keynes, *Formal Logic*, London (1906), p. 102—are in my opinion entirely wrong.

[4] *An. pr.* i. 27, 43ᵃ25–43 ἁπάντων δὴ τῶν ὄντων τὰ μέν ἐστι τοιαῦτα ὥστε κατὰ μηδενὸς ἄλλου κατηγορεῖσθαι ἀληθῶς καθόλου (οἷον Κλέων καὶ Καλλίας καὶ τὸ καθ'

There are some inexactitudes in this passage that must first be corrected. It is not correct to say that a thing may be predicated of another thing. Things cannot be predicated, because a predicate is a part of a proposition and a proposition is a series of spoken or written words having a certain meaning. The term 'Callias' may be predicated of another term, but never the thing Callias. The given classification is not a division of things but a division of terms.

It is further not correct to say that individual or singular terms, like 'Callias', cannot be truly predicated of anything else. Aristotle himself gives examples of true propositions with a singular predicate, as 'That white object is Socrates' or 'That which approaches is Callias',[1] saying that such propositions are 'incidentally' true. There are other examples of this kind which are not merely incidentally true, as 'Socrates is Socrates' or 'Sophroniscus was the father of Socrates'.

A third inexactitude concerns the conclusion drawn by Aristotle from this classification of terms. It is not true that our arguments and inquiries deal as a rule with such universal terms as may be predicated of others and others of them. It is plain that individual terms are as important as universal, not only in everyday life but also in scientific researches. This is the greatest defect of the Aristotelian logic, that singular terms and propositions have no place in it. What was the cause?

There is an opinion among philosophers that Aristotle constructed his system of logic under the influence of Plato's philosophy; for it was Plato who believed that the object of true knowledge must be stable and capable of a precise definition, which is of the universal and not of the singular. I cannot agree with this opinion. It has no confirmation in the text of the *Prior Analytics*. This purely logical work is entirely exempt from any philosophic contamination; so is the passage cited above. The argument that our inquiries are concerned with universal terms as a rule is a practical one, and though it is very weak and

ἕκαστον καὶ αἰσθητόν), κατὰ δὲ τούτων ἄλλα (καὶ γὰρ ἄνθρωπος καὶ ζῷον ἑκάτερος τούτων ἐστί)· τὰ δ' αὐτὰ μὲν κατ' ἄλλων κατηγορεῖται, κατὰ δὲ τούτων ἄλλα πρότερον οὐ κατηγορεῖται· τὰ δὲ καὶ αὐτὰ ἄλλων καὶ αὐτῶν ἕτερα, οἷον ἄνθρωπος Καλλίου καὶ ἀνθρώπου ζῷον. . . . καὶ σχεδὸν οἱ λόγοι καὶ αἱ σκέψεις εἰσὶ μάλιστα περὶ τούτων.

[1] *An. pr.* i. 27, 43ᵃ33 τῶν γὰρ αἰσθητῶν σχεδὸν ἕκαστόν ἐστι τοιοῦτον ὥστε μὴ κατηγορεῖσθαι κατὰ μηδενός, πλὴν ὡς κατὰ συμβεβηκός· φαμὲν γάρ ποτε τὸ λευκὸν ἐκεῖνο Σωκράτην εἶναι καὶ τὸ προσιὸν Καλλίαν.

Aristotle must have felt its weakness, yet it is not corroborated by any philosophical argument borrowed from Plato.

There is, however, another remarkable point that may throw some light on our problem. Aristotle emphasizes that a singular term is not suited to be a predicate of a true proposition, as a most universal term is not suited to be a subject of such a proposition. The first assertion, as we have already seen, is not generally true, and the second also seems to be false. But it does not matter whether these assertions are true or false. It suffices to know that Aristotle regarded them as true and that he eliminated from his system just those kinds of terms which in his opinion were not suited to be both subjects and predicates of true propositions. And here, as I see it, lies the chief point of our problem. It is essential for the Aristotelian syllogistic that the same term may be used as a subject and as a predicate without any restriction. In all three syllogistic figures known to Aristotle there exists one term which occurs once as a subject and then again as a predicate: in the first figure it is the middle term, in the second figure the major term, and in the third figure the minor term. In the fourth figure all three terms occur at the same time as subjects and as predicates. Syllogistic as conceived by Aristotle requires terms to be homogeneous with respect to their possible positions as subjects and predicates. This seems to be the true reason why singular terms were omitted by Aristotle.

§ 4. *Variables*

In Aristotle's systematic exposition of his syllogistic no examples are given of syllogisms with concrete terms. Only non-valid combinations of premisses are exemplified through such terms, which are of course universal, like 'animal', 'man', 'horse'. In valid syllogisms all terms are represented by letters, i.e. by variables, e.g. 'If R belongs to all S and P belongs to some S, then P belongs to some R'.[1]

The introduction of variables into logic is one of Aristotle's greatest inventions. It is almost incredible that till now, as far as I know, no one philosopher or philologist has drawn attention to

---

[1] Ibid. i. 6, 28ᵇ7 εἰ γὰρ τὸ μὲν P παντὶ τῷ Σ τὸ δὲ Π τινί, ἀνάγκη τὸ Π τινὶ τῷ P ὑπάρχειν. This is a mood of the third figure, called later Disamis, with transposed premisses.

this most important fact.[1] I venture to say that they must all have been bad mathematicians, for every mathematician knows that the introduction of variables into arithmetic began a new epoch in that science. It seems that Aristotle regarded his invention as entirely plain and requiring no explanation, for there is nowhere in his logical works any mention of variables. It was Alexander who first said explicitly that Aristotle presents his doctrine in letters, στοιχεῖα, in order to show that we get the conclusion not in consequence of the matter of the premisses, but in consequence of their form and combination; the letters are marks of universality and show that such a conclusion will follow always and for any term we may choose.[2] There is another commentator, John Philoponus, who is also fully aware of the significance and importance of variables. He says that Aristotle, after showing by examples how every premiss may be converted, states some universal rules of conversion taking letters instead of terms. For a universal sentence is disproved by one example in which it is false, but is proved either by going through all particulars (which is an endless and impossible operation) or by stating an evident universal rule. Such a rule is given here by Aristotle in letters, and the reader is allowed to substitute (ὑποβάλλειν) for the letters any concrete terms he wants.[3]

We know already that only universal terms may be substituted for the variables. In an example quoted above,[4] Aristotle performs such a substitution, saying: 'Let A be deciduous, B—broad-leaved plant, C—vine.' This is the only kind of substitution we meet in the *Prior Analytics*. Aristotle never substitutes for a variable A another variable B, although he is perfectly aware that the same syllogistic mood may be formulated with different

[1] I am glad to learn that Sir David Ross in his edition of the *Analytics*, p. 29, emphasizes that by using variables Aristotle became the founder of formal logic.

[2] Alexander 53. 28 ἐπὶ στοιχείων τὴν διδασκαλίαν ποιεῖται ὑπὲρ τοῦ ἐνδείξασθαι ἡμῖν, ὅτι οὐ παρὰ τὴν ὕλην γίνεται τὰ συμπεράσματα ἀλλὰ παρὰ τὸ σχῆμα καὶ τὴν τοιαύτην τῶν προτάσεων συμπλοκὴν καὶ τὸν τρόπον· οὐ γὰρ ὅτι ἥδε ἡ ὕλη, συνάγεται συλλογιστικῶς τόδε, ἀλλ' ὅτι ἡ συζυγία τοιαύτη. τὰ οὖν στοιχεῖα τοῦ καθόλου καὶ ἀεὶ καὶ ἐπὶ παντὸς τοῦ ληφθέντος τοιοῦτον ἔσεσθαι τὸ συμπέρασμα δεικτικά ἐστιν.

[3] Philoponus 46. 25 δείξας ὅπως ἑκάστη τῶν προτάσεων ἀντιστρέφει διὰ παραδειγμάτων . . . καθολικοὺς κανόνας παραδίδωσι τὰ στοιχεῖα παραλαμβάνων ἀντὶ τῶν ὅρων . . . τὸν μὲν γὰρ καθόλου λόγον ἐλέγχει μὲν καὶ ἐν παράδειγμα, ὡς ἤδη εἴρηται, κατασκευάζει δὲ ἢ ἡ διὰ πάντων τῶν κατὰ μέρος διέξοδος, ὅπερ ἐστὶν ἄπειρον καὶ ἀδύνατον, ἢ ἡ διὰ καθολικοῦ κανόνος πίστις· ὅπερ ποιεῖ νῦν διὰ τῶν στοιχείων διδοὺς ἑκάστῳ, ὥσπερ εἴρηται, ἐπ' ἐξουσίας χρῆσθαι καὶ ὑποβάλλειν ἀντὶ τῶν στοιχείων οἵας ἂν βούληται ὕλης ὅρους. [4] See p. 2, n.

variables. The mood Disamis, for instance, cited at the beginning of this section, is formulated with the letters R, S, P; elsewhere it is formulated with C, B, A.[1] It is evident that the validity of a syllogism does not depend on the shape of the variables used in its formulation: Aristotle knows that without saying it. It is again Alexander who states this fact explicitly.[2]

There is no passage in the *Prior Analytics* where two different variables are identified. Even where the same term is substituted for two variables, these two variables are not identified. In Book II of the *Prior Analytics* Aristotle discusses the problem whether a syllogism can be made out of opposite premisses. This can be done, he states, in the second and third figure. Let B and C, he continues, both stand for 'science' and A for 'medicine'. If one assumes that 'All medicine is science' and that 'No medicine is science', he has assumed that 'B belongs to all A' and 'C belongs to no A', so that 'Some science is not science'.[3] The syllogistic mood to which this refers runs thus: 'If B belongs to all A and C belongs to no A, then C does not belong to some B.'[4] In order to get from this mood a syllogism with opposite premisses, it suffices to identify the variables B and C, i.e. to substitute B for C. We get by this substitution: 'If B belongs to all A and B belongs to no A, then B does not belong to some B.' The heavy roundabout way by means of concrete terms, such as 'science' and 'medicine', is quite unnecessary. It seems that the straight way in this problem, i.e. the way by identifying variables, was not seen by Aristotle.

Aristotle knows that sentences like 'Some science is not science' cannot be true.[5] The generalization of such sentences 'Some A is not A' (i.e. 'A does not belong to some A') also must be false. It is not very probable that Aristotle knew this formula; it is

---

[1] *An. pr.* ii. 7, 59ᵃ17 εἰ γὰρ τὸ Γ παντὶ τῷ Β, τὸ δὲ Α τινὶ τῷ Β, ἀνάγκη τὸ Α τινὶ τῷ Γ ὑπάρχειν.

[2] Alexander 380. 2 οὐ γὰρ παρὰ τὸ τὸ μὲν Α αὐτῶν εἶναι τὸ δὲ Β ἢ Γ ἡ συναγωγή· τὸ γὰρ αὐτὸ γίνεται, κἂν ἄλλοις ἀντὶ τούτων χρησώμεθα.

[3] *An. pr.* ii. 15, 64ᵃ23 ἔστω γὰρ ἐπιστήμη ἐφ' οὗ τὸ Β καὶ Γ, ἰατρικὴ δ' ἐφ' οὗ Α. εἰ οὖν λάβοι πᾶσαν ἰατρικὴν ἐπιστήμην καὶ μηδεμίαν ἰατρικὴν ἐπιστήμην, τὸ Β παντὶ τῷ Α εἴληφε καὶ τὸ Γ οὐδενί, ὥστ' ἔσται τις ἐπιστήμη οὐκ ἐπιστήμη.

[4] This syllogism is a mood of the third figure, called later Felapton, with transposed premisses. In the systematic exposition of the syllogistic it is formulated with the letters R, S, P. See ibid. i. 6, 28ᵃ26 ἂν τὸ μὲν Ρ παντὶ τῷ Σ, τὸ δὲ Π μηδενὶ ὑπάρχῃ, ἔσται συλλογισμὸς ὅτι τὸ Π τινὶ τῷ Ρ οὐχ ὑπάρξει ἐξ ἀνάγκης.

[5] Ibid. ii. 15, 64ᵇ7 φανερὸν δὲ καὶ ὅτι ἐκ ψευδῶν μὲν ἔστιν ἀληθὲς συλλογίσασθαι, . . . , ἐκ δὲ τῶν ἀντικειμένων οὐκ ἔστιν· ἀεὶ γὰρ ἐναντίος ὁ συλλογισμὸς γίνεται τῷ πράγματι.

Alexander again who saw the falsity and applied this fact to prove the law of conversion of the universal negative premiss. The proof he gives proceeds by *reductio ad absurdum* : If the premiss 'A belongs to no B' is not convertible, let us suppose that B belongs to some A. From these two premisses we get by a syllogism of the first figure the absurd conclusion : 'A does not belong to some A.'[1] It is obvious that Alexander has in mind the mood of the first figure called later Ferio: 'If A belongs to no B and B belongs to some C, then A does not belong to some C',[2] and that in this mood he identifies the variables A and C, substituting A for C. This is perhaps the neatest example of an argument by substitution derived from an ancient source.

§ 5. *Syllogistic necessity*

The first Aristotelian syllogism, called later Barbara, may be represented, as we have already seen,[3] in the 'form of the following implication :

> If A is predicated of all B
> and B is predicated of all C,
> then A is predicated of all C.

But there is still a difference between this formulation and the genuine Greek text. The premisses are the same in the English version as in the Greek, but the exact translation of the conclusion would be 'A must be predicated of all C'. This word 'must' (ἀνάγκη) is the sign of the so-called 'syllogistic necessity'. It is used by Aristotle in almost all implications which contain variables and represent logical laws, i.e. laws of conversion or syllogisms.[4]

There are, however, some syllogisms where this word is omitted ; take, for instance, this Aristotelian form of the mood Barbara : 'If A belongs to all B and C belongs to all A, then C belongs to all B.'[5] Since it was possible to omit the word in 'some syllogisms, it must be possible to eliminate it entirely from all syllogisms. Let us see, therefore, what the word means and why it is used by Aristotle.

---

[1] Alexander 34. 15 ἔνεστι δὲ καὶ διὰ συλλογισμοῦ δεῖξαι διὰ τοῦ πρώτου σχήματος γινομένου, ὡς καὶ αὐτὸς προσχρῆται τῇ εἰς ἀδύνατον ἀπαγωγῇ· εἰ γάρ τις μὴ λέγοι ἀντιστρέφειν τὴν καθόλου ἀποφατικήν, κείσθω τὸ A μηδενὶ τῷ B· εἰ δὲ μὴ ἀντιστρέφει, ἔστω τὸ B τινὶ τῷ A· γίνεται ἐν πρώτῳ σχήματι τὸ A τινὶ τῷ A μὴ ὑπάρχον, ὅπερ ἄτοπον.
[2] *An. pr.* i. 4, 26ᵃ25 εἰ τὸ μὲν A μηδενὶ τῷ B ὑπάρχει, τὸ δὲ B τινὶ τῷ Γ, ἀνάγκη τὸ A τινὶ τῷ Γ μὴ ὑπάρχειν.   [3] See p. 3, n. 2.   [4] See p. 7, n.; p. 9, nn. 1, 4; above, n. 2.
[5] *An. pr.* ii. 11, 61ᵇ34 εἰ γὰρ τὸ A παντὶ τῷ B καὶ τὸ Γ παντὶ τῷ A, τὸ Γ παντὶ τῷ B.

The problem appears simple, and is settled implicitly by Aristotle himself incidentally in his treatment of the laws of conversion, when he says: 'If A belongs to some B, it is necessary that B should belong to some A; but if A does not belong to some B, it is not necessary that B should not belong to some A.' For if A stands for 'man' and B for 'animal', it is true that some animal is not man, but it is not true that some man is not animal, because all men are animals.[1] We see from this example that Aristotle uses the sign of necessity in the consequent of a true implication in order to emphasize that the implication is true for all values of variables occurring in the implication. We may therefore say 'If A belongs to some B, it is necessary that B should belong to some A', because it is true that 'For all A and for all B, if A belongs to some B, then B belongs to some A'. But we cannot say 'If A does not belong to some B, it is necessary that B should not belong to some A', because it is not true that 'For all A and for all B, if A does not belong to some B, then B does not belong to some A'. There exist, as we have seen, values for A and B that verify the antecedent of the last implication, but do not verify its consequent. In modern formal logic expressions like 'for all A' or 'for all B', where A and B are variables, are called universal quantifiers. The Aristotelian sign of syllogistic necessity represents a universal quantifier and may be omitted, since a universal quantifier may be omitted when it stands at the head of a true formula.

This, of course, is all known to students of modern formal logic, but some fifty years ago it was certainly not known to philosophers. It is not strange, therefore, that one of them, Heinrich Maier, has chosen our problem as the basis of what is, in my opinion, a bad philosophical speculation. He states:[2] 'The conclusion follows from the premisses with necessary consequence. This consequence arises from the syllogistic principle and its necessity reveals very properly the synthetic power of the function of reasoning.' I do not understand this last sentence, because

---

[1] Ibid. i. 2, 25ᵃ20–6 εἰ γὰρ τὸ A τινὶ τῷ B, καὶ τὸ B τινὶ τῷ A ἀνάγκη ὑπάρχειν... εἰ δέ γε τὸ A τινὶ τῷ B μὴ ὑπάρχει, οὐκ ἀνάγκη καὶ τὸ B τινὶ τῷ A μὴ ὑπάρχειν, οἷον εἰ τὸ μὲν B ἐστὶ ζῷον, τὸ δὲ A ἄνθρωπος. ἄνθρωπος μὲν γὰρ οὐ παντὶ ζῴῳ, ζῷον δὲ παντὶ ἀνθρώπῳ ὑπάρχει.

[2] H. Maier, *Die Syllogistik des Aristoteles*, vol. ii b, Tübingen (1900), p. 236: 'Aus den Prämissen folgt mit notwendiger Konsequenz der Schlußsatz. Diese Konsequenz entspringt dem syllogistischen Prinzip, und die Notwendigkeit, die ihr anhaftet, bekundet recht eigentlich die synthetische Kraft der Schlußfunktion.'

I cannot grasp the meaning of the words 'the synthetic power of the function of reasoning'. Moreover, I am not sure what is meant by 'the syllogistic principle', as I do not know whether any such principle exists at all. 'On the ground of both premisses [Maier continues his speculations[1]] which I think and express, I must also think and express the conclusion by virtue of a compulsion lying in my thinking.' This sentence I can certainly understand, but it is manifestly false. You may easily see its falsehood if you think and pronounce the premisses of a syllogism, e.g. 'All A is C' and 'Some B is not C', without pronouncing the conclusion which follows from them.

§ 6. What is formal logic?

'It is usual to say that logic is formal, in so far as it is concerned merely with the form of thought, that is with our manner of thinking irrespective of the particular objects about which we are thinking.' This is a quotation from the well-known text-book of formal logic by Keynes.[2] And here is another quotation, from the History of Philosophy by Father Copleston: 'The Aristotelian Logic is often termed formal logic. Inasmuch as the Logic of Aristotle is an analysis of the forms of thought—this is an apt characterization.'[3]

In both quotations I read the expression 'form of thought', which I do not understand. Thought is a psychical phenomenon and psychical phenomena have no extension. What is meant by the form of an object which has no extension? The expression 'form of thought' is inexact and it seems to me that this inexactitude arose from a wrong conception of logic. If you believe indeed that logic is the science of the laws of thought, you will be disposed to think that formal logic is an investigation of the forms of thought.

It is not true, however, that logic is the science of the laws of thought. It is not the object of logic to investigate how we are thinking actually or how we ought to think. The first task belongs to psychology, the second to a practical art of a similar kind to mnemonics. Logic has no more to do with thinking than mathematics has. You must think, of course, when you have to carry

---

[1] Op. cit., p. 237: 'Auf Grund der beiden Prämissen, die ich denke und ausspreche, muß ich kraft eines in meinem Denken liegenden Zwangs auch den Schlußsatz denken und aussprechen.'

[2] Op. cit., p. 2.   [3] Op. cit., p. 277.

out an inference or a proof, as you must think, too, when you have to solve a mathematical problem. But the laws of logic do not concern your thoughts in a greater degree than do those of mathematics. What is called 'psychologism' in logic is a mark of the decay of logic in modern philosophy. For this decay Aristotle is by no means responsible. Throughout the whole *Prior Analytics*, where the theory of the syllogism is systematically exposed, there exists not one psychological term. Aristotle knows with an intuitive sureness what belongs to logic, and among the logical problems treated by him there is no problem connected with a psychical phenomenon such as thinking.

What is therefore, according to Aristotle, the object of logic, and why is his logic called formal? The answer to this question is not given by Aristotle himself but by his followers, the Peripatetics.

There was a dispute among the philosophical schools of Ancient Greece about the relation of logic to philosophy. The Stoics contended that logic was a part of philosophy, the Peripatetics said that it was only an instrument of philosophy, and the Platonists were of the opinion that logic was equally a part and an instrument of philosophy. The dispute itself is of no great interest or importance, because the solution of the disputed problem seems to be for the most part a matter of convention. But an argument of the Peripatetics, preserved by Ammonius in his commentary on the *Prior Analytics*, deserves our attention.

Ammonius agrees with the Platonists and says: If you take syllogisms with concrete terms, as Plato does in proving syllogistically that the soul is immortal, then you treat logic as a part of philosophy; but if you take syllogisms as pure rules stated in letters, e.g. 'A is predicated of all B, B of all C, therefore A is predicated of all C', as do the Peripatetics following Aristotle, then you treat logic as an instrument of philosophy.[1]

---

[1] Ammonius 10. 36 κατὰ γὰρ Πλάτωνα καὶ τὸν ἀληθῆ λόγον οὔτε μέρος ἐστίν (scil. ἡ λογική), ὡς οἱ Στωϊκοί φασιν καὶ τινὲς τῶν Πλατωνικῶν, οὔτε μόνως ὄργανον, ὡς οἱ ἐκ τοῦ Περιπάτου φασίν, ἀλλὰ καὶ μέρος ἐστὶν καὶ ὄργανον φιλοσοφίας· ἐὰν μὲν γὰρ μετὰ τῶν πραγμάτων λάβῃς τοὺς λόγους, μέρος ἐστίν, ἐὰν δὲ ψιλοὺς τοὺς κανόνας ἄνευ τῶν πραγμάτων, ὄργανον. ὥστε καλῶς οἱ ἐκ τοῦ Περιπάτου τὰ παρὰ Ἀριστοτέλει ἀφορῶντες ὄργανον αὐτήν φασιν· ψιλοὺς γὰρ κανόνας παραδίδωσιν, οὐ πράγματα λαμβάνων ὑποκείμενα ἀλλὰ τοῖς στοιχείοις τοὺς κανόνας ἐφαρμόζων· οἷον τὸ Α κατὰ παντὸς τοῦ Β, τὸ Β κατὰ παντὸς τοῦ Γ, τὸ Α ἄρα κατὰ παντὸς τοῦ Γ. The syllogistic proof of the thesis that the soul is immortal is given a few lines farther on (11. 10): ἡ ψυχὴ αὐτοκίνητον, τοῦτο δὲ ἀεικίνητον, τοῦτο δὲ ἀθάνατον, ἡ ψυχὴ ἄρα ἀθάνατον.

It is important to learn from this passage that according to the Peripatetics, who followed Aristotle, only syllogistic laws stated in variables belong to logic, and not their applications to concrete terms. The concrete terms, i.e. the values of the variables, are called the matter, ὕλη, of the syllogism. If you remove all concrete terms from a syllogism, replacing them by letters, you have removed the matter of the syllogism and what remains is called its form. Let us see of what elements this form consists.

To the form of the syllogism belong, besides the number and the disposition of the variables, the so-called logical constants. Two of them, the conjunctions 'and' and 'if', are auxiliary expressions and form part, as we shall see later, of a logical system which is more fundamental than that of Aristotle. The remaining four constants, viz. 'to belong to all', 'to belong to none', 'to belong to some' and 'to not-belong to some',[1] are characteristic of Aristotelian logic. These constants represent relations between universal terms. The medieval logicians denoted them by A, E, I, and O respectively. The whole Aristotelian theory of the syllogism is built up on these four expressions with the help of the conjunctions 'and' and 'if'. We may say therefore: The logic of Aristotle is a theory of the relations A, E, I, and O in the field of universal terms.

It is obvious that such a theory has nothing more in common with our thinking than, for instance, the theory of the relations of greater and less in the field of numbers. There are, indeed, some similarities between these two theories. Compare, for example, the syllogism Barbara:

> If a belongs to all b
> and b belongs to all c,
> then a belongs to all c,

with the following arithmetical law:

> If a is greater than b
> and b is greater than c,
> then a is greater than c.

There are, of course, differences between these two laws: the range of variables is not the same, and the relations are different.

---

[1] ὑπάρχειν παντί, ὑπάρχειν οὐδενί, ὑπάρχειν τινί, οὐχ ὑπάρχειν τινί = ὑπάρχειν οὐ παντί. Instead of ὑπάρχειν Aristotle sometimes uses the verb κατηγορεῖσθαι. Syllogisms in concrete terms are formulated with εἶναι. See p. 2, n.; p. 3, n. 1, and the next section (7).

But both relations, although different and occurring between different terms, have one property in common: they are both transitive, i.e. they are particular cases of the formula:

> If *a* has the relation *R* to *b*
> and *b* has the relation *R* to *c*,
> then *a* has the relation *R* to *c*.

It is a curious thing that this very fact was observed by the logicians of the later school of the Stoics. Arguments like 'the first is greater than the second, the second is greater than the third, therefore the first is greater than the third' were called by the Stoics, as Alexander declares, 'non-methodically conclusive' and were not treated as syllogisms in the sense of their logic. Nevertheless, the Stoics regarded such arguments as similar (ὅμοιοι) to categorical syllogisms.[1] This observation of the Stoics, which Alexander tries to confute without producing convincing counter-arguments, corroborates the supposition that the logic of Aristotle was conceived as a theory of special relations, like a mathematical theory.

§ 7. *What is formalism?*

Formal logic and formalistic logic are two different things. The Aristotelian logic is formal without being formalistic, whereas the logic of the Stoics is both formal and formalistic. Let us explain what in modern formal logic is meant by 'formalism'.

Modern formal logic strives to attain the greatest possible exactness. This aim can be reached only by means of a precise language built up of stable, visually perceptible signs. Such a language is indispensable for any science. Our own thoughts not formed in words are for ourselves almost inapprehensible and the thoughts of other people, when not bearing an external shape, could be accessible only to a clairvoyant. Every scientific truth, in order to be perceived and verified, must be put into an external form intelligible to everybody. All these statements seem incontestably true. Modern formal logic gives therefore the utmost

---

[1] Alexander 21. 30 οἱ ἀμεθόδως περαίνοντες λόγοι παρὰ τοῖς Στωϊκοῖς, οἷον ' τὸ πρῶτον τοῦ δευτέρου μεῖζον, τὸ δὲ δεύτερον τοῦ τρίτου, τὸ ἄρα πρῶτον τοῦ τρίτου μεῖζον.' Ibid. 345. 13 τοιοῦτοί εἰσι καὶ οὓς λέγουσιν οἱ νεώτεροι (i.e. Στωϊκοί) ἀμεθόδως περαίνοντας. οὓς ὅτι μὲν μὴ λέγουσι συλλογιστικῶς συνάγειν, ὑγιῶς λέγουσι... ὅτι δὲ ἡγοῦνται ὁμοίους αὐτοὺς εἶναι τοῖς κατηγορικοῖς συλλογισμοῖς... τοῦ παντὸς διαμαρτάνουσιν.

attention to precision of language. What is called formalism is the consequence of this tendency. In order to understand what it is, let us analyse the following example.

There exists in logic a rule of inference, called formerly *modus ponens* and now the rule of detachment. According to this rule, if an implication of the form 'If α, then β ' is asserted and the antecedent of this implication is asserted too, we are allowed to assert its consequent β. In order to be able to apply this rule we must know that the proposition α, asserted separately, expresses 'the same' thought as the antecedent α of the implication, since only in this case are we allowed to perform the inference. We can state this only in the case where these two α's have exactly the same external form. For we cannot directly grasp the thoughts expressed by these α's, and a necessary, although not sufficient, condition for identifying two thoughts is the external equality of their expressions. When, for instance, asserting the implication 'If all philosophers are men, then all philosophers are mortal' you would also assert as second premiss the sentence 'Every philosopher is a man', you could not get from these premisses the conclusion 'All philosophers are mortal', because you would have no guarantee that the sentence 'Every philosopher is a man' represents the same thought as the sentence 'All philosophers are men'. It would be necessary to confirm by means of a definition that 'Every *A* is *B*' means the same as 'All *A*'s are *B*'s' ; on the ground of this definition replace the sentence 'Every philosopher is a man' by the sentence 'All philosophers are men', and only then will it be possible to get the conclusion. By this example you can easily comprehend the meaning of formalism. Formalism requires that the same thought should always be expressed by means of exactly the same series of words ordered in exactly the same manner. When a proof is formed according to this principle, we are able to control its validity on the basis of its external form only, without referring to the meaning of the terms used in the proof. In order to get the conclusion β from the premisses 'If α, then β ' and α, we need not know either what α or what β really means; it suffices to notice that the two α's contained in the premisses have the same external form.

Aristotle and his followers, the Peripatetics, were not formalists. As we have already seen, Aristotle is not scrupulously exact in formulating his theses. The most striking case of this inexactitude is the structural discrepancy between the abstract and concrete forms of the syllogisms. Take as an example the syllogism with opposite premisses quoted above, in our section 4.[1] Let B and C be 'science' and A 'medicine'. Aristotle states:

In variables:	In concrete terms:
If B belongs to all A	If all medicine is science
and C belongs to no A,	and no medicine is science,
then C does not belong to some B.[2]	then some science is not science.

The difference of corresponding premisses, of which the two syllogisms consist, is evident. Take, for instance, the first premiss. To the formula 'B belongs to all A' would correspond the sentence 'Science belongs to all medicine', and to the sentence 'All medicine is science' would correspond the formula 'All A is B'. The sentence in concrete terms, given by Aristotle, cannot be regarded as a substitution of the abstract formula accepted by him. What is the cause of this difference?

Alexander gives three explanations of this problem:[3] the first may be omitted as unimportant, the last is a philosophical one and is, in my opinion, wrong; only the second deserves our attention. According to this explanation, in formulae with the verb 'to be predicated of something' and, we may add, with the verb 'to belong to something', the subject and the predicate are better distinguishable (γνωριμώτεροι) than, we may add again, in formulae with the verb 'to be'. In fact, in formulae with 'to be' the subject as well as the predicate is used in the nominative; in formulae preferred by Aristotle only the predicate is in the nominative, and the subject is either in the genitive or in the dative and therefore can be more easily distinguished from the predicate. Very instructive, too, is the final remark of Alexander, from which it follows that to say 'Virtue is predicated of all justice' instead of the customary 'All justice is virtue' was felt in Ancient Greek to be as artificial as in modern languages.

---

[1] See p. 9, n. 3.

[2] The conclusion in variables is dropped in the Greek text.

[3] Alexander 54. 21 χρῆται δὲ τῷ κατὰ παντὸς καὶ τῷ κατὰ μηδενὸς ἐν τῇ διδασκαλίᾳ, ὅτι διὰ τούτων γνώριμος ἡ συναγωγὴ τῶν λόγων, καὶ ὅτι οὕτως λεγομένων γνωριμώτερος ὅ τε κατηγορούμενος καὶ ὁ ὑποκείμενος, καὶ ὅτι πρῶτον τῇ φύσει τὸ κατὰ παντὸς τοῦ ἐν ὅλῳ αὐτῷ, ὡς προείρηται. ἡ μέντοι χρῆσις ἡ συλλογιστικὴ ἐν τῇ συνηθείᾳ ἀνάπαλιν ἔχει· οὐ γὰρ ἡ ἀρετὴ λέγεται κατὰ πάσης δικαιοσύνης, ἀλλ' ἀνάπαλιν πᾶσα δικαιοσύνη ἀρετή. διὸ καὶ δεῖ κατ' ἀμφοτέρας τὰς ἐκφορὰς γυμνάζειν ἑαυτούς, ἵνα τῇ τε χρήσει παρακολουθεῖν δυνώμεθα καὶ τῇ διδασκαλίᾳ.

There are still more cases of inexactitude in Aristotelian logic. Aristotle constantly uses different phrases for the same thoughts. I shall give only a few examples of this kind. He begins his syllogistic with the words '*A* is predicated of all *B*', but shortly he changes these words into the phrase '*A* belongs to all *B*', which seems to be regular. The words 'is predicated' and 'belongs' are frequently omitted, sometimes even the important sign of the quantity 'all' is dropped. Besides the form '*A* belongs to some *B*' there are forms which may be translated '*A* belongs to some of the *B*'s'. The premisses of the syllogism are combined by means of different conjunctions. Syllogistic necessity is expressed in different ways and is sometimes entirely omitted.[1] Although these inexactitudes have no bad consequences for the system, they contribute in no way to its clearness or simplicity.

This procedure of Aristotle is probably not accidental, but seems to derive from some preconceptions. Aristotle says occasionally that we ought to exchange equivalent terms, words for words and phrases for phrases.[2] Commenting on this passage, Alexander declares that the essence of the syllogism depends not on words but on their meanings.[3] This statement, which is manifestly directed against the Stoics, can be understood thus: the syllogism does not change its essence, i.e. it remains a syllogism, if some of its expressions are replaced by other equivalent expressions, e.g. if the expression 'to be predicated of all' is replaced by the equivalent expression 'to belong to all'. The Stoics were of a directly opposite opinion. They would say that the essence of the syllogism depends on words, but not on their meanings. If therefore the words are changed, the syllogism ceases to exist. This is

---

[1] The phrase τὸ *A* κατὰ παντὸς τοῦ *B* (κατηγορεῖται is twice omitted) is used in the mood Barbara (see p. 3, n. 2), τὸ *A* παντὶ τῷ *B* (ὑπάρχει is altogether omitted) is used in another formulation of the same mood (see p. 10, n. 5). The phrase τὸ *A* τινὶ τῶν *B* appears in the laws of conversion; elsewhere, e.g. in the mood Disamis, we have τὸ *A* τινὶ τῷ *B* (see p. 9, n. 1). The logically important word παντί is altogether omitted in a formulation of the mood Barbara (see p. 2, n.). The conjunction 'and' is for the most part denoted by μέν ... δέ (see, for example, p. 7, n. or p. 10, n. 2), sometimes by καί (see p. 3, n. 2; p. 10, n. 5). Syllogistic necessity is as a rule expressed by ἀνάγκη ὑπάρχειν (see p. 7, n. or p. 9, n. 1), in the mood Felapton it is denoted by ὑπάρξει ἐξ ἀνάγκης (see p. 9, n. 4). In one case it is dropped (see p. 10, n. 5).

[2] *An. pr.* i. 39, 49ᵇ3 δεῖ δὲ καὶ μεταλαμβάνειν ἃ τὸ αὐτὸ δύναται, ὀνόματα ἀντ' ὀνομάτων καὶ λόγους ἀντὶ λόγων.

[3] Alexander 372. 29 οὐκ ἐν ταῖς λέξεσιν ὁ συλλογισμὸς τὸ εἶναι ἔχει, ἀλλ' ἐν τοῖς σημαινομένοις.

illustrated by Alexander with an example from the logic of the Stoics. The rule of inference called *modus ponens*:

> If α, then β;
> but α;
> therefore β,

is the first 'indemonstrable' syllogism of the Stoics. Both the Stoics and the Peripatetics seem mistakenly to regard the phrases 'If α, then β' and ' α entails β ' as having the same meaning. But if, in the syllogism given above, you replace the premiss 'If α, then β ' by ' α entails β ', saying:

> α entails β;
> but α;
> therefore β,

you get according to the Stoics a valid rule of inference, but not a syllogism. The logic of the Stoics is formalistic.[1]

---

[1] Alexander 373. 28 Ἀριστοτέλης μὲν οὖν οὕτως περὶ τῶν κατὰ τὰς λέξεις μεταλή-ψεων φέρεται (see p. 18, n. 2). οἱ δὲ νεώτεροι (i.e. οἱ Στωϊκοί), ταῖς λέξεσιν ἐπακο-λουθοῦντες οὐκέτι δὲ τοῖς σημαινομένοις, οὐ ταὐτόν φασι γίνεσθαι ἐν ταῖς εἰς τὰς ἰσοδυναμούσας λέξεις μεταλήψεσι τῶν ὅρων· ταὐτὸν γὰρ σημαίνοντος τοῦ ' εἰ τὸ Α τὸ Β ' τῷ ' ἀκολουθεῖ τῷ Α τὸ Β ', συλλογιστικὸν μὲν λόγον φασὶν εἶναι τοιαύτης ληφθείσης τῆς λέξεως ' εἰ τὸ Α τὸ Β, τὸ δὲ Α, τὸ ἄρα Β ', οὐκέτι δὲ συλλογιστικὸν ἀλλὰ περαντικὸν τὸ ' ἀκολουθεῖ τῷ Α τὸ Β, τὸ δὲ Α, τὸ ἄρα Β '.

CHAPTER II

THESES OF THE SYSTEM

§ 8. *Theses and rules of inference*

THE Aristotelian theory of the syllogism is a system of true propositions concerning the constants A, E, I, and O. True propositions of a deductive system I call theses. Almost all theses of the Aristotelian logic are implications, i.e. propositions of the form 'If α, then β'. There are known only two theses of this logic not beginning with 'if', viz. the so-called laws of identity: 'A belongs to all A' or 'All A is A', and 'A belongs to some A' or 'Some A is A'. Neither of these laws was explicitly stated by Aristotle, but they were known to the Peripatetics.[1]

The implications belonging to the system are either laws of conversion (and laws of the square of opposition not mentioned in the *Prior Analytics*) or syllogisms. The laws of conversion are simple implications, for instance: 'If A belongs to all B, then B belongs to some A.'[2] The antecedent of this implication is the premiss 'A belongs to all B', the consequent is 'B belongs to some A'. This implication is regarded as true for all values of the variables A and B.

All Aristotelian syllogisms are implications of the type 'If α and β, then γ', where α and β are the two premisses and γ is the conclusion. The conjunction of the premisses 'α and β' is the antecedent, the conclusion γ is the consequent. As an example take the following formulation of the mood Barbara:

> If A belongs to all B
> and B belongs to all C,
> then A belongs to all C.

In this example α means the premiss 'A belongs to all B', β the premiss 'B belongs to all C', and γ the conclusion 'A belongs to all C'. This implication is also regarded as true for all values of the variables A, B, and C.

---

[1] Cf. p. 9, n. 5, p. 10, n. 1. In the passage quoted in the latter note Alexander says that the proposition 'A does not belong to some A' is absurd. That means that the contradictory proposition 'A belongs to all A' is true.

[2] *An. pr.* i. 2, 25ᵃ17 εἰ δὲ παντὶ τὸ A τῷ B, καὶ τὸ B τινὶ τῷ A ὑπάρξει.

It must be said emphatically that no syllogism is formulated by Aristotle as an inference with the word 'therefore' (ἄρα), as is done in the traditional logic. Syllogisms of the form:

> All B is A;
> all C is B;
> therefore
> all C is A

are not Aristotelian. We do not meet them until Alexander.[1] This transference of the Aristotelian syllogisms from the implicational form into the inferential is probably due to the influence of the Stoics.

The difference between the Aristotelian and the traditional syllogism is fundamental. The Aristotelian syllogism as an implication is a proposition, and as a proposition must be either true or false. The traditional syllogism is not a proposition, but a set of propositions which are not unified so as to form one single proposition. The two premisses written usually in two different lines are stated without a conjunction, and the connexion of these loose premisses with the conclusion by means of 'therefore' does not give a new compound proposition. The famous Cartesian principle, 'Cogito, ergo sum', is not a true principle, because it is not a proposition. It is an inference, or, according to a scholastic terminology, a consequence. Inferences and consequences, not being propositions, are neither true nor false, as truth and falsity belong only to propositions. They may be valid or not. The same has to be said of the traditional syllogism. Not being a proposition the traditional syllogism is neither true nor false; it can be valid or invalid. The traditional syllogism is either an inference, when stated in concrete terms, or a rule of inference, when stated in variables. The sense of such a rule may be explained by the example given above: When you put such values for A, B, and C that the premisses 'A belongs to all B' and 'B belongs to all C' are true, then you must accept as true the conclusion 'A belongs to all C'.

If you find a book or an article where no difference is made between the Aristotelian and the traditional syllogism, you may

---

[1] In Alexander 47. 9 we find a syllogism in concrete terms with ἄρα: πᾶν ζῷον οὐσία ἐστί, πᾶν ζῷον ἔμψυχόν ἐστι, τὶς ἄρα οὐσία ἔμψυχός ἐστιν. At 382. 18 we have a complex syllogism in four variable terms with ἄρα: τὸ Α παντὶ τῷ Β, τὸ Β παντὶ τῷ Γ, τὸ Α οὐδενὶ τῷ Δ, τὸ ἄρα Δ οὐδενὶ τῷ Γ.

be sure that the author is either ignorant of logic or has never seen the Greek text of the *Organon*. Scholars like Waitz, the modern editor and commentator of the *Organon*, Trendelenburg, the compiler of the *Elementa logices Aristoteleae*, Prantl, the historian of logic, all knew the Greek text of the *Organon* well, but nevertheless they did not see the difference between the Aristotelian and the traditional syllogism. Only Maier seems to have felt for a moment that something is wrong here, when he asks for permission to replace the Aristotelian syllogism by the more familiar and more convenient form of the later logic; immediately afterwards he quotes the mood Barbara in its usual traditional form, neglecting differences he has seen between this form and that of Aristotle, and does not even say what differences he has seen.[1] When we realize that the difference between a thesis and a rule of inference is from the standpoint of logic a fundamental one, we must agree that an exposition of Aristotelian logic which disregards it cannot be sound. We have to this day no genuine exposition of Aristotelian logic.

It is always easy to deduce from an implicational thesis the corresponding rule of inference. Let us suppose that an implicational proposition 'If α, then β ' is true: if α is true, we can always get β by detachment, so that the rule 'α therefore β ' is valid. When the antecedent of an implicational thesis is a conjunction, as in the Aristotelian syllogisms, we must first change the conjunctional form 'If α and β, then γ ' into the purely implicational form 'If α, then if β, then γ '. A moment of reflection is sufficient to convince ourselves that this transformation is correct. Supposing now that α and β are true premisses of a syllogism, we get the conclusion γ, applying the rule of detachment twice to the purely implicational form of the syllogism. If, therefore, an Aristotelian syllogism of the form 'If α and β, then γ ' is true, the corresponding traditional mood of the form ' α, β, therefore γ' is valid. But conversely, it seems impossible to deduce the corre-

---

[1] Maier, op. cit., vol. ii *a*, p. 74, n. 2: 'Es ist vielleicht gestattet, hier und im Folgenden die geläufigere Darstellungsform der späteren Logik, die zugleich leichter zu handhaben ist, an die Stelle der aristotelischen zu setzen.' The mood Barbara is quoted ibid., p. 75, thus:

> alles B ist A
> alles C ist B
> alles C ist A

where the stroke replaces the word 'therefore'.

sponding Aristotelian syllogism from a valid traditional mood by known logical rules.

§ 9. *The syllogistic figures*

There are some controversial problems connected with the Aristotelian logic that are of historical interest without having any great logical importance. Among these is the problem of the syllogistic figures. The division of the syllogisms into figures has, in my opinion, only a practical aim: we want to be sure that no true syllogistic mood is omitted.

Aristotle divided the syllogistic moods into three figures. The shortest and clearest description of these figures is to be found not in the systematic part of the *Prior Analytics* but in the later chapters of that work. If we want, Aristotle says, to prove A of B syllogistically, we must take something common in relation to both, and this is possible in three ways: by predicating either A of C and C of B, or C of both, or both of C. These are the figures of which we have spoken, and it is clear that every syllogism must be made in one or other of these figures.[1]

It follows from this that A is the predicate and B the subject of the conclusion we have to prove syllogistically. A is called, as we shall see later, the major term and B the minor; C is the middle term. The position of the middle term as subject or predicate of the premisses is the principle by which Aristotle divides the syllogistic moods into figures. Aristotle says explicitly that we shall recognize the figure by the position of the middle term.[2] In the first figure the middle term is the subject of the major term and the predicate of the minor term, in the second figure it is the predicate, and in the last figure the subject, of both the other terms. Aristotle, however, is mistaken when he says that every syllogism must be in one of these three figures. There is a fourth possibility, viz. that the middle term is the predicate of the major term and the subject of the minor term. Moods of this kind are now spoken of as belonging to the fourth figure.

In the above passage Aristotle has overlooked this fourth

---

[1] *An. pr.* i. 23, 40ᵇ30 εἰ δὴ δέοι τὸ A κατὰ τοῦ B συλλογίσασθαι ἢ ὑπάρχον ἢ μὴ ὑπάρχον, ἀνάγκη λαβεῖν τι κατά τινος. 41ᵃ13 εἰ οὖν ἀνάγκη μέν τι λαβεῖν πρὸς ἄμφω κοινόν, τοῦτο δ' ἐνδέχεται τριχῶς (ἢ γὰρ τὸ A τοῦ Γ καὶ τὸ Γ τοῦ B κατηγορήσαντας, ἢ τὸ Γ κατ' ἀμφοῖν, ἢ ἄμφω κατὰ τοῦ Γ), ταῦτα δ' ἐστὶ τὰ εἰρημένα σχήματα, φανερὸν ὅτι πάντα συλλογισμὸν ἀνάγκη γίνεσθαι διὰ τούτων τινὸς τῶν σχημάτων.

[2] Ibid. 32, 47ᵇ13 τῇ τοῦ μέσου θέσει γνωριοῦμεν τὸ σχῆμα.

possibility, although a few chapters farther on he himself gives a proof by a syllogism in the fourth figure. It is the same problem again: we have to prove A of E syllogistically, where A is the major term and E the minor. Aristotle gives practical indications how to solve this problem. We must construct a list of universal propositions having the terms A and E as subjects or predicates. In this list we shall have four types of universal affirmative proposition (I omit the negative propositions), 'B belongs to all A', 'A belongs to all C', 'Z belongs to all E', and 'E belongs to all H'. Each of the letters B, C, Z, and H represents any term fulfilling the above conditions. When we find among the C's a term identical with a term among the Z's, we get two premisses with a common term, say Z: 'A belongs to all Z' and 'Z belongs to all E', and the proposition 'A belongs to all E' is proved in the mood Barbara. Let us now suppose that we cannot prove the universal proposition 'A belongs to all E', as the C's and Z's have no common term, but we want at least to prove the particular proposition 'A belongs to some E'. We can prove it in two different ways: if there is a term among the C's identical with a term among the H's, say H, we get the mood Darapti of the third figure: 'A belongs to all H', 'E belongs to all H', therefore 'A must belong to some E'. But there is still another way when we find among the H's a term identical with a term among the B's, say B; we then get a syllogism with the premisses 'E belongs to all B' and 'B belongs to all A', from which we deduce the proposition 'A belongs to some E' by converting the conclusion 'E belongs to all A' obtained from these premisses by the mood Barbara.[1]

This last syllogism: 'If E belongs to all B and B belongs to all A, then A belongs to some E', is a mood neither of the first figure nor of the second or third. It is a syllogism where the middle term

---

[1] *An. pr.* i. 28, 44ᵃ12–35 ἔστω γὰρ τὰ μὲν ἑπόμενα τῷ Α ἐφ' ὧν Β, οἷς δ' αὐτὸ ἕπεται, ἐφ' ὧν Γ . . .· πάλιν δὲ τῷ Ε τὰ μὲν ὑπάρχοντα, ἐφ' οἷς Ζ, οἷς δ' αὐτὸ ἕπεται, ἐφ' οἷς Η . . . . εἰ μὲν οὖν ταὐτό τι ἔσται τῶν Γ τινὶ τῶν Ζ, ἀνάγκη τὸ Α παντὶ τῷ Ε ὑπάρχειν· τὸ μὲν γὰρ Ζ παντὶ τῷ Ε, τῷ δὲ Γ παντὶ τὸ Α, ὥστε παντὶ τῷ Ε τὸ Α. εἰ δὲ τὸ Γ καὶ τὸ Η ταὐτόν, ἀνάγκη τινὶ τῶν Ε τὸ Α ὑπάρχειν· τῷ μὲν γὰρ Γ τὸ Α, τῷ δὲ Η τὸ Ε παντὶ ἀκολουθεῖ. . . . εἰ δὲ τῷ Η τὸ Β ταὐτόν, ἀντεστραμμένος ἔσται συλλογισμός· τὸ μὲν γὰρ Ε τῷ Α ὑπάρξει παντί, τὸ γὰρ Β τῷ Α, τὸ δὲ Ε τῷ Β (ταὐτὸ γὰρ ἦν τῷ Η)· τὸ δὲ Α τῷ Ε παντὶ μὲν οὐκ ἀνάγκη ὑπάρχειν, τινὶ δ' ἀνάγκη διὰ τὸ ἀντιστρέφειν τὴν καθόλου κατηγορίαν τῇ κατὰ μέρος. I read τὴν καθόλου κατηγορίαν τῇ with codex B (see Waitz, i. 196; the footnote in Bekker to 44ᵃ34 seems to be a misprint) and Alexander 306. 16 against τῇ καθόλου κατηγορίᾳ τὴν in Bekker and Waitz. I am glad to see that this reading is also accepted by Sir David Ross.

B is the predicate of the major term *A* and the subject of the minor term *E*. It is the mood Bramantip of the fourth figure. Nevertheless it is as valid as any other Aristotelian mood. Aristotle calls it a 'converted syllogism' (ἀντεστραμμένος συλλογισμός) because he proves this mood by converting the conclusion of the mood Barbara. There are two other moods, Camestres of the second figure and Disamis of the third, which Aristotle proves in the same manner, by converting the conclusion of moods of the first figure. Let us consider the proof of Disamis: 'If *R* belongs to all *S* and *P* belongs to some *S*, then *P* belongs to some *R*'. As the second premiss can be converted into '*S* belongs to some *P*', we get by the mood Darii the conclusion '*R* belongs to some *P*'. By converting this conclusion into '*P* belongs to some *R*' we get the proof of Disamis. Aristotle here applies the conversion to the conclusion of the mood Darii, which gives another syllogism of the fourth figure called Dimaris: 'If *R* belongs to all *S* and *S* belongs to some *P*, then *P* belongs to some *R*.'[1]

All these deductions are logically correct, and so are the moods obtained by their means. Aristotle knows, indeed, that besides the fourteen moods of the first, second, and third figures established by him systematically in the early chapters of the *Prior Analytics* there are still other true syllogisms. Two of them are quoted by him at the end of this systematic exposition. It is evident, he says, that in all the figures, whenever a syllogism does not result, if both the terms are affirmative or negative nothing necessary follows at all, but if one is affirmative, the other negative, and if the negative is stated universally, a syllogism always results linking the minor to the major term, e.g. if *A* belongs to all or some *B*, and *B* belongs to no *C*; for if the premisses are converted it is necessary that *C* does not belong to some *A*.[2] From the second premiss

---

[1] *An. pr.* i. 6, 28ᵇ7 εἰ γὰρ τὸ μὲν *P* παντὶ τῷ *Σ* τὸ δὲ *Π* τινί, ἀνάγκη τὸ *Π* τινὶ τῷ *P* ὑπάρχειν. ἐπεὶ γὰρ ἀντιστρέφει τὸ καταφατικόν, ὑπάρξει τὸ *Σ* τινὶ τῷ *Π*, ὥστ' ἐπεὶ τὸ μὲν *P* παντὶ τῷ *Σ*, τὸ δὲ *Σ* τινὶ τῷ *Π*, καὶ τὸ *P* τινὶ τῷ *Π* ὑπάρξει· ὥστε τὸ *Π* τινὶ τῷ *P*. This passage refutes the assertion of Friedrich Solmsen that Aristotle was not willing to apply the procedure of conversion to the conclusion. *Die Entstehung der aristotelischen Logik und Rhetorik*, Berlin (1929), p. 55: 'Die Umkehrung dringt in die conclusio ein, in der Aristoteles sie nicht kennen wollte.'

[2] *An. pr.* i. 7, 29ᵃ19 δῆλον δὲ καὶ ὅτι ἐν ἅπασι τοῖς σχήμασιν, ὅταν μὴ γίνηται συλλογισμός, κατηγορικῶν μὲν ἢ στερητικῶν ἀμφοτέρων ὄντων τῶν ὅρων οὐδὲν ὅλως γίνεται ἀναγκαῖον, κατηγορικοῦ δὲ καὶ στερητικοῦ, καθόλου ληφθέντος τοῦ στερητικοῦ, ἀεὶ γίνεται συλλογισμὸς τοῦ ἐλάττονος ἄκρου πρὸς τὸ μεῖζον, οἷον εἰ τὸ μὲν *A* παντὶ τῷ *B* ἢ τινί, τὸ δὲ *B* μηδενὶ τῷ *Γ*· ἀντιστρεφομένων γὰρ τῶν προτάσεων ἀνάγκη τὸ *Γ* τινὶ τῷ *A* μὴ ὑπάρχειν.

given here by Aristotle we get by conversion the proposition 'C belongs to no B', from the first premiss we get 'B belongs to some A', and from these two propositions results, according to the mood Ferio of the first figure, the conclusion 'C does not belong to some A'. Two new syllogistic moods are thus proved, called later Fesapo and Fresison:

If A belongs to all B
and B belongs to no C,
then C does not belong to some A.

If A belongs to some B
and B belongs to no C,
then C does not belong to some A.

Aristotle calls the minor term C and the major term A because he treats the premisses from the point of view of the first figure. He says, therefore, that from the given premisses a conclusion results in which the minor term is predicated of the major.

Three other syllogisms belonging to the fourth figure are mentioned by Aristotle at the beginning of Book II of the *Prior Analytics*. Aristotle states here that all universal syllogisms (i.e. syllogisms with a universal conclusion) give more than one result, and of particular syllogisms the affirmative yield more than one, the negative yield only one conclusion. For all premisses are convertible except the particular negative; and the conclusion states something about something. Consequently all syllogisms except the particular negative yield more than one conclusion, e.g. if A has been proved to belong to all or to some B, then B must belong to some A; and if A has been proved to belong to no B, then B belongs to no A. This is a different conclusion from the former. But if A does not belong to some B, it is not necessary that B should not belong to some A, for it may possibly belong to all A.[1]

We see from this passage that Aristotle knows the moods of the fourth figure, called later Bramantip, Camenes, and Dimaris, and that he gets them by conversion of the conclusion of the moods Barbara, Celarent, and Darii. The conclusion of a syllogism is a proposition stating something about something, i.e. a premiss, and therefore the laws of conversion can be applied to it.

---

[1] *An. pr.* ii. 1, 53ª4 οἱ μὲν καθόλου (scil. συλλογισμοί) πάντες ἀεὶ πλείω συλλογίζονται, τῶν δ' ἐν μέρει οἱ μὲν κατηγορικοὶ πλείω, οἱ δ' ἀποφατικοὶ τὸ συμπέρασμα μόνον. αἱ μὲν γὰρ ἄλλαι προτάσεις ἀντιστρέφουσιν, ἡ δὲ στερητικὴ οὐκ ἀντιστρέφει· τὸ δὲ συμπέρασμα τὶ κατά τινός ἐστιν. ὥσθ' οἱ μὲν ἄλλοι συλλογισμοὶ πλείω συλλογίζονται, οἷον εἰ τὸ Α δέδεικται παντὶ τῷ Β ἢ τινί, καὶ τὸ Β τινὶ τῷ Α ἀναγκαῖον ὑπάρχειν· καὶ εἰ μηδενὶ τῷ Β τὸ Α, οὐδὲ τὸ Β οὐδενὶ τῷ Α. τοῦτο δ' ἕτερον τοῦ ἔμπροσθεν. εἰ δὲ τινὶ μὴ ὑπάρχει, οὐκ ἀνάγκη καὶ τὸ Β τινὶ τῷ Α μὴ ὑπάρχειν· ἐνδέχεται γὰρ παντὶ ὑπάρχειν.

It is important that propositions of the type 'A belongs to no B' and 'B belongs to no A' are regarded by Aristotle as different.

It follows from these facts that Aristotle knows and accepts all the moods of the fourth figure. This must be emphasized against the opinion of some philosophers that he rejected these moods. Such a rejection would be a logical error which cannot be imputed to Aristotle. His only mistake is the omission of these moods in the systematic division of the syllogisms. We do not know why he did so. Philosophical reasons, as we shall see later, must be excluded. The most probable explanation is given, in my opinion, by Bocheński,[1] who supposes that Book I, chapter 7 and Book II, chapter 1 of the *Prior Analytics*, where these new moods are mentioned, were composed by Aristotle later than the systematic exposition of chapters 4–6 of Book I. This hypothesis seems to me the more probable, as there are many other points in the *Prior Analytics* suggesting that the contents of this work grew during its composition. Aristotle did not have time to draw up systematically all the new discoveries he had made, and left the continuation of his logical work to his pupil Theophrastus. Theophrastus, indeed, found for the moods of the fourth figure which are 'homeless' in Aristotle's system a place among the moods of the first figure.[2] For this purpose he had to introduce a slight modification into the Aristotelian definition of the first figure. Instead of saying that in the first figure the middle term is the subject of the major and the predicate of the minor, as Aristotle does,[3] he said generally that in the first figure the middle term is the subject of one premiss and the predicate of another. Alexander repeats this definition, which probably comes from Theophrastus, and seems not to see that it differs from the Aristotelian description of the first figure.[4] The correction of

---

[1] I. M. Bocheński, O.P., *La Logique de Théophraste*, Collectanea Friburgensia, Nouvelle Série, fasc. xxxii, Fribourg en Suisse (1947), p. 59.

[2] Alexander 69. 27 Θεόφραστος δὲ προστίθησιν ἄλλους πέντε τοῖς τέσσαρσι τούτοις οὐκέτι τελείους οὐδ᾽ ἀναποδείκτους ὄντας, ὧν μνημονεύει καὶ ὁ Ἀριστοτέλης, τῶν μὲν ἐν τούτῳ τῷ βιβλίῳ προελθών, τῶν δὲ ἐν τῷ μετὰ τοῦτο τῷ δευτέρῳ κατ᾽ ἀρχάς. Cf. ibid. 110. 12.

[3] Cf. p. 23, n. 1.

[4] Alexander 258. 17 (ad i. 23) ἡ δὲ τοῦ μέσου σχέσις πρὸς τά, ὧν λαμβάνεται μέσον, τριχῶς γίνεται (ἢ γὰρ ἐν μέσῳ τίθεται αὐτῶν τῷ μὲν ὑποκείμενος αὐτῶν τοῦ δὲ κατηγορούμενος, ἢ ἀμφοτέρων κατηγορεῖται, ἢ ἀμφοτέροις ὑπόκειται). Ibid. 349. 5 (ad i. 32) ἂν μὲν γὰρ ὁ μέσος ἐν ἀμφοτέραις ὢν ταῖς προτάσεσιν οὕτως ᾖ ὡς τοῦ μὲν κατηγορεῖσθαι αὐτῶν τῷ δὲ ὑποκεῖσθαι, πρῶτον ἔσται σχῆμα.

Theophrastus is as good a solution of the problem of the syllogistic figures as the addition of a new figure.

§ 10. *The major, middle, and minor terms*

There is still another error committed by Aristotle in the *Prior Analytics*, with more serious consequences. It concerns the definition of the major, minor, and middle terms as given in his characterization of the first figure. This begins with the words: 'Whenever three terms are so related to one another that the last is contained in the middle and the middle is contained or not in the first, the extremes must form a perfect syllogism.' This is how he begins; in the next sentence he explains what he means by the middle term: 'I call that term the middle which is itself contained in another and contains another in itself, which by position also becomes the middle.'[1] Aristotle then investigates the syllogistic forms of the first figure with universal premisses without using the expressions 'major term' and 'minor term'. These expressions occur for the first time when he comes to the moods of the first figure with particular premisses. Here we find the following explanations: 'I call that term the major in which the middle term is contained and that term the minor which comes under the middle.'[2] These explanations of the major and the minor term, like that of the middle term, are expressed quite generally. It would seem that Aristotle intends to apply them to all moods of the first figure.[3] If he thought, however, that they are capable of covering all cases, he was mistaken.

In fact these explanations can be applied only to syllogisms of the mood Barbara with concrete terms and true premisses, e.g.:

> (1)   If all birds are animals
>   and all crows are birds,
>   then all crows are animals.

In this syllogism there is a term, 'bird', which is itself contained in another term, 'animal', and contains in itself a third term,

---

[1] *An. pr.* i. 4, 25ᵇ32 ὅταν οὖν ὅροι τρεῖς οὕτως ἔχωσι πρὸς ἀλλήλους ὥστε τὸν ἔσχατον ἐν ὅλῳ εἶναι τῷ μέσῳ καὶ τὸν μέσον ἐν ὅλῳ τῷ πρώτῳ ἢ εἶναι ἢ μὴ εἶναι, ἀνάγκη τῶν ἄκρων εἶναι συλλογισμὸν τέλειον. καλῶ δὲ μέσον μὲν ὃ καὶ αὐτὸ ἐν ἄλλῳ καὶ ἄλλο ἐν τούτῳ ἐστίν, ὃ καὶ τῇ θέσει γίνεται μέσον.

[2] Ibid., 26ᵃ21 λέγω δὲ μεῖζον μὲν ἄκρον ἐν ᾧ τὸ μέσον ἐστίν, ἔλαττον δὲ τὸ ὑπὸ τὸ μέσον ὄν.

[3] Maier, op. cit., vol. ii *a*, pp. 49, 55, really treats them as definitions valid for all the moods of the first figure.

'crow'. According to the given explanation 'bird' would be the middle term. Consequently 'animal' would be the major term and 'crow' the minor term. It is evident that the major term is so called because it is the largest in extent, as the minor term is the smallest.

We know, however, that syllogisms with concrete terms are only applications of logical laws, but do not belong to logic themselves. The mood Barbara as a logical law must be stated with variables:

$$(2) \quad \text{If all } B \text{ is } A$$
$$\text{and all } C \text{ is } B,$$
$$\text{then all } C \text{ is } A.$$

To this logical law the given explanations are not applicable, because it is not possible to determine extensional relations between variables. It may be said that B is the subject in the first premiss and the predicate in the second, but it cannot be stated that B is contained in A or that it contains C; for the syllogism (2) is true for all values of the variables A, B, and C, even for those which do not verify its premisses. Take 'bird' for A, 'crow' for B, and 'animal' for C: you get a true syllogism:

$$(3) \quad \text{If all crows are birds}$$
$$\text{and all animals are crows,}$$
$$\text{then all animals are birds.}$$

The extensional relations of the terms 'crow', 'bird', and 'animal' are of course independent of syllogistic moods and remain the same in syllogism (3) as they were in (1). But the term 'bird' is no longer the middle term in (3) as it was in (1); 'crow' is the middle term in (3) because it occurs in both premisses, and the middle term must be common to both premisses. This is the definition of the middle term accepted by Aristotle for all figures.[1] This general definition is incompatible with the special explanation given by Aristotle for the first figure. The special explanation of the middle term is obviously wrong. It is evident also that the explanations of the major and minor terms which Aristotle gives for the first figure are wrong, too.

Aristotle does not give a definition of the major and minor terms valid for all figures; but practically he treats the predicate

---

[1] *An. pr.* i. 32, 47ᵃ38 μέσον δὲ θετέον τῶν ὅρων τὸν ἐν ἀμφοτέραις ταῖς προτάσεσι λεγόμενον· ἀνάγκη γὰρ τὸ μέσον ἐν ἀμφοτέραις ὑπάρχειν ἐν ἅπασι τοῖς σχήμασιν.

of the conclusion as the major term and the subject of the conclusion as the minor term. It is easy to see how misleading this
terminology is: in syllogism (3) the major term 'bird' is smaller
in extension than the minor term 'animal'. If the reader feels
a difficulty in accepting syllogism (3) because of its false minor,
he may read 'some animals' instead of 'all animals'. The syllogism:

> (4)   If all crows are birds
> and some animals are crows,
> then some animals are birds

is a valid syllogism of the mood Darii with true premisses. And
here again, as in syllogism (3), the largest term 'animal' is the
minor term; 'bird', middle in extension, is the major term; and
the smallest term, 'crow', is the middle term.

The difficulties we have already met are still greater when we
take as examples syllogisms with negative premisses, e.g. the mood
Celarent:

> If no B is A
> and all C is B,
> then no C is A.

B is the middle term; but does it fulfil the conditions laid down
by Aristotle for the middle term of the first figure? Certainly not.
And which of the terms, C or A, is the major and which is the
minor? How can we compare these terms with respect to their
extension? There is no positive answer to these last questions, as
they spring from a mistaken origin.[1]

§ 11. *The history of an error*

The faulty definition of the major and the minor terms, given
by Aristotle for the first figure, and the misleading terminology
he adopts, were already in antiquity a source of difficulty. The
problem arose in the case of the second figure. All the moods of

---

[1] We have no guarantee, as Keynes (op. cit., p. 286) justly remarks, that the
major term will be the largest in extension and the minor the smallest, when one of
the premisses is negative or particular. Thus, Keynes continues, 'the syllogism—
No M is P, All S is M, therefore, No S is P—yields as one case [here there follows
a diagram representing three circles M, P, and S, a large S included in a larger M,
outside of them a small P] where the major term may be the smallest in extent,
and the middle the largest.' Keynes forgets that it is not the same to draw a small
circle P outside of a large circle S and to maintain that the term P is smaller in
extent than the term S. Terms can be compared with respect to their extent only
in the case when one of them is contained in the other.

this figure have a negative conclusion and the first two moods, called later Cesare and Camestres, yield a universal negative conclusion. From the premisses 'M belongs to all N' and 'M belongs to no X' follows the conclusion 'X belongs to no N', and by conversion of this result we get a second conclusion, 'N belongs to no X'. In both syllogisms M is the middle term; but how are we to decide which of the two remaining terms, N and X, is the major term and which is the minor? Do major and minor terms exist 'by nature' (φύσει) or only 'by convention' (θέσει)?[1]

Such problems, according to Alexander, were raised by the later Peripatetics. They saw that in universal affirmative premisses there can be a major term by nature, because in such premisses the predicate is larger in extension (ἐπὶ πλέον) than the subject, but the same is not true in universal negative premisses.[2] We cannot know, for instance, which of the terms 'bird' or 'man' is major, because it is equally true that 'no bird is a man' and that 'no man is a bird'. Herminus, the teacher of Alexander, tried to answer this question by modifying the meaning of the expression 'major term'. He says that of two such terms, 'bird' and 'man', that is the major which in a systematic classification of the animals is nearer to the common genus 'animal'. In our example it is the term 'bird'.[3] Alexander is right when he rejects this theory and its further elaboration given by Herminus, but he also rejects the opinion that the major term is the predicate of the conclusion. The major term, he says, would not be fixed in this case, as the universal negative premiss is convertible, and what till now has been a major term instantly becomes a minor, and it would depend upon us to make the same term major and minor.[4] His own solution is based on the assumption that when we are forming a syllogism we are choosing premisses for a given problem

[1] Alexander 72. 17 ζητεῖται, εἰ φύσει ἐν δευτέρῳ σχήματι μείζων τίς ἐστι καὶ ἐλάττων ἄκρος, καὶ τίνι οὗτος κριθήσεται.

[2] Ibid. 72. 24 ἐπὶ μὲν γὰρ τῶν καταφατικῶν μείζων ὁ κατηγορούμενος καθόλου, ὅτι καὶ ἐπὶ πλέον· διὰ τούτου γὰρ οὐδὲ ἀντιστρέφει· ὥστε φύσει αὐτῷ τὸ μείζονα εἶναι ὑπάρχει. ἐπὶ δὲ τῶν καθόλου ἀποφατικῶν οὐκέτι τοῦτο ἀληθές.

[3] Ibid. 27 Ἑρμῖνος οἴεται, ἐν δευτέρῳ σχήματι τὸν μείζονα ἄκρον εἶναι ... τὸν ἐγγύτερον τοῦ κοινοῦ γένους αὐτῶν (ἂν γὰρ ὦσιν οἱ ἄκροι ὄρνεον καὶ ἄνθρωπος, ἐγγυτέρω τοῦ κοινοῦ γένους αὐτῶν, τοῦ ζῴου, τὸ ὄρνεον τοῦ ἀνθρώπου καὶ ἐν τῇ πρώτῃ διαιρέσει, διὸ καὶ μείζων ἄκρος τὸ ὄρνεον).

[4] Ibid. 75. 10 ἀλλ' οὐδὲ ἁπλῶς πάλιν ῥητέον μείζονα τὸν ἐν τῷ συμπεράσματι τοῦ συλλογισμοῦ κατηγορούμενον, ὡς δοκεῖ τισιν· οὐδὲ γὰρ οὗτος δῆλος· ἄλλοτε γὰρ ἄλλος ἔσται καὶ οὐχ ὡρισμένος τῷ ἀντιστρέφειν τὴν καθόλου ἀποφατικήν, καὶ ὁ τέως μείζων αὖθις ἐλάττων, καὶ ἐφ' ἡμῖν ἔσται τὸν αὐτὸν καὶ μείζω καὶ ἐλάττω ποιεῖν.

conceived as the conclusion. The predicate of this conclusion is the major term, and it does not matter whether we afterwards convert this conclusion or not: in the problem as first given the major term was and remains the predicate.[1] Alexander forgets that when we are forming a syllogism we are not always choosing premisses for a given conclusion, but sometimes we are deducing new conclusions from given premisses.

The problem was settled only after Alexander. What John Philoponus writes on the subject deserves to be regarded as classic. According to him we may define the major and the minor term either for the first figure alone or for all the three figures together. In the first figure the major term is the predicate of the middle and the minor is the subject of the middle. Such a definition cannot be given for the other two figures because the relations of the extremes to the middle term are in the other figures the same. We must therefore accept as a common rule for all figures that the major term is the predicate of the conclusion and the minor term is the subject of the conclusion.[2] That this rule is only a convention follows from another passage of Philoponus, where we read that the universal moods of the second figure have a major and a minor term only by convention, but not by nature.[3]

§ 12. *The order of the premisses*

Around the Aristotelian logic arose some queer philosophical prejudices which cannot be explained rationally. One of them is directed against the fourth figure, disclosing sometimes a strange aversion to it, another is the odd opinion that in all syllogisms the major premiss should be stated first.

---

[1] Alexander 75. 26 τὸν δὴ ἐν τῷ προκειμένῳ προβλήματι εἰς τὴν δεῖξιν κατηγορούμενον τοῦτο θετέον μείζονα· καὶ γὰρ εἰ ἀντιστρέφει καὶ διὰ τοῦτο γίνεται ὁ αὐτὸς καὶ ὑποκείμενος, ἀλλ' ἔν γε τῷ ἡμῖν εἰς τὸ δεῖξαι προκειμένῳ κατηγορούμενος ἦν τε καὶ μένει.

[2] Philoponus 67. 19 ἴδωμεν πρότερον καὶ τίς ἐστι μείζων ὅρος καὶ τίς ἐλάττων. τοῦτο δὲ δυνατὸν μὲν καὶ κοινῶς ἐπὶ τῶν τριῶν σχημάτων διορίσασθαι καὶ ἰδίᾳ ἐπὶ τοῦ πρώτου. καὶ ἰδίᾳ μὲν ἐπὶ τοῦ πρώτου σχήματος μείζων ὅρος ἐστὶν ὁ τοῦ μέσου κατηγορούμενος, ἐλάττων δὲ ὁ τῷ μέσῳ ὑποκείμενος. καὶ τοῦτο μὲν ἰδιαζόντως ἐπὶ τοῦ πρώτου λέγομεν, ἐπειδὴ ὁ μέσος ἐν τῷ πρώτῳ τοῦ μὲν κατηγορεῖται τῷ δὲ ὑπόκειται. ἀλλ' ἐπειδὴ κατ' οὐδέτερον τῶν ἄλλων σχημάτων διάφορον ἔχουσι σχέσιν οἱ ἄκροι πρὸς τὸν μέσον, δῆλον ὅτι οὐκέτι ἁρμόσει ἡμῖν οὗτος ὁ προσδιορισμὸς ἐπ' ἐκείνων. χρηστέον οὖν κοινῷ κανόνι ἐπὶ τῶν τριῶν σχημάτων τούτῳ, ὅτι μείζων ἐστὶν ὅρος ὁ ἐν τῷ συμπεράσματι κατηγορούμενος, ἐλάττων δὲ ὁ ἐν τῷ συμπεράσματι ὑποκείμενος.

[3] Ibid. 87. 10 τὸ δὲ μεῖζον ἄκρον ἐν τούτῳ τῷ σχήματι τῶν δύο προτάσεων καθόλου οὐσῶν οὐκ ἔστι φύσει ἀλλὰ θέσει.

From the standpoint of logic the order of the premisses in the Aristotelian syllogisms is arbitrary, because the premisses of the syllogism form a conjunction and the members of a conjunction are commutable. It is only a convention that the major premiss is stated first. Nevertheless, some philosophers, like Waitz or Maier, maintain that the order of the premisses is fixed. Waitz censures Apuleius for having changed this order,[1] and Maier rejects Trendelenburg's opinion that Aristotle does not tie it down.[2] No arguments are given in either case.

I do not know who is the author of the opinion that the order of the premisses is fixed. Certainly it is not Aristotle. Although Aristotle has not given a definition of the major and minor terms valid for all the three figures, it is always easy to determine which term and which premiss are regarded by him as the major and which as the minor. Aristotle, in his systematic exposition of the syllogistic, uses different letters to denote different terms; for each figure he puts them in alphabetical order (θέσις) and says explicitly which term is denoted by a given letter. We have thus for the first figure the letters A, B, C; A is the major term, B the middle, and C the minor.[3] For the second figure we have the letters M, N, X, where M is the middle term, N the major, and X the minor.[4] For the third figure we have the letters P, R, S, where P is the major term, R the minor, and S the middle.[5]

[1] Waitz, op. cit., vol. i, p. 380: 'Appuleius in hunc errorem se induci passus est, ut propositionum ordinem immutaverit.'

[2] Maier, op. cit., vol. ii a, p. 63: 'Darnach is Trendelenburg's Auffassung, dass Aristoteles die Folge der Prämissen frei lasse, falsch. Die Folge der Prämissen ist vielmehr festgelegt.' It is not clear to me what reasons he refers to by darnach.

[3] This follows from the definition given by Aristotle for the first figure; see p. 28, n. 1. Cf. Alexander 54. 12 ἔστω γὰρ μείζων μὲν ἄκρος τὸ A, μέσος δὲ ὅρος τὸ B, ἐλάττων δὲ ἄκρος τὸ Γ.

[4] An. pr. i. 5, 26ᵇ34 ὅταν δὲ τὸ αὐτὸ τῷ μὲν παντὶ τῷ δὲ μηδενὶ ὑπάρχῃ, ἢ ἑκατέρῳ παντὶ ἢ μηδενί, τὸ μὲν σχῆμα τὸ τοιοῦτον καλῶ δεύτερον, μέσον δὲ ἐν αὐτῷ λέγω τὸ κατηγορούμενον ἀμφοῖν, ἄκρα δὲ καθ' ὧν λέγεται τοῦτο, μεῖζον δὲ ἄκρον τὸ πρὸς τῷ μέσῳ κείμενον, ἔλαττον δὲ τὸ πορρωτέρω τοῦ μέσου. τίθεται δὲ τὸ μέσον ἔξω μὲν τῶν ἄκρων, πρῶτον δὲ τῇ θέσει. Cf. Alexander 78. 1 χρῆται γὰρ στοιχείοις οὐ τοῖς A, B, Γ, οἷς ἐν τῷ πρώτῳ σχήματι, ἀλλὰ τοῖς M, N, Ξ, μέσον μὲν λαμβάνων τὸ M τὸ ἀμφοτέρων κατηγορούμενον καὶ τὴν πρώτην ἔχον τάξιν ἐν τῇ καταγραφῇ, μείζονα δὲ ἄκρον τὸ N ἐφεξῆς κείμενον μετὰ τὸν μέσον, ἔσχατον δὲ καὶ ἐλάττονα τὸ Ξ.

[5] An. pr. i. 6, 28ᵃ10 ἐὰν δὲ τῷ αὐτῷ τὸ μὲν παντὶ τὸ δὲ μηδενὶ ὑπάρχῃ, ἢ ἄμφω παντὶ ἢ μηδενί, τὸ μὲν σχῆμα τὸ τοιοῦτον καλῶ τρίτον, μέσον δ' ἐν αὐτῷ λέγω καθ' οὗ ἄμφω τὰ κατηγορούμενα, ἄκρα δὲ τὰ κατηγορούμενα, μεῖζον δ' ἄκρον τὸ πορρώτερον τοῦ μέσου, ἔλαττον δὲ τὸ ἐγγύτερον. τίθεται δὲ τὸ μέσον ἔξω μὲν τῶν ἄκρων, ἔσχατον δὲ τῇ θέσει. Cf. Alexander 98. 20 ἐπὶ τούτου τοῦ σχήματος πάλιν χρῆται στοιχείοις

Aristotle states the major premiss first in all the moods of the first and the second figure, and in two moods of the third figure, Darapti and Ferison.[1] In the remaining moods of the third figure, Felapton, Disamis, Datisi, and Bocardo, the minor premiss is stated first.[2] The most conspicuous example is the mood Datisi. This mood is formulated in the same chapter twice; in both formulations the letters are the same, but the premisses are inverted. The first formulation runs: 'If R belongs to some S, and P to all S, P must belong to some R.'[3] The first premiss of this syllogism is the minor premiss, for it contains the minor term R. The second formulation reads: 'If P belongs to all S, and R to some S, then P will belong to some R.'[4] The first premiss of this second syllogism is the major premiss, as it contains the major term P. Attention must be called to the fact that this second formulation is given only occasionally, while the standard formula of this mood, belonging to the systematic exposition, is enunciated with transposed premisses.

In Book II of the *Prior Analytics* we meet other moods with transposed premisses, as Darii,[5] Camestres,[6] Baroco.[7] Even Barbara, the main syllogism, is occasionally quoted by Aristotle with the minor premiss first.[8] I can hardly understand, in view of these examples, how some philosophers knowing the Greek text of the *Organon* could have formed and maintained the opinion that the order of the premisses is fixed and the major premiss must be stated first. It seems that philosophical prejudices may sometimes destroy not only common sense but also the faculty of seeing facts as they are.

§ 13. *Errors of some modern commentators*

The story of the fourth figure may serve as another example to

τοῖς Π, Ρ, Σ, καὶ ἔστιν αὐτῷ τοῦ μὲν μείζονος ἄκρου σημαντικὸν τὸ Π, τοῦ δὲ ἐλάττονος καὶ ὀφείλοντος ὑποκεῖσθαι ἐν τῷ γινομένῳ συμπεράσματι τὸ Ρ, τοῦ δὲ μέσου τὸ Σ.

[1] See, for instance, p. 3, n. 2 (Barbara) and p. 10, n. 2 (Ferio).

[2] See p. 9, n. 4 (Felapton), and p. 7, n. (Disamis).

[3] *An. pr.* i. 6, 28^{b}12 εἰ τὸ μὲν Ρ τινὶ τῷ Σ τὸ δὲ Π παντὶ ὑπάρχει, ἀνάγκη τὸ Π τινὶ τῷ Ρ ὑπάρχειν.

[4] Ibid. 28^{b}26 εἰ γὰρ παντὶ τὸ Π τῷ Σ ὑπάρχει, τὸ δὲ Ρ τινὶ τῷ Σ, καὶ τὸ Π τινὶ τῷ Ρ ὑπάρξει.

[5] Ibid. ii. 11, 61^{b}41 εἰ γὰρ τὸ Α τινὶ τῷ Β, τὸ δὲ Γ παντὶ τῷ Α, τινὶ τῷ Β τὸ Γ ὑπάρξει.

[6] Ibid. ii. 8, 60^{a}3 εἰ τὸ Α μηδενὶ τῷ Γ, τῷ δὲ Β παντί, οὐδενὶ τῷ Γ τὸ Β.

[7] Ibid. 60^{a}5 εἰ γὰρ τὸ Α τινὶ τῷ Γ μὴ ὑπάρχει, τῷ δὲ Β παντί, τὸ Β τινὶ τῷ Γ οὐχ ὑπάρξει.   [8] See p. 10, n. 5.

show how strange philosophical prejudices sometimes are. Carl
Prantl, the well-known historian of logic, begins his consideration
of this figure with the following words: 'The question why silly
playthings, as, for instance, the so-called Galenian fourth figure,
are not to be found in Aristotle, is one we do not put at all; it
plainly cannot be our task to declare at every step of the Aristotelian logic that this or that nonsense does not occur in it.'[1] Prantl
does not see that Aristotle knows and accepts the moods of the
so-called Galenian fourth figure and that it would be a logical
error not to regard these moods as valid. But let us go farther.
Commenting upon the passage where Aristotle speaks of the two
moods later called Fesapo and Fresison,[2] Prantl first states these
moods as rules of inference:

All B is A Some B is A
No C is B No C is B
———————   ———————
Some A is not C Some A is not C

—he does not, of course, see the difference between the Aristotelian
and the traditional syllogism—and then he says: 'By transposition of the major premiss and the minor it becomes possible
for the act of reasoning to begin'; and further: 'Such kinds of
reasoning are, of course, not properly valid, because the premisses
ordered as they were before the transposition are simply nothing
for the syllogism.'[3] This passage reveals, in my opinion, Prantl's
entire ignorance of logic. He seems not to understand that
Aristotle proves the validity of these moods not by transposing
the premisses, i.e. by inverting their order, but by converting
them, i.e. by changing the places of their subjects and predicates.

---

[1] Carl Prantl, *Geschichte der Logik im Abendlande*, vol. i, p. 272: 'Die Frage aber,
warum einfältige Spielereien, wie z. B. die sog. Galenische vierte Figur, sich bei
Aristoteles nicht finden, werfen wir natürlich gar nicht auf; . . . wir können
selbstverständlicher Weise nicht die Aufgabe haben, bei jedem Schritte der
aristotelischen Logik eigens anzugeben, dass dieser oder jener Unsinn sich bei
Aristoteles nicht finde.'

[2] See p. 25, n. 2.

[3] Prantl, op. cit., vol. i, p. 276:

'Alles B ist A   Einiges B ist A
Kein C ist B   Kein C ist B
———————   ———————
Einiges A ist nicht C   Einiges A ist nicht C

woselbst durch Vertauschung des Untersatzes mit dem Obersatze es möglich wird,
dass die Thätigkeit des Schliessens beginne; . . . natürlich aber sind solches keine
eigenen berechtigten Schlussweisen, denn in solcher Anordnung vor der Vornahme
der Vertauschung sind die Prämissen eben einfach nichts für den Syllogismus.'

Moreover, it is out of place to say that, two premisses being given, the act of reasoning begins when one premiss is stated first, but no syllogism results when the other precedes. From the standpoint of logic Prantl's work is useless.

The same may be said of Heinrich Maier's work. His treatise on the syllogistic figures generally and the fourth figure in particular is in my opinion one of the most obscure chapters of his laborious but unfortunate book.[1] Maier writes that two opinions of the criterion for the syllogistic figures stand opposed to each other: one (especially Ueberweg) sees this criterion in the position of the middle term as subject or predicate, the other (especially Trendelenburg) sees it in the extensional relations of the middle term to the extremes. It is not yet settled, Maier says, which of these opinions is right.[2] He adopts the second as his own, relying on Aristotle's characterization of the first figure. We know already that this characterization is logically untenable. Maier not only accepts it, but modifies the Aristotelian characterizations of the two other figures according to the first. Aristotle describes the second figure somewhat carelessly as follows: 'Whenever the same term belongs to all of one subject and to none of the other, or to all of each subject, or to none of either, I call such a figure the second; by "middle term" in it I mean that which is predicated of both subjects, by "extremes" the terms of which this is said.'[3] Maier remarks: 'When we reflect that the expressions "*B* is included in *A*", "*A* belongs to *B*", and "*A* is predicated of *B*" are interchangeable, then we may put this characterization according to the description of the first figure in the following words.'[4] Maier commits here his first error: it is not true that the three expressions he quotes can be exchanged for each other. Aristotle states explicitly: 'To say that one term is included in another is the same as to say that the other is predicated of all of the first.'[5] The expression '*B* is included in *A*' means, therefore,

---

[1] See Maier, op. cit., vol. ii *a*, 'Die drei Figuren', pp. 47–71, and vol. ii *b*, 'Ergänzung durch eine 4. Figur mit zwei Formen', pp. 261–9.

[2] Op. cit., vol. ii *a*, p. 48, n. 1.

[3] See the Greek text on p. 33, n. 4.

[4] Op. cit., vol. ii *a*, p. 49: 'Erwägt man nämlich, dass die Ausdrücke "B liegt im Umfang von A", "A kommt dem Begriff B zu" und "A wird von B ausgesagt" mit einander vertauscht werden können, so lässt sich die Charakteristik der zweiten Figur, welche der Beschreibung der ersten parallel gedacht ist, auch so fassen.'

[5] *An. pr.* i. 1, 24^{b}26 τὸ δὲ ἐν ὅλῳ εἶναι ἕτερον ἑτέρῳ καὶ τὸ κατὰ παντὸς κατηγορεῖσθαι θατέρου θάτερον ταὐτόν ἐστιν.

the same as '*A* is predicated of all *B*' or '*A* belongs to all *B*', but does not mean '*A* is predicated of *B*' or '*A* belongs to *B*'. With this first error is connected a second: Maier maintains that the negative premiss also has the external form of subordination of one term to another, like the affirmative universal premiss.[1] What is here meant by 'external form'? When *A* belongs to all *B*, then *B* is subordinated to *A*, and the external form of this relation is just the proposition '*A* belongs to all *B*'. But in a negative premiss, e.g. '*A* belongs to no *B*', the subordination of terms does not exist, nor does its form. Maier's assertion is logically nonsense.

Let us now quote Maier's description of the second figure. It runs thus: 'Whenever of two terms one is included, and the other is not included, in the same third term, or both are included in it, or neither of them, we have the second figure before us. The middle term is that which includes both remaining terms, and the extremes are the terms which are included in the middle.'[2] This would-be characterization of the second figure is again logically nonsense. Take the following example: Two premisses are given: '*A* belongs to all *B*' and '*C* belongs to no *A*'. If *A* belongs to all *B*, then *B* is included in *A*, and if *C* belongs to no *A*, it is not included in *A*. We have therefore two terms, *B* and *C*, one of which, *B*, is included, and the other, *C*, is not included in the same third term *A*. According to Maier's description we should have the second figure before us. What we have, however, is not the second figure, but only two premisses '*A* belongs to all *B*' and '*C* belongs to no *A*', from which we can get by the mood Celarent of the first figure the conclusion '*C* belongs to no *B*', and by the mood Camenes of the fourth figure the conclusion '*B* belongs to no *C*'.

The peak, however, of logical absurdity Maier attains by his assertion that there exists a fourth syllogistic figure consisting of only two moods, Fesapo and Fresison. He supports this assertion by the following argument: 'The Aristotelian doctrine overlooks one possible position of the middle term. This term may be less

[1] Op. cit., vol. ii *a*, p. 60, n. 1: 'auch der negative syllogistische Satz hat wenigstens die äussere Form der Subordination.' Cf. also ibid., p. 50.
[2] Ibid., p. 49: 'Wenn im Umfang eines und desselben Begriffes der eine der beiden übrigen Begriffe liegt, der andere nicht liegt, oder aber beide liegen oder endlich beide nicht liegen, so haben wir die zweite Figur vor uns. Mittelbegriff ist derjenige Begriff, in dessen Umfang die beiden übrigen, äußere Begriffe aber diejenigen, die im Umfang des mittleren liegen.'

general than the major and more general than the minor, it may
secondly be more general, and thirdly less general, than the
extremes, but it may be also more general than the major term
and at the same time less general than the minor.'¹ When we
remind ourselves that according to Maier the major term is
always more general than the minor,² and that the relation 'more
general than' is transitive, we cannot avoid the strange consequence of his argument that the middle term of his fourth figure
should be at the same time more and less general than the minor
term. From the standpoint of logic Maier's work is useless.

§ 14. *The four Galenian figures*

In almost every text-book of logic you may find the remark that
the inventor of the fourth figure was Galen, a Greek physician and
philosopher living in Rome in the second century A.D. The source of
this remark is suspect. We do not find it either in the extant works
of Galen or in the works of the Greek commentators (including
Philoponus). According to Prantl the medieval logicians received
the information from Averroes, who says that the fourth figure
was mentioned by Galen.³ To this vague information we may add
two late Greek fragments found in the nineteenth century, and
also very vague. One of them was published in 1844 by Mynas in
the preface to his edition of Galen's *Introduction to Dialectic*, and
republished by Kalbfleisch in 1897. This fragment of unknown
authorship tells us that some later scholars transformed the moods
added by Theophrastus and Eudemus to the first figure into a
new fourth figure, referring to Galen as the father of this doctrine.⁴
The other Greek fragment was found by Prantl in a logical work

¹ Op. cit., vol. ii *b*, p. 264: 'Die aristotelische Lehre läßt eine mögliche Stellung
des Mittelbegriffs unbeachtet. Dieser kann specieller als der Ober- und allgemeiner
als der Unterbegriff, er kann ferner allgemeiner, er kann drittens specieller als die
beiden äußeren Begriffe: aber er kann auch allgemeiner als der Ober- und zugleich
specieller als der Unterbegriff sein.'
² Ibid., vol. ii *a*, p. 56: 'Oberbegriff ist stets, wie in der 1. Figur ausdrücklich
festgestellt ist, der allgemeinere, Unterbegriff der weniger allgemeine.'
³ Prantl, i. 571, n. 99, quotes Averroes in a Latin translation edited in
Venice (1553): 'Et ex hoc planum, quod figura quarta, de qua meminit Galenus,
non est syllogismus super quem cadat naturaliter cogitatio.' Cf. also Prantl, ii.
390, n. 322.
⁴ K. Kalbfleisch, *Über Galens Einleitung in die Logik*, 23. Supplementband der
Jahrbücher für klassische Philologie, Leipzig (1897), p. 707: Θεόφραστος δὲ καὶ
Εὔδημος καί τινας ἑτέρας συζυγίας παρὰ τὰς ἐκτεθείσας τῷ Ἀριστοτέλει προσέθηκασι
τῷ πρώτῳ σχήματι . . ., ἃς καὶ τέταρτον ἀποτελεῖν σχῆμα τῶν νεωτέρων ᾠήθησάν τινες
ὡς πρὸς πατέρα τὴν δόξαν τὸν Γαληνὸν ἀναφέροντες.

of Ioannes Italus (eleventh century A.D.). This author says sar-
castically that Galen maintained the existence of a fourth figure
in opposition to Aristotle, and, thinking that he would appear
cleverer than the old logical commentators, fell very far short.[1]
That is all. In view of such a weak basis of sources, Ueberweg
suspected a misunderstanding in the matter, and Heinrich Scholz
writes in his *History of Logic* that Galen is probably not responsible
for the fourth figure.[2]

For fifty years there has existed a Greek scholium in print
which clears up the whole matter in an entirely unexpected way.
Although printed, it seems to be unknown. Maximilian Wallies,
one of the Berlin editors of the Greek commentaries on Aristotle,
published in 1899 the extant fragments of Ammonius' commentary on the *Prior Analytics*, and has inserted in the preface a
scholium of an unknown author found in the same codex as that
in which the fragments of Ammonius are preserved. The scholium
is entitled 'On all the kinds of syllogism', and begins thus:

'There are three kinds of syllogism: the categorical, the hypothetical,
and the syllogism κατὰ πρόσληψιν. Of the categorical there are two
kinds: the simple and the compound. Of the simple syllogism there
are three kinds: the first, the second, and the third figure. Of the compound syllogism there are four kinds: the first, the second, the third,
and the fourth figure. For Aristotle says that there are only three
figures, because he looks at the simple syllogisms, consisting of three
terms. Galen, however, says in his *Apodeictic* that there are four figures, because he looks at the compound syllogisms consisting of four
terms, as he has found many such syllogisms in Plato's dialogues.'[3]

The unknown scholiast further gives us some explanations, from

---

[1] Prantl, ii. 302, n. 112: τὰ δὲ σχήματα τῶν συλλογισμῶν ταῦτα· ὁ Γαληνὸς δὲ καὶ
τέταρτον ἐπὶ τούτοις ἔφασκεν εἶναι, ἐναντίως πρὸς τὸν Σταγειρίτην φερόμενος, ὃς λαμ-
πρότερον ἀναφανῆναι οἰόμενος τῶν τὴν λογικὴν πραγματείαν ἐξηγουμένων παλαιῶν ὡς
πορρωτάτω εὐθέως ἐκπέπτωκε.

[2] Fr. Ueberweg, *System der Logik*, Bonn (1882), 341. Cf. also Kalbfleisch, op. cit.,
p. 699; H. Scholz, *Geschichte der Logik*, Berlin (1931), p. 36.

[3] M. Wallies, *Ammonii in Aristotelis Analyticorum Priorum librum I Commentarium*,
Berlin (1899), p. ix: Περὶ τῶν εἰδῶι πάντων τοῦ συλλογισμοῦ. τρία εἴδη ἐστὶ τοῦ
[ἁπλοῦ] συλλογισμοῦ· τὸ κατηγορικόν, τὸ ὑποθετικόν, τὸ κατὰ πρόσληψιν. τοῦ δὲ
κατηγορικοῦ δύο ἐστὶν εἴδη· ἁπλοῦν, σύνθετον. καὶ τοῦ μὲν ἁπλοῦ τρία ἐστὶν εἴδη·
πρῶτον σχῆμα, δεύτερον σχῆμα, τρίτον σχῆμα. τοῦ δὲ συνθέτου τέσσαρά ἐστιν εἴδη·
πρῶτον σχῆμα, δεύτερον σχῆμα, τρίτον, τέταρτον σχῆμα. Ἀριστοτέλης μὲν γὰρ τρία
τὰ σχήματά φησιν πρὸς τοὺς ἁπλοῦς συλλογισμοὺς ἀποβλέπων τοὺς ἐκ τριῶν ὅρων
συγκειμένους. Γαληνὸς δ' ἐν τῇ οἰκείᾳ Ἀποδεικτικῇ δ τὰ σχήματα λέγει πρὸς τοὺς
συνθέτους συλλογισμοὺς ἀποβλέπων τοὺς ἐκ δ ὅρων συγκειμένους πολλοὺς τοιούτους
εὑρὼν ἐν τοῖς Πλάτωνος διαλόγοις.

which we can gather how Galen may have found these four figures. Compound syllogisms consisting of four terms may be formed by combinations of the three figures I, II, and III of simple syllogisms in nine different ways: I to I, I to II, I to III, II to II, II to I, II to III, III to III, III to I, III to II. Two of these combinations, viz. II to II and III to III, do not give syllogisms at all, and of the remaining combinations II to I gives the same figure as I to II, III to I the same as I to III, and III to II the same as II to III. We get thus only four figures, I to I, I to II, I to III, and II to III.[1] Examples are given, of which three are taken from Plato's dialogues, two from the *Alcibiades*, and one from the *Republic*.

This precise and minute account must be explained and examined. Compound syllogisms of four terms have three premisses and two middle terms, say B and C, which form the premiss $B–C$ or $C–B$. Let us call this the middle premiss. B forms together with A, the subject of the conclusion, the minor premiss, and C forms together with D, the predicate of the conclusion, the major premiss. We thus obtain the following eight combinations (in all the premisses the first term is the subject, the second the predicate):

Figure	Minor	Middle	Major		Conclusion
		Premiss		Conclusion	
F1	$A–B$	$B–C$	$C–D$	$A–D$	I to I
F2	$A–B$	$B–C$	$D–C$	$A–D$	I to II
F3	$A–B$	$C–B$	$C–D$	$A–D$	II to III
F4	$A–B$	$C–B$	$D–C$	$A–D$	II to I
F5	$B–A$	$B–C$	$C–D$	$A–D$	III to I
F6	$B–A$	$B–C$	$D–C$	$A–D$	III to II
F7	$B–A$	$C–B$	$C–D$	$A–D$	I to III
F8	$B–A$	$C–B$	$D–C$	$A–D$	I to I

If we adopt the principle of Theophrastus that in the first

---

[1] Wallies, op. cit., pp. ix–x: ὁ κατηγορικὸς συλλογισμὸς ἁπλοῦς, ὡς Ἀριστοτέλης· σχῆμα Α Β Γ. σύνθετος, ὡς Γαληνός· Α πρὸς Α, Α πρὸς Β, Α πρὸς Γ, Β πρὸς Β, Β πρὸς Α, Β πρὸς Γ, Γ πρὸς Γ, Γ πρὸς Α, Γ πρὸς Β.

συλλογιστικόν·   Α πρὸς Α,   Α πρὸς Β,   Α πρὸς Γ,   Β πρὸς Γ.
              Α   Β   Γ   Δ

ἀσυλλόγιστον· Β πρὸς Β, Γ πρὸς Γ, (οὐ γὰρ γίνεται συλλογισμὸς οὔτε ἐκ δύο ἀποφατικῶν οὔτε ἐκ δύο μερικῶν)·

              Β πρὸς Α,   Γ πρὸς Α,   Γ πρὸς Β,
              Β   Γ   Δ

οἱ αὐτοί εἰσιν τοῖς συλλογισμοῖς ὡς ὑπογέγραπται.

Aristotelian figure the middle term is the subject of one premiss—
it does not matter of which, the major or the minor—and the
predicate of another, and define by this principle which figure is
formed by the minor and middle premisses on the one hand, and
by the middle and major premisses on the other, we get the combinations of figures shown in the last column. Thus, for instance,
in the compound figure F2 the minor premiss together with the
middle forms the figure I, as the middle term B is the predicate
of the first premiss and the subject of the second, and the middle
premiss together with the major forms the figure II, as the middle
term C is the predicate of both premisses. This was probably how
Galen has got his four figures. Looking at the last column we see
at once that, as Galen held, the combinations II to II and III to
III do not exist, not for the reason, as the scholiast mistakenly
says, that no conclusion results either from two negative or two
particular premisses, but because no term can occur in the
premisses three times. It is obvious also that if we extend the
principle of Theophrastus to compound syllogisms and include
in the same figure all the moods that from the same combination
of premisses yield either the conclusion A–D or the conclusion
D–A, we get as Galen does the same figure from the combination
I to II as from the combination II to I. For, interchanging in
figure F4 the letters B and C as well as the letters A and D, we
get the scheme:

$$\text{F4} \qquad D\text{–}C \qquad B\text{–}C \qquad A\text{–}B \qquad D\text{–}A,$$

and as the order of the premisses is irrelevant we see that the
conclusion D–A results in F4 from the same premisses as A–D
in F2. For the same reason figure F1 does not differ from figure
F8, F3 from F6, or F5 from F7. It is possible, therefore, to divide
the compound syllogisms of four terms into four figures.

The scholium edited by Wallies explains all historical problems
connected with the alleged invention of the fourth figure by
Galen. Galen divided syllogisms into four figures, but these were
the compound syllogisms of four terms, not the simple syllogisms
of Aristotle. The fourth figure of the Aristotelian syllogisms was
invented by someone else, probably very late, perhaps not before
the sixth century A.D. This unknown scholar must have heard
something about the four figures of Galen, but he either did not
understand them or did not have Galen's text at hand. Being in

opposition to Aristotle and to the whole school of the Peripatetics, he eagerly seized the occasion to back up his opinion by the authority of an illustrious name.

REMARK. The problem of compound syllogisms raised by Galen has considerable interest from the systematic point of view. Investigating the number of valid moods of the syllogisms consisting of three premisses, I have found that there are forty-four valid moods, the figures F1, F2, F4, F5, F6, and F7 having six moods each, and figure F8 eight. Figure F3 is empty. It has no valid moods, for it is not possible to find premisses of the form $A–B$, $C–B$, $C–D$ such that a conclusion of the form $A–D$ would follow from them. This result, if known, would certainly be startling for students of the traditional logic. Mr. C. A. Meredith, who attended my lectures delivered on this subject in 1949 at University College, Dublin, has found some general formulae concerning the number of figures and valid moods for syllogisms of n terms, including expressions of 1 and 2 terms. I publish these formulae here with his kind permission :

Number of terms . . . . n
Number of figures . . . . 2^{n-1}
Number of figures with valid moods . $\frac{1}{2}(n^2-n+2)$
Number of valid moods . . . $n(3n-1)$

For all n every non-empty figure has 6 valid moods, except one that has $2n$ valid moods.

Examples :

Number of terms . . . . 1, 2, 3, 4,..., 10
Number of figures . . . . 1, 2, 4, 8,..., 512
Number of figures with valid moods . 1, 2, 4, 7,..., 46
Number of valid moods . . . 2, 10, 24, 44,..., 290

It is obvious that for large n's the number of figures with valid moods is comparatively small against the number of all figures. For $n = 10$ we have 46 against 512 respectively, i.e. 466 figures are empty. For $n = 1$ there is only 1 figure, $A–A$, with 2 valid moods, i.e. the laws of identity. For $n = 2$ there are 2 figures :

	Premiss	Conclusion
F1	$A–B$	$A–B$
F2	$B–A$	$A–B$

with 10 valid moods, 6 in F1 (viz. four substitutions of the propositional law of identity, e.g. 'if all A is B, then all A is B', and two laws of subordination), and 4 moods in F2 (viz. four laws of conversion).

CHAPTER III

THE SYSTEM

§ 15. *Perfect and imperfect syllogisms*

IN the introductory chapter to the syllogistic Aristotle divides all syllogisms into perfect and imperfect. 'I call that a perfect syllogism', he says, 'which needs nothing other than what has been stated to make the necessity evident; a syllogism is imperfect, if it needs either one or more components which are necessary by the terms set down, but have not been stated by the premisses.'[1] This passage needs translation into logical terminology. Every Aristotelian syllogism is a true implication, the antecedent of which is the joint premisses and the consequent the conclusion. What Aristotle says means, therefore, that in a perfect syllogism the connexion between the antecedent and the consequent is evident of itself without an additional proposition. Perfect syllogisms are self-evident statements which do not possess and do not need a demonstration; they are indemonstrable, ἀναπόδεικτοι.[2] Indemonstrable true statements of a deductive system are now called axioms. The perfect syllogisms, therefore, are the axioms of the syllogistic. On the other hand, the imperfect syllogisms are not self-evident; they must be proved by means of one or more propositions which result from the premisses, but are different from them.

Aristotle knows that not all true propositions are demonstrable.[3] He says that a proposition of the form '*A* belongs to *B*' is demonstrable if there exists a middle term, i.e. a term which forms with *A* and *B* true premisses of a valid syllogism having the above proposition as the conclusion. If such a middle term does

---

[1] *An. pr.* i. 1, 24^b22 τέλειον μὲν οὖν καλῶ συλλογισμὸν τὸν μηδενὸς ἄλλου προσδεόμενον παρὰ τὰ εἰλημμένα πρὸς τὸ φανῆναι τὸ ἀναγκαῖον, ἀτελῆ δὲ τὸν προσδεόμενον ἢ ἑνὸς ἢ πλειόνων, ἃ ἔστι μὲν ἀναγκαῖα διὰ τῶν ὑποκειμένων ὅρων, οὐ μὴν εἴληπται διὰ προτάσεων.

[2] Commenting upon the above passage Alexander uses the expression ἀναπόδεικτος, 24. 2: ἑνὸς μὲν οὖν προσδέονται οἱ ἀτελεῖς συλλογισμοὶ οἱ μιᾶς ἀντιστροφῆς δεόμενοι πρὸς τὸ ἀναχθῆναι εἴς τινα τῶν ἐν τῷ πρώτῳ σχήματι τῶν τελείων καὶ ἀναποδείκτων, πλειόνων δὲ ὅσοι διὰ δύο ἀντιστροφῶν εἰς ἐκείνων τινὰ ἀνάγονται. Cf. also p. 27, n. 2.

[3] *An. post.* i. 3, 72^b18 ἡμεῖς δέ φαμεν οὔτε πᾶσαν ἐπιστήμην ἀποδεικτικὴν εἶναι, ἀλλὰ τὴν τῶν ἀμέσων ἀναπόδεικτον.

not exist, the proposition is called 'immediate', ἄμεσος, i.e. without a middle term. Immediate propositions are indemonstrable; they are basic truths, ἀρχαί.[1] To these statements of the *Posterior Analytics* may be added a passage of the *Prior Analytics* which states that every demonstration and every syllogism must be formed by means of the three syllogistical figures.[2]

This Aristotelian theory of proof has a fundamental flaw: it supposes that all problems can be expressed by the four kinds of syllogistic premiss and that therefore the categorical syllogism is the only instrument of proof. Aristotle did not realize that his own theory of the syllogism is an instance against this conception. The syllogistic moods, being implications, are propositions of another kind than the syllogistic premisses, but nevertheless they are true propositions, and if any of them is not self-evident and indemonstrable it requires a proof to establish its truth. The proof, however, cannot be done by means of a categorical syllogism, because an implication does not have either a subject or a predicate, and it would be useless to look for a middle term between non-existent extremes. This is perhaps a subconscious cause of the special terminology Aristotle uses in the doctrine of the syllogistic figures. He does not speak of 'axioms' or 'basic truths' but of 'perfect syllogisms', and does not 'demonstrate' or 'prove' the imperfect syllogisms but 'reduces' them (ἀνάγει or ἀναλύει) to the perfect. The effects of this improper terminology persist till today. Keynes devotes to this matter a whole section of his *Formal Logic*, entitled 'Is Reduction an essential part of the Doctrine of the Syllogism?', and comes to the conclusion 'that reduction is not a necessary part of the doctrine of the syllogism, so far as the establishment of the validity of the different moods is concerned'.[3] This conclusion cannot be applied to the Aristotelian theory of the syllogism, as this theory is an axiomatized deductive system, and the reduction of the other syllogistic moods to those of the first figure, i.e. their proof as theorems by means of the axioms, is an indispensable part of the system.

Aristotle accepts as perfect syllogisms the moods of the first

---

[1] *An. post.* i. 23, 84ᵇ19 φανερὸν δὲ καὶ ὅτι, ὅταν τὸ Α τῷ Β ὑπάρχῃ, εἰ μὲν ἔστι τι μέσον, ἔστι δεῖξαι ὅτι τὸ Α τῷ Β ὑπάρχει . . ., εἰ δὲ μή ἐστιν, οὐκέτι ἐστιν ἀπόδειξις, ἀλλ' ἡ ἐπὶ τὰς ἀρχὰς ὁδὸς αὕτη ἐστίν.

[2] *An. pr.* i. 23, 41ᵇ1 πᾶσαν ἀπόδειξιν καὶ πάντα συλλογισμὸν ἀνάγκη γίνεσθαι διὰ τριῶν τῶν προειρημένων σχημάτων.   [3] Op. cit., pp. 325–7.

figure, called Barbara, Celarent, Darii, and Ferio.[1] Yet in the
last chapter of his systematic exposition he reduces the third and
fourth moods to the first two, and takes therefore as axioms of his
theory the most clearly evident syllogisms, Barbara and Celarent.[2] This detail is of no little interest. Modern formal logic tends
to reduce the number of axioms in a deductive theory to a
minimum, and this is a tendency which has its first exponent in
Aristotle.

Aristotle is right when he says that only two syllogisms are
needed as axioms to build up the whole theory of the syllogism.
He forgets, however, that the laws of conversion, which he uses
to reduce the imperfect moods to the perfect ones, also belong to
his theory and cannot be proved by means of the syllogisms.
There are three laws of conversion mentioned in the *Prior
Analytics*: the conversion of the *E*-premiss, of the *A*-premiss, and
of the *I*-premiss. Aristotle proves the first of these laws by what
he calls ecthesis, which requires, as we shall see later, a logical
process lying outside the limits of the syllogistic. As it cannot be
proved otherwise, it must be stated as a new axiom of the system.
The conversion of the *A*-premiss is proved by a thesis belonging
to the square of opposition of which there is no mention in the
Prior Analytics. We must therefore accept as a fourth axiom either
this law of conversion or the thesis of the square of opposition,
from which this law follows. Only the law of conversion of the
I-premisses can be proved without a new axiom.

There are still two theses that have to be taken into account,
although neither of them is explicitly stated by Aristotle, viz. the
laws of identity: '*A* belongs to all *A*' and '*A* belongs to some *A*'.
The first of these laws is independent of all other theses of the
syllogistic. If we want to have this law in the system, we must
accept it axiomatically. The second law of identity can be
derived from the first.

Modern formal logic distinguishes in a deductive system not
only between primitive and derivative propositions, but also
between primitive and defined terms. The constants of the
Aristotelian syllogistic are the four relations: 'to belong to all'

---

[1] At the end of chapter 4, containing the moods of the first figure, Aristotle says,
An. Pr. i. 4, 26^{b}29 δῆλον δὲ καὶ ὅτι πάντες οἱ ἐν αὐτῷ συλλογισμοὶ τέλειοί εἰσιν.
[2] Ibid. 7, 29^{b}1 ἔστι δὲ καὶ ἀναγαγεῖν πάντας τοὺς συλλογισμοὺς εἰς τοὺς ἐν τῷ
πρώτῳ σχήματι καθόλου συλλογισμούς.

or A, 'to belong to none' or E, 'to belong to some' or I, and 'to not-belong to some' or O. Two of them may be defined by the other two by means of propositional negation in the following way: 'A does not belong to some B' means the same as 'It is not true that A belongs to all B', and 'A belongs to no B' means the same as 'It is not true that A belongs to some B'. In the same manner A could be defined by O, and I by E. Aristotle does not introduce these definitions into his system, but he uses them intuitively as arguments of his proofs. Let us quote as only one example the proof of conversion of the I-premiss. It runs as follows: 'If A belongs to some B, then B must belong to some A. For if B should belong to no A, A would belong to no B.'[1] It is obvious that in this indirect proof Aristotle treats the negation of 'B belongs to some A' as equivalent to 'B belongs to no A'. As to the other pair, A and O, Alexander says explicitly that the phrases 'to not-belong to some' and 'to not-belong to all' are different only in words, but have equivalent meanings.[2]

If we accept as primitive terms of the system the relations A and I, defining E and O by means of them, we may, as I stated many years ago,[3] build up the whole theory of the Aristotelian syllogism on the following four axioms:

1. A belongs to all A.
2. A belongs to some A.
3. If A belongs to all B and B belongs to all C, then A belongs to all C.   Barbara
4. If A belongs to all B and C belongs to some B, then A belongs to some C.   Datisi

It is impossible to reduce the number of these axioms. In particular they cannot be derived from the so-called *dictum de omni et nullo*. This principle is differently formulated in different text-books of logic, and always very vaguely. The classic formulation, 'quidquid de omnibus valet, valet etiam de quibusdam et de singulis' and 'quidquid de nullo valet, nec de quibusdam nec de

---

[1] *An. pr.* i. 2, 25ᵃ20 εἰ γὰρ τὸ A τινὶ τῷ B, καὶ τὸ B τινὶ τῷ A ἀνάγκη ὑπάρχειν. εἰ γὰρ μηδενί, οὐδὲ τὸ A οὐδενὶ τῷ B. [Corr. by W. D. Ross.]

[2] Alexander 84. 6 τὸ τινὶ μὴ ὑπάρχειν ἴσον δυνάμενον τῷ μὴ παντὶ κατὰ τὴν λέξιν διαφέρει.

[3] J. Łukasiewicz, *Elementy logiki matematycznej* (Elements of Mathematical Logic), edited by M. Presburger (mimeographed), Warsaw (1929), p. 172; 'Znaczenie analizy logicznej dla poznania' (Importance of Logical Analysis for Knowledge), *Przegl. Filoz.* (*Philosophical Review*), vol. xxxvii, Warsaw (1934), p. 373.

singulis valet', cannot be strictly applied to the Aristotelian logic, as singular terms and propositions do not belong to it. Besides, I do not see how it would be possible to deduce from this principle the laws of identity and the mood Datisi, if anything at all can be deduced from it. Moreover, it is evident that it is not one single principle but two. It must be emphasized that Aristotle is by no means responsible for this obscure principle. It is not true that the *dictum de omni et nullo* was given by Aristotle as the axiom on which all syllogistic inference is based, as Keynes asserts.[1] It is nowhere formulated in the *Prior Analytics* as a principle of syllogistic. What is sometimes quoted as a formulation of this principle is only an explanation of the words 'to be predicated of all' and 'of none'.[2]

It is a vain attempt to look for the principle of the Aristotelian logic, if 'principle' means the same as 'axiom'. If it has another meaning, I do not understand the problem at all. Maier, who has devoted to this subject another obscure chapter of his book,[3] spins out philosophic speculations that neither have a basis in themselves nor are supported by texts of the *Prior Analytics*. From the standpoint of logic they are useless.

§ 16. *The logic of terms and the logic of propositions*

To this day there exists no exact logical analysis of the proofs Aristotle gives to reduce the imperfect syllogisms to the perfect. The old historians of logic, like Prantl and Maier, were philosophers and knew only the 'philosophical logic' which in the nineteenth century, with very few exceptions, was below a scientific level. Prantl and Maier are now dead, but perhaps it would not be impossible to persuade living philosophers that they should cease to write about logic or its history before having acquired a solid knowledge of what is called 'mathematical logic'. It would otherwise be a waste of time for them as well as for their readers. It seems to me that this point is of no small practical importance.

No one can fully understand Aristotle's proofs who does not know that there exists besides the Aristotelian system another system of logic more fundamental than the theory of the syllogism.

---

[1] Op. cit., p. 301.

[2] *An. pr.* i. 1, 24^{b}28 λέγομεν δὲ τὸ κατὰ παντὸς κατηγορεῖσθαι, ὅταν μηδὲν ᾖ λαβεῖν [τοῦ ὑποκειμένου (secl. W. D. Ross)], καθ' οὗ θάτερον οὐ λεχθήσεται· καὶ τὸ κατὰ μηδενὸς ὡσαύτως.   [3] Op. cit., vol. ii *b*, p. 149.

It is the logic of propositions. Let us explain by an example the difference between the logic of terms, of which the Aristotelian logic is only a part, and the logic of propositions. Besides the Aristotelian law of identity 'A belongs to all A' or 'All A is A', we have still another law of identity of the form 'If p, then p'. Let us compare these two, which are the simplest logical formulae:

$$\text{All } A \text{ is } A \qquad \text{and} \qquad \text{If } p, \text{ then } p.$$

They differ in their constants, which I call functors: in the first formula the functor reads 'all—is', in the second 'if—then'. Both are functors of two arguments which are here identical. But the main difference lies in the arguments. In both formulae the arguments are variables, but of a different kind: the values which may be substituted for the variable A are terms, like 'man' or 'plant'. From the first formula we get thus the propositions 'All men are men' or 'All plants are plants'. The values of the variable p are not terms but propositions, like 'Dublin lies on the Liffey' or 'Today is Friday'; we get, therefore, from the second formula the propositions: 'If Dublin lies on the Liffey, then Dublin lies on the Liffey' or 'If today is Friday, then today is Friday'. This difference between term-variables and proposition-variables is the primary difference between the two formulae and consequently between the two systems of logic, and, as propositions and terms belong to different semantical categories, the difference is a fundamental one.

The first system of propositional logic was invented about half a century after Aristotle: it was the logic of the Stoics. This logic is not a system of theses but of rules of inference. The so-called *modus ponens*, now called the rule of detachment: 'If α, then β; but α; therefore β' is one of the most important primitive rules of the Stoic logic. The variables α and β are propositional variables, as only propositions can be significantly substituted for them.[1] The modern system of the logic of propositions was created only in 1879 by the great German logician Gottlob Frege. Another outstanding logician of the nineteenth century, the American Charles Sanders Peirce, made important contributions to this logic by his discovery of logical matrices (1885). The authors of *Principia Mathematica*, Whitehead and Russell, later put this

[1] Cf. Łukasiewicz, 'Zur Geschichte des Aussagenkalküls', *Erkenntnis*, vol. v, Leipzig (1935), pp. 111–31.

system of logic at the head of all mathematics under the title 'Theory of Deduction'. All this was entirely unknown to philosophers of the nineteenth century. To this day they seem to have no idea of the logic of propositions. Maier says that the Stoic logic, which in fact is a masterpiece equal to the logic of Aristotle, yields a poor and barren picture of formalistic-grammatical unsteadiness and lack of principle, and adds in a footnote that the unfavourable judgement of Prantl and Zeller on this logic must be maintained.[1] The *Encyclopaedia Britannica* of 1911 says briefly of the logic of the Stoics that 'their corrections and fancied improvements of the Aristotelian logic are mostly useless and pedantic'.[2]

It seems that Aristotle did not suspect the existence of another system of logic besides his theory of the syllogism. Yet he uses intuitively the laws of propositional logic in his proofs of imperfect syllogisms, and even sets forth explicitly three statements belonging to this logic in Book II of the *Prior Analytics*. The first of these is a law of transposition : 'When two things', he says, 'are so related to one another, that if the one is, the other necessarily is, then if the latter is not, the former will not be either.'[3] That means, in terms of modern logic, that whenever an implication of the form 'If α, then β ' is true, then there must also be true another implication of the form 'If not-β, then not-α'. The second is the law of the hypothetical syllogism. Aristotle explains it by an example : 'Whenever if *A* is white, then *B* should be necessarily great, and if *B* is great, then *C* should not be white, then it is necessary if *A* is white that *C* should not be white.'[4] That means : whenever two implications of the form 'If α, then β ' and 'If β, then γ ' are true, then there must also be true a third implication 'If α, then γ '. The third statement is an application of the two foregoing laws to a new example and, curiously enough, it is false. This very interesting passage runs thus :

'It is impossible that the same thing should be necessitated by the being and by the not-being of the same thing. I mean, for example,

---

[1] Maier, op. cit., vol. ii *b*, p. 384: 'In der Hauptsache jedoch bietet die Logik der Stoiker . . . ein dürftiges, ödes Bild formalistisch-grammatischer Prinzip- und Haltlosigkeit.' Ibid., n. 1 : 'In der Hauptsache wird es bei dem ungünstigen Urteil, das Prantl und Zeller über die stoische Logik fällen, bleiben müssen.'

[2] 11th ed., Cambridge (1911), vol. xxv, p. 946 (s.v. 'Stoics').

[3] *An. pr.* ii. 4, 57ᵇ1 ὅταν δύο ἔχῃ οὕτω πρὸς ἄλληλα ὥστε θατέρου ὄντος ἐξ ἀνάγκης εἶναι θάτερον, τούτου μὴ ὄντος μὲν οὐδὲ θάτερον ἔσται.

[4] Ibid. 6 ὅταν γὰρ τουδὶ ὄντος λευκοῦ τοῦ *A* τοδὶ ἀνάγκη μέγα εἶναι τὸ *B*, μεγάλου δὲ τοῦ *B* ὄντος τὸ *Γ* μὴ λευκόν, ἀνάγκη, εἰ τὸ *A* λευκόν, τὸ *Γ* μὴ εἶναι λευκόν.

that it is impossible that B should necessarily be great if A is white, and that B should necessarily be great if A is not white. For if B is not great A cannot be white. But if, when A is not white, it is necessary that B should be great, it necessarily results that if B is not great, B itself is great. But this is impossible.'[1]

Although the example chosen by Aristotle is unfortunate, the sense of his argument is clear. In terms of modern logic it can be stated thus : Two implications of the form 'If α, then β ' and 'If not-α, then β ' cannot be together true. For by the law of transposition we get from the first implication the premiss 'If not-β, then not-α', and this premiss yields together with the second implication the conclusion 'If not-β, then β ' by the law of the hypothetical syllogism. According to Aristotle this conclusion is impossible.

Aristotle's final remark is erroneous. The implication 'If not-β, then β ', the antecedent of which is the negation of the consequent, is not impossible; it may be true, and yields as conclusion the consequent β, according to the law of the logic of propositions : 'If (if not-p, then p), then p.'[2] Commenting upon this passage, Maier says that there would here result a connexion contrary to the law of contradiction and therefore absurd.[3] This comment again reveals Maier's ignorance of logic. It is not the implication 'If not-β, then β ' that is contrary to the law of contradiction, but only the conjunction ' β and not-β '.

A few years after Aristotle, the mathematician Euclid gave a proof of a mathematical theorem which implies the thesis 'If (if not-p, then p), then p'.[4] He states first that 'If the product of two

---

[1] *An. pr.* ii. 4, 57ᵇ3 τοῦ δ' αὐτοῦ ὄντος καὶ μὴ ὄντος, ἀδύνατον ἐξ ἀνάγκης εἶναι τὸ αὐτό. λέγω δ' οἷον τοῦ A ὄντος λευκοῦ τὸ B εἶναι μέγα ἐξ ἀνάγκης, καὶ μὴ ὄντος λευκοῦ τοῦ A τὸ B εἶναι μέγα ἐξ ἀνάγκης. Here follows the example of the hypothetical syllogism quoted in p. 49, n. 4, and a second formulation of the law of transposition. The conclusion reads, 11 τοῦ δὴ B μὴ ὄντος μεγάλου τὸ A οὐχ οἷόν τε λευκὸν εἶναι. τοῦ δὲ A μὴ ὄντος λευκοῦ, εἰ ἀνάγκη τὸ B μέγα εἶναι, συμβαίνει ἐξ ἀνάγκης τοῦ B μεγάλου μὴ ὄντος αὐτὸ τὸ B εἶναι μέγα. τοῦτο δ' ἀδύνατον.

[2] See A. N. Whitehead and B. Russell, *Principia Mathematica*, vol. i, Cambridge (1910), p. 1 08, thesis *2·18.

[3] Op. cit., vol. ii *a*, p. 331 : 'Es ergäbe sich also ein Zusammenhang, der dem Gesetze des Widerspruchs entgegenstünde und darum absurd wäre.'

[4] See *Scritti di G. Vailati*, Leipzig-Firenze, cxv. 'A proposito d'un passo del Teeteto e di una dimostrazione di Euclide', pp. 516–27; cf. Łukasiewicz, 'Philosophische Bemerkungen zu mehrwertigen Systemen des Aussagenkalküls', *Comptes Rendus des séances de la Société des Sciences et des Lettres de Varsovie*, xxiii (1930), Cl. III, p. 67.

integers, *a* and *b*, is divisible by a prime number *n*, then if *a* is not divisible by *n*, *b* should be divisible by *n'*. Let us now suppose that *a* = *b* and the product *a* × *a* (*a*²) is divisible by *n*. It results from this supposition that 'If *a* is not divisible by *n*, then *a* is divisible by *n'*. Here we have an example of a true implication the antecedent of which is the negation of the consequent. From this implication Euclid derives the theorem: 'If *a*² is divisible by a prime number *n*, then *a* is divisible by *n*.'

§ 17. *The proofs by conversion*

The proofs of imperfect syllogisms by conversion of a premiss are both the simplest and those most frequently employed by Aristotle. Let us analyse two examples. The proof of the mood Festino of the second figure runs thus: 'If *M* belongs to no *N*, but to some *X*, then it is necessary that *N* should not belong to some *X*. For since the negative premiss is convertible, *N* will belong to no *M*; but *M* was admitted to belong to some *X*; therefore *N* will not belong to some *X*. The conclusion is reached by means of the first figure.'[1]

The proof is based on two premisses: one of them is the law of conversion of the *E*-propositions:

(1) If *M* belongs to no *N*, then *N* belongs to no *M*,

and the other is the mood Ferio of the first figure:

(2) If *N* belongs to no *M* and *M* belongs to some *X*, then *N* does not belong to some *X*.

From these premisses we have to derive the mood Festino:

(3) If *M* belongs to no *N* and *M* belongs to some *X*, then *N* does not belong to some *X*.

Aristotle performs the proof intuitively. Analysing his intuitions we find two theses of the propositional calculus: one of them is the above-mentioned law of the hypothetical syllogism, which may be stated in the following form:

(4) If (if *p*, then *q*), then [if (if *q*, then *r*), then (if *p*, then *r*)];[2]

---

[1] *An. pr.* i. 5, 27ᵃ32 εἰ γὰρ τὸ *M* τῷ μὲν *N* μηδενὶ τῷ δὲ *Ξ* τινὶ ὑπάρχει, ἀνάγκη τὸ *N* τινὶ τῷ *Ξ* μὴ ὑπάρχειν. ἐπεὶ γὰρ ἀντιστρέφει τὸ στερητικόν, οὐδενὶ τῷ *M* ὑπάρξει τὸ *N·* τὸ δέ γε *M* ὑπέκειτο τινὶ τῷ *Ξ* ὑπάρχειν· ὥστε τὸ *N* τινὶ τῷ *Ξ* οὐχ ὑπάρξει. γίνεται γὰρ συλλογισμὸς διὰ τοῦ πρώτου σχήματος.

[2] See *Principia Mathematica*, p. 104, thesis *2·06.

The other thesis reads:

(5) If (if p, then q), then (if p and r, then q and r).

This thesis is called in *Principia Mathematica*, following Peano, the principle of the factor. It shows that we may 'multiply' both sides of an implication by a common factor, i.e. we may add, by means of the word 'and', to p and to q a new proposition r.[1]

We start with thesis (5). As p, q, and r are propositional variables, we may substitute for them premisses of the Aristotelian logic. Putting 'M belongs to no N' for p, 'N belongs to no M' for q, and 'M belongs to some X' for r, we get from the antecedent of (5) the law of conversion (1), and we may detach the consequent of (5) as a new thesis. This new thesis has the form:

(6) If M belongs to no N and M belongs to some X, then N belongs to no M and M belongs to some X.

The consequent of this thesis is identical with the antecedent of thesis (2). Therefore we may apply to (6) and (2) the law of the hypothetical syllogism, substituting for p the conjunction 'M belongs to no N and M belongs to some X', for q the conjunction 'N belongs to no M and M belongs to some X', and for r the proposition 'N does not belong to some X'. By applying the rule of detachment twice we get from this new thesis the mood Festino.

The second example I want to analyse is somewhat different. It is the above-mentioned proof of the mood Disamis.[2] We have to prove the following imperfect syllogism:

(7) If R belongs to all S and P belongs to some S, then P belongs to some R.

The proof is based on the mood Darii of the first figure:

(8) If R belongs to all S and S belongs to some P, then R belongs to some P,

and on the law of conversion of the I-propositions applied twice, once in the form:

(9) If P belongs to some S, then S belongs to some P,

and for the second time in the form:

(10) If R belongs to some P, then P belongs to some R.

As auxiliary theses of the propositional logic we have the law of

---

[1] See *Principia Mathematica*, p. 119, thesis *3.45. The conjunction 'p and r' is called in the *Principia* 'logical product'.   [2] See the Greek text in p. 25, n. 1.

the hypothetical syllogism, and the following thesis, which is slightly different from thesis (5), but also may be called the principle of the factor:

(11) If (if p, then q), then (if r and p, then r and q).

The difference between (5) and (11) consists in this, that the common factor r is not in the second place, as in (5), but in the first. As conjunction is commutable and 'p and r' is equivalent to 'r and p', this difference does not affect the validity of the thesis.

The proof given by Aristotle begins with the conversion of the premiss 'P belongs to some S'. Following this procedure, let us substitute for p in (11) the premiss 'P belongs to some S', for q the premiss 'S belongs to some P', and for r the premiss 'R belongs to all S'. By this substitution we get from the antecedent of (11) the law of conversion (9), and therefore we may detach the consequent of (11) which reads:

(12) If R belongs to all S and P belongs to some S, then R belongs to all S and S belongs to some P.

The consequent of (12) is identical with the antecedent of (8). By applying the law of the hypothetical syllogism we can get from (12) and (8) the syllogism:

(13) If R belongs to all S and P belongs to some S, then R belongs to some P.

This syllogism, however, is not the required mood Disamis, but Datisi. Of course, the mood Disamis could be derived from Datisi by converting its consequent according to thesis (10), i.e. by applying the hypothetical syllogism to (13) and (10). It seems, however, that Aristotle took another course: instead of deriving Datisi and converting its conclusion, he converts the conclusion of Darii, getting the syllogism:

(14) If R belongs to all S and S belongs to some P, then P belongs to some R,

and then he applies intuitively the law of the hypothetical syllogism to (12) and (14). The syllogism (14) is a mood of the fourth figure called Dimaris. As we already know, Aristotle mentions this mood at the beginning of Book II of the *Prior Analytics*.

In a similar way we could analyse all the other proofs by conversion. It follows from this analysis that if we add to the perfect syllogisms of the first figure and to the laws of conversion three laws of the logic of propositions, viz. the law of the hypothetical syllogism and two laws of the factor, we get strictly formalized proofs of all imperfect syllogisms except Baroco and Bocardo. These two moods require other theses of the propositional logic.

§ 18. *The proofs by* reductio ad impossibile

The moods Baroco and Bocardo cannot be reduced to the first figure by conversion. The conversion of the *A*-premiss would yield an *I*-proposition, from which together with the *O*-premiss nothing results, and the *O*-premiss cannot be converted. Aristotle tries to prove these two moods by a *reductio ad impossibile*, ἀπαγωγή εἰς τὸ ἀδύνατον. The proof of Baroco runs thus: 'If *M* belongs to all *N*, but not to some *X*, it is necessary that *N* should not belong to some *X*; for if *N* belongs to all *X*, and *M* is predicated also of all *N*, *M* must belong to all *X*; but it was assumed that *M* does not belong to some *X*.'[1] This proof is very concise and needs an explanation. Usually it is explained in the following way:[2]

We have to prove the syllogism:

(1) If *M* belongs to all *N* and *M* does not belong to some *X*, then *N* does not belong to some *X*.

It is admitted that the premisses '*M* belongs to all *N*' and '*M* does not belong to some *X*' are true; then the conclusion '*N* does not belong to some *X*' must also be true. For if it were false, its contradictory, '*N* belongs to all *X*', would be true. This last proposition is the starting-point of our reduction. As it is admitted that the premiss '*M* belongs to all *N*' is true, we get from this premiss and the propostion '*N* belongs to all *X*' the conclusion '*M* belongs to all *X*' by the mood Barbara. But this conclusion is false, for it is admitted that its contradictory '*M* does not belong to some *X*' is true. Therefore the starting-point of our reduction, '*N* belongs to all *X*', which leads to a false conclusion, must be false, and its contradictory, '*N* does not belong to some *X*', must be true.

This argument is only apparently convincing; in fact it does not prove the above syllogism. It can be applied only to the traditional mood Baroco (I quote this mood in its usual form

---

[1] *An. pr.* i. 5, 27ᵃ37 εἰ τῷ μὲν Ν παντὶ τὸ Μ, τῷ δὲ Ξ τινὶ μὴ ὑπάρχει, ἀνάγκη τὸ Ν τινὶ τῷ Ξ μὴ ὑπάρχειν· εἰ γὰρ παντὶ ὑπάρχει, κατηγορεῖται δὲ καὶ τὸ Μ παντὸς τοῦ Ν, ἀνάγκη τὸ Μ παντὶ τῷ Ξ ὑπάρχειν· ὑπέκειτο δὲ τινὶ μὴ ὑπάρχειν.

[2] Cf., for instance, Maier, op. cit., vol. ii *a*, p. 84.

with the verb 'to be', and not in the Aristotelian form with 'to belong') :

$$(2) \quad \text{All } N \text{ is } M,$$
$$\text{Some } X \text{ is not } M,$$
$$\text{therefore}$$
$$\text{Some } X \text{ is not } N.$$

This is a rule of inference and allows us to assert the conclusion provided the premisses are true. It does not say what happens when the premisses are not true. This is irrelevant for a rule of inference, as it is evident that an inference based on false premisses cannot be valid. But Aristotelian syllogisms are not rules of inference, they are propositions. The syllogism (1) is an implication which is true for all values of the variables M, N, and X, and not only for those values that verify the premisses. If we apply this mood Baroco to the terms $M =$ 'bird', $N =$ 'animal', and $X =$ 'owl', we get a true syllogism (I use forms with 'to be', as does Aristotle in examples) :

$$(3) \quad \text{If all animals are birds}$$
$$\text{and some owls are not birds,}$$
$$\text{then some owls are not animals.}$$

This is an example of the mood Baroco, because it results from it by substitution. The above argument, however, cannot be applied to this syllogism. We cannot admit that the premisses are true, because the propositions 'All animals are birds' and 'Some owls are not birds' are certainly false. We need not suppose that the conclusion is false; it is false whether we suppose its falsity or not. But the main point is that the contradictory of the conclusion, i.e. the proposition 'All owls are animals', yields together with the first premiss 'All animals are birds' not a false conclusion, but a true one: 'All owls are birds'. The *reductio ad impossibile* is in this case impossible.

The proof given by Aristotle is neither sufficient nor a proof by *reductio ad impossibile*. Aristotle describes indirect proof or the demonstration *per impossibile*, by contrast with direct or ostensive proof, as a proof that posits what it wishes to refute, i.e. to refute by reduction to a statement admitted to be false, whereas ostensive proof starts from propositions admitted to be true.[1] Accordingly,

---

[1] *An. pr.* ii. 14, 62ᵇ29 διαφέρει δ' ἡ εἰς τὸ ἀδύνατον ἀπόδειξις τῆς δεικτικῆς τῷ τιθέναι ὃ βούλεται ἀναιρεῖν, ἀπάγουσα εἰς ὁμολογούμενον ψεῦδος· ἡ δὲ δεικτικὴ ἄρχεται ἐξ ὁμολογουμένων θέσεων (ἀληθῶν).

if we have to prove a proposition by *reductio ad impossibile*, we must start from its negation and derive thence a statement obviously false. The indirect proof of the mood Baroco should start from the negation of this mood, and not from the negation of its conclusion, and this negation should lead to an unconditionally false statemen⸲, and not to a proposition that is admitted to be false only under certain conditions. I shall here give a sketch of such a proof. Let α denote the proposition '*M* belongs to all *N*', β '*N* belongs to all *X*', and γ '*M* belongs to all *X*'. As the negation of an *A*-premiss is an *O*-premiss, 'not-β '[1] will have the meaning '*N* does not belong to some *X*', and 'not-γ ' '*M* does not belong to some *X*'. According to the mood Baroco the implication 'If α and not-γ, then not-β ' is true, or in other words, α and not-γ are not true together with β. The negation, therefore, of this proposition would mean that ' α and β and not-γ ' are together true. But from ' α and β ', ' γ ' results by the mood Barbara; we get therefore ' γ and not-γ ', i.e. a proposition obviously false, being a contradiction *in forma*. It can easily be seen that this genuine proof of the mood Baroco by *reductio ad impossibile* is quite different from that given by Aristotle.

The mood Baroco can be proved from the mood Barbara by a very simple ostensive proof which requires one and only one thesis of the propositional logic. It is the following compound law of transposition :

(4) If (if *p* and *q*, then *r*), then if *p* and it is not true that *r*, then it is not true that *q*.[2]

Put for *p* '*M* belongs to all *N*', for *q* '*N* belongs to all *X*', and for *r* '*M* belongs to all *X*'. By this substitution we get in the antecedent of (4) the mood Barbara, and therefore we can detach the consequent, which reads :

(5) If *M* belongs to all *N* and it is not true that *M* belongs to all *X*, then it is not true that *N* belongs to all *X*.

As the *O*-premiss is the negation of the *A*-premiss, we may replace in (5) the forms 'it is not true that belongs to all' by 'does not belong to some', getting thus the mood Baroco.

There can be no doubt that Aristotle knew the law of transposition referred to in the above proof. This law is closely con-

[1] I am using 'not-' as an abbreviation for the propositional negation 'it is not true that'.   [2] See *Principia Mathematica*, p. 118, thesis *3·37.

nected with the so-called 'conversion' of the syllogism, which he investigated thoroughly.[1] To convert a syllogism means to take the contrary or the contradictory (in proofs *per impossibile* only the contradictory) of the conclusion together with one premiss, thereby destroying the other premiss. 'It is necessary,' Aristotle says, 'if the conclusion has been converted and one of the premisses stands, that the other premiss should be destroyed. For if it should stand, the conclusion must also stand.'[2] This is a description of the compound law of transposition. Aristotle therefore knows this law; moreover, he applies it to obtain from the mood Barbara the moods Baroco and Bocardo. Investigating in the same chapter the conversion of the moods of the first figure, he says: 'Let the syllogism be affirmative (i.e. Barbara), and let it be converted as stated (i.e. by the contradictory denial). Then if *A* does not belong to all *C*, but to all *B*, *B* will not belong to all *C*. And if *A* does not belong to all *C*, but *B* belongs to all *C*, *A* will not belong to all *B*.'[3] The proofs of Baroco and Bocardo are here given in their simplest form.

In the systematic exposition of the syllogistic these valid proofs are replaced by insufficient demonstrations *per impossibile*. The reason is, I suppose, that Aristotle does not recognize arguments ἐξ ὑποθέσεως as instruments of genuine proof. All demonstration is for him proof by categorical syllogisms; he is anxious to show that the proof *per impossibile* is a genuine proof in so far as it contains at least a part that is a categorical syllogism. Analysing the proof of the theorem that the side of a square is incommensurable with its diagonal, he states explicitly: We know by a syllogism that the contradictory of this theorem would lead to an absurd consequence, viz. that odd numbers should be equal to evens, but the theorem itself is proved by an hypothesis, since a falsehood results when it is denied.[4] Of the same kind, Aristotle

---

[1] *An. pr.* ii. 8–10.

[2] Ibid. 8, 59^{b}3 ἀνάγκη γὰρ τοῦ συμπεράσματος ἀντιστραφέντος καὶ τῆς ἑτέρας μενούσης προτάσεως ἀναιρεῖσθαι τὴν λοιπήν· εἰ γὰρ ἔσται, καὶ τὸ συμπέρασμα ἔσται. Cf. *Top.* viii. 14, 163^{a}34 ἀνάγκη γάρ, εἰ τὸ συμπέρασμα μή ἐστι, μίαν τινα ἀναιρεῖσθαι τῶν προτάσεων, εἴπερ πασῶν τεθεισῶν ἀνάγκη ἦν τὸ συμπέρασμα εἶναι.

[3] *An. pr.* ii. 8, 59^{b}28 ἔστω γὰρ κατηγορικὸς ὁ συλλογισμός, καὶ ἀντιστρεφέσθω οὕτως (i.e. ἀντικειμένως). οὐκοῦν εἰ τὸ Α οὐ παντὶ τῷ Γ, τῷ δὲ Β παντί, τὸ Β οὐ παντὶ τῷ Γ· καὶ εἰ τὸ μὲν Α μὴ παντὶ τῷ Γ, τὸ δὲ Β παντί, τὸ Α οὐ παντὶ τῷ Β.

[4] Ibid. i. 23, 41^{a}23 πάντες γὰρ οἱ διὰ τοῦ ἀδυνάτου περαίνοντες τὸ μὲν ψεῦδος συλλογίζονται, τὸ δ' ἐξ ἀρχῆς ἐξ ὑποθέσεως δεικνύουσιν, ὅταν ἀδύνατόν τι συμβαίνῃ τῆς ἀντιφάσεως τεθείσης, οἷον ὅτι ἀσύμμετρος ἡ διάμετρος διὰ τὸ γίνεσθαι τὰ περιττὰ ἴσα

concludes, are all other hypothetical arguments; for in every case the syllogism leads to a proposition that is different from the original thesis, and the original thesis is reached by an admission or some other hypothesis.[1] All this is, of course, not true; Aristotle does not understand the nature of hypothetical arguments. The proof of Baroco and Bocardo by the law of transposition is not reached by an admission or some other hypothesis, but performed by an evident logical law; besides, it is certainly a proof of one categorical syllogism on the ground of another, but it is not performed by a categorical syllogism.

At the end of Book I of the *Prior Analytics* Aristotle remarks that there are many hypothetical arguments that ought to be considered and described, and promises to do so in the sequel.[2] This promise he nowhere fulfils.[3] It was reserved for the Stoics to include the theory of hypothetical arguments in their system of propositional logic, in which the compound law of transposition found its proper place. On the occasion of an argument of Aenesidemus (which is irrelevant for our purpose) the Stoics analysed the following rule of inference which corresponds to the compound law of transposition: 'If the first and the second, then the third; but not the third, yet the first; therefore not the second.'[4] This rule is reduced to the second and third indemonstrable syllogisms of the Stoic logic. We already know the first indemonstrable syllogism, it is the *modus ponens*; the second is the *modus tollens*: 'If the first, then the second; but not the second; therefore not the first.' The third indemonstrable syllogism starts from a denied conjunction and reads: 'Not (the first and the second); but the first; therefore not the second.' According to Sextus Empiricus the analysis runs thus: By the second indemonstrable syllogism we get from the implication 'if the first and the second,

τοῖς ἀρτίοις συμμέτρου τεθείσης. τὸ μὲν οὖν ἴσα γίνεσθαι τὰ περιττὰ τοῖς ἀρτίοις συλλογίζεται, τὸ δ' ἀσύμμετρον εἶναι τὴν διάμετρον ἐξ ὑποθέσεως δείκνυσιν, ἐπεὶ ψεῦδος συμβαίνει διὰ τὴν ἀντίφασιν.

[1] *An. pr.* i. 23, 41ᵃ37 ὡσαύτως δὲ καὶ οἱ ἄλλοι πάντες οἱ ἐξ ὑποθέσεως· ἐν ἅπασι γὰρ ὁ μὲν συλλογισμὸς γίνεται πρὸς τὸ μεταλαμβανόμενον, τὸ δ' ἐξ ἀρχῆς περαίνεται δι' ὁμολογίας ἤ τινος ἄλλης ὑποθέσεως.

[2] *Ibid.* 44, 50ᵃ39 πολλοὶ δὲ καὶ ἕτεροι περαίνονται ἐξ ὑποθέσεως, οὓς ἐπισκέψασθαι δεῖ καὶ διασημῆναι καθαρῶς. τίνες μὲν οὖν αἱ διαφοραὶ τούτων, καὶ ποσαχῶς γίνεται τὸ ἐξ ὑποθέσεως, ὕστερον ἐροῦμεν.

[3] Alexander 389. 32, commenting on this passage says: λέγει καὶ ἄλλους πολλοὺς ἐξ ὑποθέσεως περαίνεσθαι, περὶ ὧν ὑπεντίθεται μὲν ὡς ἐρῶν ἐπιμελέστερον, οὐ μὴν φέρεται αὐτοῦ σύγγραμμα περὶ αὐτῶν.

[4] The Stoics denote proposition-variables by ordinal numbers.

then the third', and the negation of its consequent 'not the third', the negation of its antecedent 'not (the first and the second)'. From this proposition, which is virtually contained in the premisses, but not explicitly expressed in words, together with the premiss 'the first', there follows the conclusion 'not the second' by the third indemonstrable syllogism.[1] This is one of the neatest arguments we owe to the Stoics. We see that competent logicians reasoned 2,000 years ago in the same way as we are doing today.

§ 19. *The proofs by ecthesis*

The proofs by conversion and *per impossibile* are sufficient to reduce all imperfect syllogisms to perfect ones. But there is still a third kind of proof given by Aristotle, viz. the so-called proofs by exposition or ἔκθεσις. Although of little importance for the system, they have an interest in themselves, and it is worth while to study them carefully.

There are only three passages in the *Prior Analytics* where Aristotle gives a short characterization of this kind of proof. The first is connected with the proof of conversion of the *E*-premiss, the second is a proof of the mood Darapti, the third of the mood Bocardo. The word ἐκθέσθαι occurs only in the second passage, but there can be no doubt that the other two passages also are meant as proofs by ecthesis.[2]

Let us begin with the first passage, which runs thus: 'If *A*

---

[1] Sextus Empiricus (ed. Mutschmann), *Adv. math.* viii. 235–6 συνέστηκε γὰρ ὁ τοιοῦτος λόγος (scil. ὁ παρὰ τῷ Αἰνησιδήμῳ ἐρωτηθείς) ἐκ δευτέρου ἀναποδείκτου καὶ τρίτου, καθὼς πάρεστι μαθεῖν ἐκ τῆς ἀναλύσεως, ἥτις σαφεστέρα μᾶλλον γενήσεται ἐπὶ τοῦ τρόπου ποιησαμένων ἡμῶν τὴν διδασκαλίαν, ἔχοντος οὕτως· ' εἰ τὸ πρῶτον καὶ τὸ δεύτερον, τὸ τρίτον· οὐχὶ δέ γε τὸ τρίτον, ἀλλὰ καὶ τὸ πρῶτον· οὐκ ἄρα τὸ δεύτερον.' ἐπεὶ γὰρ ἔχομεν συνημμένον ἐν ᾧ ἡγεῖται συμπεπλεγμένον ⟨τὸ⟩ ' τὸ πρῶτον καὶ τὸ δεύτερον ', λήγει δὲ ⟨τὸ⟩ ' τὸ τρίτον ', ἔχομεν δὲ καὶ τὸ ἀντικείμενον τοῦ λήγοντος τὸ ' οὐ τὸ τρίτον ', συναχθήσεται ἡμῖν καὶ τὸ ἀντικείμενον τοῦ ἡγουμένου τὸ ' οὐκ ἄρα τὸ πρῶτον καὶ τὸ δεύτερον ' δευτέρῳ ἀναποδείκτῳ. ἀλλὰ δὴ τοῦτο αὐτὸ κατὰ μὲν τὴν δύναμιν ἔγκειται τῷ λόγῳ, ἐπεὶ ἔχομεν τὰ συνακτικὰ αὐτοῦ λήμματα, κατὰ δὲ τὴν προφορὰν παρεῖται. ὅπερ τάξαντες μετὰ τοῦ λειπομένου λήμματος τοῦ ' τὸ πρῶτον ',* ἔξομεν συναγόμενον τὸ συμπέρασμα τὸ ' οὐκ ἄρα τὸ δεύτερον ' τρίτῳ ἀναποδείκτῳ. [* τοῦ πρώτου codd., τοῦ τρόπου Kochalsky, τοῦ ' τὸ πρῶτον ' scripsi. (τρόπος = mood expressed in variables, συνημμένον = implication, ἡγούμενον = antecedent, λῆγον = consequent, συμπεπλεγμένον = conjunction.)]

[2] There are two other passages dealing with ecthesis, *An. pr.* 30ᵃ6–14 and 30ᵇ31–40 (I owe this remark to Sir David Ross), but both are related to the scheme of modal syllogisms.

belongs to no *B*, neither will *B* belong to any *A*. For if it should belong to some, say *C*, it would not be true that *A* belongs to no *B*; for *C* is some of the *B*'s.'[1] The conversion of the *E*-premiss is here proved *per impossibile*, but this proof *per impossibile* is based on the conversion of the *I*-premiss which is proved by exposition. The proof by exposition requires the introduction of a new term, called the 'exposed term'; here it is *C*. Owing to the obscurity of the passage the very meaning of this *C* and of the logical structure of the proof can be reached only by conjecture. I shall try to explain the matter on the ground of modern formal logic.

We have to prove the law of conversion of the *I*-premiss: 'If *B* belongs to some *A*, then *A* belongs to some *B*.' Aristotle introduces for this purpose a new term, *C*; it follows from his words that *C* is included in *B* as well as in *A*, so that we get two premisses: '*B* belongs to all *C*' and '*A* belongs to all *C*'. From these premisses we can deduce syllogistically (by the mood Darapti) the conclusion '*A* belongs to some *B*'. This is the first interpretation given by Alexander.[2] But it may be objected that this interpretation presupposes the mood Darapti which is not yet proved. Alexander prefers, therefore, another interpretation which is not based on a syllogism: he maintains that the term *C* is a singular term given by perception, and the proof by exposition consists in a sort of perceptual evidence.[3] This explanation, however, which is accepted by Maier,[4] has no support in the text of the *Prior Analytics*: Aristotle does not say that *C* is an individual term. Moreover, a proof by perception is not a logical proof. If we

---

[1] *An. pr.* i. 2, 25ª15 εἰ οὖν μηδενὶ τῷ Β τὸ Α ὑπάρχει, οὐδὲ τῷ Α οὐδενὶ ὑπάρξει τὸ Β. εἰ γάρ τινι, οἷον τῷ Γ, οὐκ ἀληθὲς ἔσται τὸ μηδενὶ τῷ Β τὸ Α ὑπάρχειν· τὸ γὰρ Γ τῶν Β τί ἐστιν. [Corr. W. D. Ross.]

[2] Alexander 32. 12 εἰ γὰρ τὸ Β τινὶ τῷ Α ὑπάρχει ... ὑπαρχέτω τῷ Γ· ἔστω γὰρ τοῦτο τὶ τοῦ Α, ᾧ ὑπάρχει τὸ Β. ἔσται δὴ τὸ Γ ἐν ὅλῳ τῷ Β καὶ τὶ αὐτοῦ, καὶ τὸ Β κατὰ παντὸς τοῦ Γ· ταὐτὸν γὰρ τὸ ἐν ὅλῳ καὶ κατὰ παντός. ἀλλ' ἦν τὸ Γ τὶ τοῦ Α· ἐν ὅλῳ ἄρα καὶ τῷ Α τὸ Γ ἐστίν· εἰ δὲ ἐν ὅλῳ, κατὰ παντὸς αὐτοῦ ῥηθήσεται τὸ Α. ἦν δὲ τὸ Γ τὶ τοῦ Β· καὶ τὸ Α ἄρα κατὰ τινὸς τοῦ Β κατηγορηθήσεται.

[3] Ibid. 32 ἢ ἄμεινόν ἐστι καὶ οἰκειότατον τοῖς λεγομένοις τὸ δι' ἐκθέσεως καὶ αἰσθητικῶς λέγειν τὴν δεῖξιν γεγονέναι, ἀλλὰ μὴ τὸν εἰρημένον τρόπον μηδὲ συλλογιστικῶς. ὁ γὰρ διὰ τῆς ἐκθέσεως τρόπος δι' αἰσθήσεως γίνεται καὶ οὐ συλλογιστικῶς· τοιοῦτον γάρ τι λαμβάνεται τὸ Γ τὸ ἐκτιθέμενον, ὃ αἰσθητὸν ὂν μόριόν ἐστι τοῦ Α· εἰ γὰρ κατὰ μορίου τοῦ Α ὄντος τοῦ Γ αἰσθητοῦ τινος καὶ καθ' ἕκαστα λέγοιτο τὸ Β, εἴη ἂν καὶ τοῦ Β μόριον τὸ αὐτὸ Γ ὄν γε ἐν αὐτῷ· ὥστε τὸ Γ εἴη ἂν ἀμφοτέρων μόριον καὶ ἐν ἀμφοτέροις αὐτοῖς.

[4] Op. cit., vol. ii *a*, p. 20: 'Die Argumentation bedient sich also nicht eines Syllogismus, sondern des Hinweises auf den Augenschein.'

want to prove logically that the premiss '*B* belongs to some *A*' may be converted, and the proof is to be performed by means of a third term *C*, we must find a thesis that connects the above premiss with a proposition containing *C*.

It would not, of course, be true to say simply that if *B* belongs to some *A*, then *B* belongs to all *C* and *A* belongs to all *C*; but a little modification of the consequent of this implication easily solves our problem. We must put before the consequent an existential quantifier, the words 'there exists', binding the variable *C*. For if *B* belongs to some *A*, there always exists a term *C* such that *B* belongs to all *C* and *A* belongs to all *C*. *C* may be the common part of *A* and *B* or a term included in this common part. If, for example, some Greeks are philosophers, there exists a common part of the terms 'Greek' and 'philosopher', viz. 'Greek philosopher', and it is evident that all Greek philosophers are Greeks, and all Greek philosophers are philosophers. We may state, therefore, the following thesis:

(1) If *B* belongs to some *A*, then there exists a *C* such that *B* belongs to all *C* and *A* belongs to all *C*.

This thesis is evident. But also the converse of (1) is evident. If there exists a common part of *A* and *B*, *B* must belong to some *A*. We get, therefore:

(2) If there exists a *C* such that *B* belongs to all *C* and *A* belongs to all *C*, then *B* belongs to some *A*.

It is probable that Aristotle intuitively felt the truth of these theses without being able to formulate them explicitly, and that he grasped their connexion with the conversion of the *I*-premiss without seeing all the deductive steps leading to this result. I shall give here the full formal proof of the conversion of the *I*-premiss, starting from theses (1) and (2), and applying to them some laws of the propositional logic and the rules of existential quantifiers.

The following thesis of the propositional logic was certainly known to Aristotle:

(3) If *p* and *q*, then *q* and *p*.

It is the commutative law of conjunction.[1] Applying this law to the premisses '*B* belongs to all *C*' and '*A* belongs to all *C*', we get:

(4) If *B* belongs to all *C* and *A* belongs to all *C*, then *A* belongs to all *C* and *B* belongs to all *C*.

[1] See *Principia Mathematica*, p. 116, thesis *3·22.

To this thesis I shall apply the rules of existential quantifiers. There are two such rules; both are stated with respect to a true implication. The first rule reads: It is permissible to put before a consequent of a true implication an existential quantifier, binding a free variable occurring in the consequent. It results from this rule that:

(5) If B belongs to all C and A belongs to all C, then there exists a C such that A belongs to all C and B belongs to all C.

The second rule reads: It is permissible to put before the antecedent of a true implication an existential quantifier, binding a free variable occurring in the antecedent, provided that this variable does not occur as a free variable in the consequent. In (5) C is already bound in the consequent; therefore according to this rule we may bind C in the antecedent, thus getting the formula:

(6) If there exists a C such that B belongs to all C and A belongs to all C, then there exists a C such that A belongs to all C and B belongs to all C.

The antecedent of this formula is identical with the consequent of thesis (1); it results, therefore, by the law of the hypothetical syllogism that:

(7) If B belongs to some A, then there exists a C such that A belongs to all C and B belongs to all C.

From (2) by interchanging B and A we get the thesis:

(8) If there exists a C such that A belongs to all C and B belongs to all C, then A belongs to some B,

and from (7) and (8) we may deduce by the hypothetical syllogism the law of conversion of the I-premiss:

(9) If B belongs to some A, then A belongs to some B.

We see from the above that the true reason of the convertibility of the I-premiss is the commutability of the conjunction. The perception of an individual term belonging to both A and B may intuitively convince us of the convertibility of this premiss, but is not sufficient for a logical proof. There is no need to assume C as a singular term given by perception.

The proof of the mood Darapti by exposition can now be easily understood. Aristotle reduces this mood to the first figure by conversion, and then he says: 'It is possible to demonstrate this also *per impossibile* and by exposition. For if both P and R belong to all S, should some of the S's, e.g. N, be taken, both P and R will belong to this, and then P will belong to some R.'[1] Alexander's commentary on this passage deserves our attention. It begins with a critical remark. If N were a universal term included in S, we should get as premisses 'P belongs to all N' and 'R belongs to all N'. But this is just the same combination of premisses, συζυγία, as 'P belongs to all S' and 'R belongs to all S', and the problem remains the same as before. Therefore, Alexander continues, N cannot be a universal term; it is a singular term given by perception, a term evidently existing in P as well as in R, and the whole proof by ecthesis is a proof by perception.[2] We have already met this opinion above. In support of it Alexander adduces three arguments: First, if his explanation were rejected, we should have no proof at all; secondly, Aristotle does not say that P and R belong to all N, but simply to N; thirdly, he does not convert the propositions with N.[3] None of these arguments is convincing: in our example there is no need of conversion; Aristotle often omits the mark of universality where it should be used,[4] and as to the first argument, we know already that there exists another and a better explanation.

The mood Darapti:

(10) If P belongs to all S and R belongs to all S, then P belongs to some R,

---

[1] *An. pr.* i. 5, 28ᵃ22 ἔστι δὲ καὶ διὰ τοῦ ἀδυνάτου καὶ τῷ ἐκθέσθαι ποιεῖν τὴν ἀπόδειξιν· εἰ γὰρ ἄμφω (scil. Π καὶ Ρ) παντὶ τῷ Σ ὑπάρχει, ἂν ληφθῇ τι τῶν Σ, οἷον τὸ Ν, τούτῳ καὶ τὸ Π καὶ τὸ Ρ ὑπάρξει, ὥστε τινὶ τῷ Ρ τὸ Π ὑπάρξει.

[2] Alexander 99. 28 τί γὰρ διαφέρει τῷ Σ ὑπάρχειν λαβεῖν παντὶ τό τε Π καὶ τὸ Ρ καὶ μέρει τινὶ τοῦ Σ τῷ Ν; τὸ γὰρ αὐτὸ καὶ ἐπὶ τοῦ Ν ληφθέντος μένει· ἡ γὰρ αὐτὴ συζυγία ἐστίν, ἄν τε κατὰ τοῦ Ν παντὸς ἐκείνων ἑκάτερον, ἄν τε κατὰ τοῦ Σ κατηγορῆται. ἢ οὐ τοιαύτη ἡ δεῖξις, ᾗ χρῆται· ὁ γὰρ δι᾽ ἐκθέσεως τρόπος δι᾽ αἰσθήσεως γίνεται. οὐ γὰρ ἵνα τοιοῦτόν τι τοῦ Σ λάβωμεν, καθ᾽ οὗ ῥηθήσεται παντὸς καὶ τὸ Π καὶ τὸ Ρ, λέγει ... ἀλλ᾽ ἵνα τι τῶν ὑπ᾽ αἴσθησιν πιπτόντων, ὃ φανερόν ἐστιν ὂν καὶ ἐν τῷ Π καὶ ἐν τῷ Ρ.

[3] Ibid. 100. 7 ὅτι γὰρ αἰσθητὴ ἡ διὰ τῆς ἐκθέσεως δεῖξις, σημεῖον πρῶτον μὲν τὸ εἰ μὴ οὕτως λαμβάνοιτο, μηδεμίαν γίνεσθαι δεῖξιν· ἔπειτα δὲ καὶ τὸ αὐτὸ μηκέτι χρήσασθαι ἐπὶ τοῦ Ν, ὃ ἦν τι τοῦ Σ, τῷ παντὶ αὐτῷ ὑπάρχειν τό τε Π καὶ τὸ Ρ, ἀλλ᾽ ἁπλῶς θεῖναι τὸ ὑπάρχειν· ἀλλὰ καὶ τὸ μηδετέραν ἀντιστρέψαι.

[4] See, for instance, p. 2, n.

results from a substitution of thesis (2)—take P for B, and R for A:

(11) If there exists a C such that P belongs to all C and R belongs to all C, then P belongs to some R,

and from the thesis:

(12) If P belongs to all S and R belongs to all S, then there exists a C such that P belongs to all C and R belongs to all C.

Thesis (12) we may prove by applying to the identity:

(13) If P belongs to all C and R belongs to all C, then P belongs to all C and R belongs to all C,

the second rule of existential quantifiers, getting thus:

(14) If P belongs to all C and R belongs to all C, then there exists a C such that P belongs to all C and R belongs to all C,

and substituting in (14) the letter S for the free variable C, i.e. performing the substitution in the antecedent only, as it is not permissible to substitute anything for a bound variable.

From (12) and (11) the mood Darapti results by the hypothetical syllogism. We see again that the exposed term C is a universal term like A or B. It is of no consequence, of course, to denote this term by N rather than by C.

Of greater importance seems to be the third passage, containing the proof by exposition of the mood Bocardo. This passage reads: 'If R belongs to all S, but P does not belong to some S, it is necessary that P should not belong to some R. For if P belongs to all R, and R belongs to all S, then P will belong to all S; but we assumed that it did not. Proof is possible also without reduction *ad impossibile*, if some of the S's be taken to which P does not belong.'[1] I shall analyse this proof in the same way as the other proofs by exposition.

Let us denote the part of S to which P does not belong by C; we get two propositions: 'S belongs to all C' and 'P belongs to no C'. From the first of these propositions and the premiss 'R

[1] *An. pr.* i. 6, 28^{b}17 εἰ γὰρ τὸ P παντὶ τῷ Σ, τὸ δὲ Π τινὶ μὴ ὑπάρχει, ἀνάγκη τὸ Π τινὶ τῷ P μὴ ὑπάρχειν. εἰ γὰρ παντί, καὶ τὸ P παντὶ τῷ Σ, καὶ τὸ Π παντὶ τῷ Σ ὑπάρξει· ἀλλ' οὐχ ὑπῆρχεν. δείκνυται δὲ καὶ ἄνευ τῆς ἀπαγωγῆς, ἐὰν ληφθῇ τι τῶν Σ ᾧ τὸ Π μὴ ὑπάρχει.

belongs to all S' we get by the mood Barbara the consequence 'R belongs to all C', which yields together with the second proposition 'P belongs to no C' the required conclusion 'P does not belong to some R' by the mood Felapton. The problem is how we can get the propositions with C from the original premisses 'R belongs to all S' and 'P does not belong to some S'. The first of these premisses is useless for our purpose as it does not contain P; from the second premiss we cannot get our propositions in the ordinary way, since it is particular, and our propositions are universal. But if we introduce the existential quantifier we can get them, for the following thesis is true:

(15) If P does not belong to some S, then there exists a C such that S belongs to all C and P belongs to no C.

The truth of this thesis will be obvious if we realize that the required condition for C is always fulfilled by that part of S to which P does not belong.

Starting from thesis (15) we can prove the mood Bocardo on the basis of the moods Barbara and Felapton by means of some laws of propositional logic and the second rule of existential quantifiers. As the proof is rather long, I shall give here only a sketch.

We take as premisses, besides (15), the mood Barbara with transposed premisses:

(16) If S belongs to all C and R belongs to all S, then R belongs to all C,

and the mood Felapton, also with transposed premisses:

(17) If R belongs to all C and P belongs to no C, then P does not belong to some R.

To these premisses we may apply a complicated thesis of propositional logic which, curiously enough, was known to the Peripatetics and is ascribed by Alexander to Aristotle himself. It is called the 'synthetic theorem', συνθετικὸν θεώρημα, and runs thus: 'If α and β imply γ, and γ together with δ implies ϵ, then α and β together with δ imply ϵ.'[1] Take for α, β, and γ the first

---

[1] Alexander 274. 19 δι' ὧν δὲ λέγει νῦν, ὑπογράφει ἡμῖν φανερώτερον τὸ λεγόμενον ' συνθετικὸν θεώρημα ', οὗ αὐτός ἐστιν εὑρετής. ἔστι δὲ ἡ περιοχὴ αὐτοῦ τοιαύτη· ' ὅταν ἔκ τινων συνάγηταί τι, τὸ δὲ συναγόμενον μετά τινος ἢ τινῶν συνάγῃ τι, καὶ τὰ συνακτικὰ αὐτοῦ μεθ' οὗ ἢ μεθ' ὧν συνάγεται ἐκεῖνο, καὶ αὐτὰ τὸ αὐτὸ συνάξει.' The following example is given ibid. 26 ἐπεὶ γὰρ τὸ ' πᾶν δίκαιον ἀγαθὸν ' συναγόμενον ὑπὸ τῶν ' πᾶν δίκαιον καλόν, πᾶν καλὸν ἀγαθὸν ' συνάγει μετὰ τοῦ ' πᾶν ἀγαθὸν συμφέρον '

premiss, the second premiss, and the conclusion respectively of Barbara, for δ and ε the second premiss and the conclusion respectively of Felapton; we get the formula:

(18) If S belongs to all C and R belongs to all S and P belongs to no C, then P does not belong to some R.

This formula may be transformed by another law of propositional logic into the following:

(19) If S belongs to all C and P belongs to no C, then if R belongs to all S, P does not belong to some R.

To this formula may be applied the second rule of existential quantifiers. For C is a free variable occurring in the antecedent of (19), but not in the consequent. According to this rule we get the thesis:

(20) If there exists a C such that S belongs to all C and P belongs to no C, then if R belongs to all S, P does not belong to some R.

From premiss (15) and thesis (20) there results by the hypothetical syllogism the consequence:

(21) If P does not belong to some S, then if R belongs to all S, P does not belong to some R,

and this is the implicational form of the mood Bocardo.

It is, of course, highly improbable that Aristotle saw all the steps of this deduction; but it is important to know that his intuitions with regard to the proof by ecthesis were right. Alexander's commentary on this proof of the mood Bocardo is worthy of quotation. 'It is possible', he says, 'to prove this mood without assuming some S given by perception and singular, but taking such an S, to none of which P would belong. For P will belong to none of this S, and R to all, and this combination of premisses yields as conclusion that P does not belong to some R.'[1] Here at last Alexander concedes that the exposed term may be universal.

The proofs by exposition have no importance for Aristotle's

τὸ ' πᾶν δίκαιον συμφέρον ', καὶ τὰ ' πᾶν δίκαιον καλόν, πᾶν καλὸν ἀγαθὸν ' ὄντα συνακτικὰ τοῦ ' πᾶν δίκαιον ἀγαθὸν ' μετὰ τοῦ ' πᾶν ἀγαθὸν συμφέρον ' συνάξει τὸ ' πᾶν δίκαιον συμφέρον '.

[1] Alexander 104. 3 δύναται δ' ἐπὶ τῆς συζυγίας ταύτης δεικνύναι, καὶ εἰ μὴ αἰσθητόν τι τοῦ Σ λαμβάνοιτο καὶ καθ' ἕκαστα, ἀλλὰ τοιοῦτον, οὗ κατὰ μηδενὸς κατηγορηθήσεται τὸ Π. ἔσται γὰρ τὸ μὲν Π κατ' οὐδενὸς αὐτοῦ, τὸ δὲ Ρ κατὰ παντός· ἡ δ' οὕτως ἔχουσα συζυγία συλλογιστικῶς δέδεικται συνάγουσα τὸ τινὶ τῷ Ρ τὸ Π μὴ ὑπάρχειν.

syllogistic as a system. All theorems proved by ecthesis can be proved by conversion or *per impossibile*. But they are highly important in themselves, as they contain a new logical element the meaning of which was not entirely clear for Aristotle. This was perhaps the reason why he dropped this kind of proof in his final chapter (7) of Book I of the *Prior Analytics*, where he sums up his systematic investigation of syllogistic.[1] Nobody after him understood these proofs. It was reserved for modern formal logic to explain them by the idea of the existential quantifier.

§ 20. *The rejected forms*

Aristotle in his systematic investigation of syllogistic forms not only proves the true ones but also shows that all the others are false, and must be rejected. Let us see by means of an example how Aristotle proceeds to reject false syllogistic forms. The following two premisses are given: *A* belongs to all *B* and *B* belongs to no *C*. It is the first figure: *A* is the first or the major term, *B* is the middle, and *C* is the last or the minor term. Aristotle writes:

'If the first term belongs to all the middle, but the middle to none of the last, there will be no syllogism of the extremes; for nothing necessary follows from the terms being so related; for it is possible that the first should belong to all as well as to none of the last, so that neither a particular nor a universal conclusion is necessary. But if there is no necessary consequence by means of these premisses, there cannot be a syllogism. Terms of belonging to all: animal, man, horse; to none: animal, man, stone.'[2]

In contrast to the shortness and obscurity of the proofs by ecthesis, the above passage is rather full and clear. Nevertheless I am afraid it has not been properly understood by the commentators. According to Alexander, Aristotle shows in this passage that from the same combination of premisses there can be

---

[1] Cf. the comment of Alexander, who maintains to the end his idea of the perceptual character of proofs by ecthesis, 112. 33: ὅτι δὲ ἡ δι' ἐκθέσεως δεῖξις ἦν αἰσθητικὴ καὶ οὐ συλλογιστική, δῆλον καὶ ἐκ τοῦ νῦν αὐτὸν μηκέτι μνημονεύειν αὐτῆς ὡς διὰ συλλογισμοῦ τινος γινομένης.

[2] *An. pr.* i. 4, 26ᵃ2 εἰ δὲ τὸ μὲν πρῶτον παντὶ τῷ μέσῳ ἀκολουθεῖ, τὸ δὲ μέσον μηδενὶ τῷ ἐσχάτῳ ὑπάρχει, οὐκ ἔσται συλλογισμὸς τῶν ἄκρων· οὐδὲν γὰρ ἀναγκαῖον συμβαίνει τῷ ταῦτα εἶναι· καὶ γὰρ παντὶ καὶ μηδενὶ ἐνδέχεται τὸ πρῶτον τῷ ἐσχάτῳ ὑπάρχειν, ὥστε οὔτε τὸ κατὰ μέρος οὔτε τὸ καθόλου γίνεται ἀναγκαῖον· μηδενὸς δὲ ὄντος ἀναγκαίου διὰ τούτων οὐκ ἔσται συλλογισμός. ὅροι τοῦ παντὶ ὑπάρχειν ζῷον, ἄνθρωπος, ἵππος· τοῦ μηδενὶ ζῷον, ἄνθρωπος, λίθος.

derived (δυνάμενον συνάγεσθαι) for some concrete terms a universal affirmative conclusion, and for some other concrete terms a universal negative conclusion. This is, Alexander asserts, the most obvious sign that such a combination of premisses has no syllogistic force, since opposite and contradictory propositions which destroy each other are proved by it (δείκνυται).[1] What Alexander says is certainly misleading, for nothing can be formally derived from an asyllogistic combination of premisses, and nothing can be proved by it. Besides, propositions with different concrete subjects and predicates are neither opposite to each other nor contradictory. Maier again puts the terms pointed out by Aristotle into a syllogistical form:

all men are animals	all men are animals
no horse is a man	no stone is a man
all horses are animals	no stone is an animal

(the premisses are underlined by him, as in a syllogism), and says that there results (*ergibt sich*) from logically equivalent premisses a universal affirmative proposition as well as a universal negative.[2] We shall see below that the terms given by Aristotle are not intended to be put into the form of a syllogism, and that nothing results formally from the premisses of the would-be syllogisms quoted by Maier. In view of these misunderstandings a logical analysis of the matter seems to be necessary.

If we want to prove that the following syllogistic form:

(1) If A belongs to all B and B belongs to no C, then A does not belong to some C,

is not a syllogism, and consequently not a true logical theorem, we must show that there exist such values of the variables A, B, and C as verify the premisses without verifying the conclusion. For an implication containing variables is true only when all the

---

[1] Alexander 55. 22 καὶ γὰρ καθόλου καταφατικὸν ἐπί τινος ὕλης δείξει δυνάμενον συνάγεσθαι καὶ πάλιν ἐπ' ἄλλης καθόλου ἀποφατικόν, ὃ ἐναργέστατον σημεῖον τοῦ μηδεμίαν ἔχειν τὴν συζυγίαν ταύτην ἰσχὺν συλλογιστικήν, εἴ γε τά τε ἐναντία καὶ τὰ ἀντικείμενα ἐν αὐτῇ δείκνυται, ὄντα ἀλλήλων ἀναιρετικά.

[2] Op. cit., vol. ii. *a*, p. 76: 'Es handelt sich also um folgende Kombinationen:

aller Mensch ist Lebewesen   aller Mensch ist Lebewesen
kein Pferd ist Mensch   kein Stein ist Mensch
alles Pferd ist Lebewesen   kein Stein ist Lebewesen

So wird an Beispielen gezeigt, dass bei der in Frage stehenden Prämissenzusammenstellung von logisch völlig gleichen Vordersätzen aus sowohl ein allgemein bejahender, als ein allgemein verneinender Satz sich ergeben könne.'

values of variables that verify the antecedent verity the consequent also. The easiest way of showing this is to find concrete terms verifying the premisses 'A belongs to all B' and 'B belongs to no C', but not verifying the conclusion 'A does not belong to some C'. Aristotle found such terms: take 'animal' for A, 'man' for B, 'horse' for C. The premisses 'Animal belongs to all man' or 'All men are animals', and 'Man belongs to no horse' or 'No horses are men', are verified; but the conclusion 'Animal does not belong to some horse' or 'Some horses are not animals' is false. Formula (1), therefore, is not a syllogism. For the same reason neither will the following form:

(2) If A belongs to all B and B belongs to no C, then A belongs to no C,

be a syllogism, because the premisses are verified for the same concrete terms as before, but the conclusion 'Animal belongs to no horse' or 'No horses are animals' is false. It follows from the falsity of (1) and (2) that no negative conclusion can be drawn from the given premisses.

Nor can an affirmative conclusion be drawn from them. Take the next syllogistical form:

(3) If A belongs to all B and B belongs to no C, then A belongs to some C.

There exist values for A, B, and C, i.e. concrete terms, that verify the premisses without verifying the conclusion. Aristotle again gives such terms: take 'animal' for A, 'man' for B, 'stone' for C. The premisses are verified, for it is true that 'All men are animals' and 'No stone is a man', but the conclusion 'Some stone is an animal' is obviously false. Formula (3), therefore, is not a syllogism. Neither can the last form:

(4) If A belongs to all B and B belongs to no C, then A belongs to all C,

be a syllogism, since for the given terms the premisses are verified as before, but the conclusion 'All stones are animals' is not verified. It results from the above that no conclusion whatever can be derived from the combination of premisses 'A belongs to all B' and 'B belongs to no C', where A is the predicate and B is the subject of the conclusion. This combination of premisses is useless for syllogistic.

The main point of this process of rejection is to find a true universal affirmative proposition (like 'All horses are animals') and a true universal negative proposition (like 'No stone is an animal'), both compatible with the premisses. It is not sufficient to find, for instance, for some terms a true universal affirmative statement, and for some other terms a true particular negative statement. This opinion was put forward by Alexander's teacher Herminus and some older Peripatetics, and was rightly refuted by Alexander.[1] This is again a proof that Aristotle's ideas of rejection have not been properly understood.

The syllogistic forms (1)–(4) are rejected by Aristotle on the basis of some concrete terms that verify the premisses without verifying the conclusion. Aristotle, however, knows yet another kind of proof for rejection. Investigating the syllogistic forms of the second figure, Aristotle states generally that in this figure neither two affirmative nor two negative premisses yield a necessary conclusion, and then continues thus:

'Let M belong to no N, and not to some X. It is possible then for N to belong either to all X or to no X. Terms of belonging to none: black, snow, animal. Terms of belonging to all cannot be found, if M belongs to some X, and does not belong to some X. For if N belonged to all X, and M to no N, then M would belong to no X; but it is assumed that it belongs to some X. In this way, then, it is not possible to take terms, and the proof must start from the indefinite nature of the particular premiss. For since it is true that M does not belong to some X, even if it belongs to no X, and since if it belongs to no X a syllogism is not possible, clearly it will not be possible either.'[2]

Aristotle here begins the proof of rejection by giving concrete terms, as in the first example. But then he breaks off his proof, as he cannot find concrete terms that would verify the premisses

[1] Cf. Alexander 89. 34–90. 27. The words of Herminus are quoted 89. 34: Ἑρμῖνος δὲ λέγει ' ἐφ' ἧς γὰρ συζυγίας τὴν ἀντίφασιν ἔνεστι συναγομένην δεῖξαι, εὔλογον ταύτην μηδὲν ἔλαττον ἀσυλλόγιστον λέγειν τῆς ἐν ᾗ τὰ ἐναντία συνάγεται· ἀσυνύπαρκτα γὰρ καὶ ταῦτα ὁμοίως ἐκείνοις.'

[2] An. pr. i. 5, 27ᵇ12–23 ἔστωσαν γάρ . . . στερητικαί, οἷον τὸ Μ τῷ μὲν Ν μηδενὶ τῷ δὲ Ξ τινὶ μὴ ὑπαρχέτω· ἐνδέχεται δὴ καὶ παντὶ καὶ μηδενὶ τῷ Ξ τὸ Ν ὑπάρχειν. ὅροι τοῦ μὲν μὴ ὑπάρχειν· μέλαν, χιών, ζῷον· τοῦ δὲ παντὶ ὑπάρχειν οὐκ ἔστι λαβεῖν, εἰ τὸ Μ τῷ Ξ τινὶ μὲν ὑπάρχει, τινὶ δὲ μή. εἰ γὰρ παντὶ τῷ Ξ τὸ Ν, τὸ δὲ Μ μηδενὶ τῷ Ν, τὸ Μ οὐδενὶ τῷ Ξ ὑπάρξει· ἀλλ' ὑπέκειτο τινὶ ὑπάρχειν. οὕτω μὲν οὖν οὐκ ἐγχωρεῖ λαβεῖν ὅρους, ἐκ δὲ τοῦ ἀδιορίστου δεικτέον· ἐπεὶ γὰρ ἀληθεύεται τὸ τινὶ μὴ ὑπάρχειν τὸ Μ τῷ Ξ καὶ εἰ μηδενὶ ὑπάρχει, μηδενὶ δὲ ὑπάρχοντος οὐκ ἦν συλλογισμός, φανερὸν ὅτι οὐδὲ νῦν ἔσται.

'M belongs to no N' and 'M does not belong to some X', without verifying the proposition 'N does not belong to some X', provided M, which does not belong to some X, belongs at the same time to some (other) X. The reason is that from the premisses 'M belongs to no N' and 'M belongs to some X' the proposition 'N does not belong to some X' follows by the mood Festino. But it is not necessary that M should belong to some X, when it does not belong to some (other) X; M might belong to no X. Concrete terms verifying the premisses 'M belongs to no N' and 'M belongs to no X', and not verifying the proposition 'N does not belong to some X', can easily be chosen, and in fact Aristotle found them, rejecting the syllogistic form of the second figure with universal negative premisses; the required terms are: M—'line', N—'animal', X—'man'.[1] The same terms may be used to disprove the syllogistic form:

(5) If M belongs to no N and M does not belong to some X, then N does not belong to some X.

For the premiss 'No animal is a line' is true, and the second premiss 'Some man is not a line' is also true, as it is true that 'No man is a line', but the conclusion 'Some man is not an animal' is false. Aristotle, however, does not finish his proof in this way,[2] because he sees another possibility: if the form with universal negative premisses:

(6) If M belongs to no N and M belongs to no X, then N does not belong to some X,

is rejected, (5) must be rejected too. For if (5) stands, (6), having a stronger premiss than (5), must also stand.

Modern formal logic, as far as I know, does not use 'rejection' as an operation opposed to Frege's 'assertion'. The rules of rejection are not yet known. On the ground of the above proof of Aristotle we may state the following rule:

(c) If the implication 'If α, then β' is asserted, but its consequent β is rejected, then its antecedent α must be rejected too.

---

[1] Ibid. 27ª20 οὐδ' (scil. ἔσται συλλογισμός) ὅταν μήτε τοῦ N μήτε τοῦ $\varXi$ μηδενὸς κατηγορῆται τὸ M. ὅροι τοῦ ὑπάρχειν γραμμή, ζῷον, ἄνθρωπος, τοῦ μὴ ὑπάρχειν γραμμή, ζῷον, λίθος.

[2] Alexander completed this proof, 88. 12: τοῦ παντὶ τὸ N τῷ $\varXi$ ὑπάρχειν ὅροι· γραμμὴ τὸ M, ζῷον τὸ N, ἄνθρωπος τὸ $\varXi$· ἡ μὲν γὰρ γραμμὴ οὐδενὶ ζῴῳ καὶ τινὶ οὐχ ὑπάρχει ἀνθρώπῳ ἐπεὶ καὶ μηδενί, ζῷον δὲ παντὶ ἀνθρώπῳ.

This rule can be applied not only to reject (5) if (6) is rejected, but also to reject (2) if (1) is rejected. For from an *E*-premiss an *O*-premiss follows, and if (2) is true, then (1) must be true. But if (1) is rejected, so must (2) be rejected.

The rule (*c*) for rejection corresponds to the rule of detachment for assertion. We may accept another rule for rejection corresponding to the rule of substitution for assertion. It can be formulated thus:

(*d*) If α is a substitution for β, and α is rejected, then β must be rejected too.

Example: suppose that '*A* does not belong to some *A*' is rejected; then '*A* does not belong to some *B*' must be rejected too, since, if the second expression were asserted, we should obtain from it by substitution the first expression, which is rejected.

The first of these rules was anticipated by Aristotle, the second was unknown to him. Both enable us to reject some forms, provided that some other forms have already been rejected. Aristotle rejects some forms by means of concrete terms, as 'man', 'animal', 'stone'. This procedure is correct, but it introduces into logic terms and propositions not germane to it. 'Man' and 'animal' are not logical terms, and the proposition 'All men are animals' is not a logical thesis. Logic cannot depend on concrete terms and statements. If we want to avoid this difficulty, we must reject some forms axiomatically. I have found that if we reject the two following forms of the second figure axiomatically:

(7) If *A* belongs to all *B* and *A* belongs to all *C*, then *B* belongs to some *C*, and
(8) If *A* belongs to no *B* and *A* belongs to no *C*, then *B* belongs to some *C*,

all the other forms may be rejected by the rules (*c*) and (*d*).

§ 21. *Some unsolved problems*

The Aristotelian system of non-modal syllogisms is a theory of four constants which may be denoted by 'All — is', 'No — is', 'Some — is', and 'Some — is not'. These constants are functors of two arguments which are represented by variables having as values only concrete universal terms. Singular, empty, and also negative terms are excluded as values. The constants together with their arguments form four kinds of proposition called pre-misses, viz. 'All A is B', 'No A is B', 'Some A is B', and 'Some A is not B'. The system may be called 'formal logic', as concrete terms, like 'man' or 'animal', belong not to it but only to its applications. The system is not a theory of the forms of thought, nor is it dependent on psychology; it is similar to a mathematical theory of the relation 'greater than', as was rightly observed by the Stoics.

The four kinds of premiss form theses of the system by means of two functors 'if — then' and 'and'. These functors belong to pro-positional logic, which is an auxiliary theory of the system. In some proofs we meet a third propositional functor, viz. the propositional negation 'It is not true that', denoted shortly by 'not'. The four Aristotelian constants 'All — is', 'No — is', 'Some — is' and 'Some — is not', together with the three propositional constants 'if — then', 'and', and 'not', are the sole elements of the syllogistic.

All theses of the system are propositions regarded as true for all values of the variables that occur in them. No Aristotelian syllo-gism is formulated as a rule of inference with the word 'therefore', as is done in the traditional logic. The traditional logic is a system different from the Aristotelian syllogistic, and should not be mixed up with the genuine logic of Aristotle. Aristotle divided syllogisms into three figures, but he knew and accepted all the syllogistic moods of the fourth figure. The division of syllogisms into figures is of no logical importance and has only a practical aim: we want to be sure that no valid syllogistical mood is omitted.

The system is axiomatized. As axioms Aristotle takes the two first moods of the first figure, Barbara and Celarent. To these two axioms we have to add two laws of conversion, as these can-not be proved syllogistically. If we wish to have the law of identity, 'All A is A,' in the system we have to assume it axiomatic-ally. The simplest basis we can get is to take the constants 'All — is' and 'Some — is' as primitive terms, to define the two other con-stants by means of those terms with the help of propositional negation, and to assume as axioms four theses, viz. the two laws of identity and the moods Barbara and Datisi, or Barbara and Dimaris. It is not possible to build up the system on one axiom only. To look for the principle of the Aristotelian syllogistic is a vain attempt, if 'principle' means the same as 'axiom'. The so-called *dictum de omni et nullo* cannot be the principle of syllogistic in this sense, and was never stated to be such by Aristotle himself.

Aristotle reduces the so-called imperfect syllogisms to the perfect, i.e. to the axioms. Reduction here means proof or deduction of a theorem from the axioms. He uses three kinds of proof: by conversion, by *reductio ad impossibile*, and by ecthesis. Logical analysis shows that in all the proofs of the first two kinds there are involved theses of the most elementary part of propositional logic, the theory of deduction. Aristotle uses them intuitively, but soon after him the Stoics, who were the inventors of the first system of propositional logic, stated some of them explicitly—the compound law of transposition and the so-called 'synthetic theorem', which is ascribed to Aristotle but does not exist in his extant logical works. A new logical element seems to be implied by the proofs by ecthesis: they can be explained with the help of existential quantifiers. The systematic introduction of quantifiers into the syllogistic would completely change this system: the primitive term 'Some — is' could be defined by the term 'All — is', and many new theses would arise not known to Aristotle. As Aristotle himself has dropped the proofs by ecthesis in his final summary of the syllogistic, there is no need to introduce them into his system.

Another new logical element is contained in Aristotle's investigation of the inconclusive syllogistic forms: it is rejection. Aristotle rejects invalid forms by exemplification through concrete terms. This procedure is logically correct, but it introduces into the system terms and propositions not germane to it. There are, however, cases where he applies a more logical procedure, reducing one invalid form to another already rejected. On the basis of this remark a rule of rejection could be stated corresponding to the rule of detachment by assertion; this can be regarded as the commencement of a new field of logical inquiries and of new problems that have to be solved.

Aristotle does not systematically investigate the so-called polysyllogisms, i.e. syllogisms with more than three terms and two premisses. As we have seen, Galen studied compound syllogisms consisting of four terms and three premisses. It is an old error to ascribe to Galen the authorship of the fourth figure:

Galen divided the compound syllogisms of four terms into four figures, but not the simple ones known to us by their medieval names. His investigations were entirely forgotten. But compound syllogisms also belong to the syllogistic and have to be taken into account, and here is another problem that has to be studied systematically. An essential contribution to this problem is the set of formulae given by C. A. Meredith, and mentioned above at the end of section 14.

There still remains one problem not seen by Aristotle, but of the utmost importance for his whole system: it is the problem of decision. The number of significant expressions of the syllogistic is infinite; most of them are certainly false, but some of them may be true, like valid polysyllogisms of n terms where n is any integer whatever. Can we be sure that our axioms together with our rules of inference are sufficient to prove all the true expressions of the syllogistic? And similarly, can we be sure that our rules of rejection, formulated at the end of section 20, are sufficient to reject all the false expressions, provided that a finite number of them is rejected axiomatically? I raised these problems in 1938 in my Seminar on Mathematical Logic at the University of Warsaw. One of my former pupils, now Professor of Logic and Methodology at the University of Wrocław, J. Słupecki, found the solution to both problems. His answer to the first question was positive, to the second negative. According to Słupecki it is not possible to reject all the false expressions of the syllogistic by means of the rules (c) and (d) quoted in section 20, provided a finite number of them is rejected axiomatically. However many false expressions we may reject axiomatically, there always exist other false expressions that cannot be rejected otherwise than axiomatically. But it is impossible to establish an infinite set of axioms. A new rule of rejection must be added to the system to complete the insufficient characterization of the Aristotelian logic given by the four axioms. This rule was found by Słupecki.

Słupecki's rule of rejection peculiar to Aristotle's syllogistic can be formulated in the following way: Let α and β denote negative premisses of the Aristotelian logic, i.e. premisses of the type 'No A is B' or 'Some A is not B', and let γ denote either a simple premiss (of any kind) or an implication the consequent of which is a simple premiss and the antecedent a conjunction of such premisses: if the expressions 'If α, then γ' and 'If β, then γ'

are rejected, then the expression 'If α and β, then γ' must be rejected too.[1] This rule, together with the rules of rejection (c) and (d) and the axiomatically rejected expression 'If all C is B and all A is B, then some A is C', enables us to reject any false expression of the system. Besides, we suppose as given the four asserted axioms of the syllogistic, the definitions of the E- and the O-premiss, the rules of inference for asserted expressions, and the theory of deduction as an auxiliary system. In this way the problem of decision finds its solution: for any given significant expression of the system we can decide whether it is true and may be asserted or whether it is false and must be rejected.

By the solution of this problem the main investigations on Aristotle's syllogistic are brought to an end. There remains only one problem, or rather one mysterious point waiting for an explanation: in order to reject all the false expressions of the system it is necessary and sufficient to reject axiomatically only one false expression, viz. the syllogistic form of the second figure with universal affirmative premisses and a particular affirmative conclusion. There exists no other expression suitable for this purpose. The explanation of this curious logical fact may perhaps lead to new discoveries in the field of logic.

[1] J. Słupecki, 'Z badań nad sylogistyką Arystotelesa' (Investigation on Aristotle's Syllogistic), *Travaux de la Société des Sciences et des Lettres de Wrocław*, Sér. B, No. 9, Wrocław (1948). See chapter v, devoted to the problem of decision.

CHAPTER IV

ARISTOTLE'S SYSTEM IN SYMBOLIC FORM

§ 22. *Explanation of the symbolism*

THIS chapter does not belong to the history of logic. Its purpose is to set out the system of non-modal syllogisms according to the requirements of modern formal logic, but in close connexion with the ideas set forth by Aristotle himself.

Modern formal logic is strictly formalistic. In order to get an exactly formalized theory it is more convenient to employ a symbolism invented for this purpose than to make use of ordinary language which has its own grammatical laws. I have therefore to start from the explanation of such a symbolism. As the Aristotelian syllogistic involves the most elementary part of the propositional logic called theory of deduction, I shall explain the symbolic notation of both these theories.

In both theories there occur variables and constants. Variables are denoted by small Latin letters, constants by Latin capitals. By the initial letters of the alphabet a, b, c, d, ..., I denote term-variables of the Aristotelian logic. These term-variables have as values universal terms, as 'man' or 'animal'. For the constants of this logic I employ the capital letters A, E, I, and O, used already in this sense by the medieval logicians. By means of these two kinds of letters I form the four functions of the Aristotelian logic, writing the constants before the variables:

Aab means	All *a* is *b*	or	*b* belongs to all *a*,
Eab „	No *a* is *b*	„	*b* belongs to no *a*,
Iab „	Some *a* is *b*	„	*b* belongs to some *a*,
Oab „	Some *a* is not *b*	„	*b* does not belong to some *a*.

The constants A, E, I, and O are called functors, a and b their arguments. All Aristotelian syllogisms are composed of these four types of function connected with each other by means of the words 'if' and 'and'. These words also denote functors, but of a different kind from the Aristotelian constants: their arguments are not term-expressions, i.e. concrete terms or term-variables, but propositional expressions, i.e. propositions like

'All men are animals', propositional functions like '*Aab*', or propositional variables. I denote propositional variables by p, q, r, s, ..., the functor 'if' by C, the functor 'and' by K. The expression Cpq means 'if p, then q' ('then' may be omitted) and is called 'implication' with p as the antecedent and q as the consequent. C does not belong to the antecedent, it only combines the antecedent with the consequent. The expression Kpq means 'p and q' and is called 'conjunction'. We shall meet in some proofs a third functor of propositional logic, propositional negation. This is a functor of one argument and is denoted by N. It is difficult to render the function Np either in English or in any other modern language, as there exists no single word for the propositional negation.[1] We have to say by circumlocution 'it-is-not-true-that p' or 'it-is-not-the-case-that p'. For the sake of brevity I shall use the expression 'not-p'.

The principle of my notation is to write the functors before the arguments. In this way I can avoid brackets. This symbolism without brackets, which I invented and have employed in my logical papers since 1929,[2] can be applied to mathematics as well as to logic. The associative law of addition runs in the ordinary notation thus:

$$(a+b)+c = a+(b+c),$$

and cannot be stated without brackets. If you write, however, the functor $+$ before its arguments, you get:

$$(a+b)+c = ++abc \quad \text{and} \quad a+(b+c) = +a+bc.$$

The law of association can be now written without brackets:

$$++abc = +a+bc.$$

Now I shall explain some expressions written down in this symbolic notation. The symbolic expression of a syllogism is easy to understand. Take, for instance, the mood Barbara:

If all b is c and all a is b, then all a is c.

It reads in symbols:

$CKAbcAabAac$.

---

[1] The Stoics used for propositional negation the single word οὐχί.

[2] See, for instance, Łukasiewicz and Tarski, 'Untersuchungen über den Aussagenkalkül', *Comptes Rendus des séances de la Société des Sciences et des Lettres de Varsovie*, xxiii (1930), Cl. III, pp. 31–2.

The conjunction of the premisses *Abc* and *Aab*, viz. *KAbcAab*, is the antecedent of the formula, the conclusion *Aac* is its consequent.

Some expressions of the theory of deduction are more complicated. Take the symbolic expression of the hypothetical syllogism:

If (if *p*, then *q*), then [if (if *q*, then *r*), then (if *p*, then *r*)].

It reads:

CCpqCCqrCpr.

In order to understand the construction of this formula you must remember that *C* is a functor of two propositional arguments which follow immediately after *C*, forming together with *C* a new compound propositional expression. Of this kind are the expressions *Cpq*, *Cqr*, and *Cpr* contained in the formula. Draw brackets around each of them; you will get the expression:

C(*Cpq*)*C*(*Cqr*)(*Cpr*).

Now you can easily see that (*Cpq*) is the antecedent of the whole formula, and the rest, i.e. *C*(*Cqr*)(*Cpr*), is the consequent, having (*Cqr*) as its antecedent and (*Cpr*) as its consequent.

In the same way we may analyse all the other expressions, for instance the following, which contains *N* and *K* besides *C*:

CCKpqrCKNrqNp.

Remember that *K*, like *C*, is a functor of two arguments, and that *N* is a functor of one argument. By using different kinds of brackets we get the expression:

C[*C*(*Kpq*)*r*]{*C*[*K*(*Nr*)*q*](*Np*)}.

[*C*(*Kpq*)*r*] is here the antecedent of the whole formula while {*C*[*K*(*Nr*)*q*](*Np*)} is its consequent, having the conjunction [*K*(*Nr*)*q*] as its antecedent and the negation (*Np*) as its consequent.

§ 23. *Theory of deduction*

The most fundamental logical system on which all the other logical systems are built up is the theory of deduction. As every logician is bound to know this system, I shall here describe it in brief.

The theory of deduction can be axiomatized in several different ways, according to which functors are chosen as primitive terms. The simplest way is to follow Frege, who takes as primitive terms the functors of implication and negation, in our symbolism C and N. There exist many sets of axioms of the C–N-system; the simplest of them and the one almost universally accepted was discovered by myself before 1929.[1] It consists of three axioms:

T1. *CCpqCCqrCpr*
T2. *CCNppp*
T3. *CpCNpq.*

The first axiom is the law of the hypothetical syllogism already explained in the foregoing section. The second axiom, which reads in words 'If (if not-p, then p), then p', was applied by Euclid to the proof of a mathematical theorem.[2] I call it the law of Clavius, as Clavius (a learned Jesuit living in the second half of the sixteenth century, one of the constructors of the Gregorian calendar) first drew attention to this law in his commentary on Euclid. The third axiom, in words 'If p, then if not-p, then q', occurs for the first time, as far as I know, in a commentary on Aristotle ascribed to Duns Scotus; I call it the law of Duns Scotus.[3] This law contains the venom usually imputed to contradiction: if two contradictory sentences, like α and $N\alpha$, were true together, we could derive from them by means of this law the arbitrary proposition q, i.e. any proposition whatever.

There belong to the system two rules of inference: the rule of substitution and the rule of detachment.

The rule of substitution allows us to deduce new theses from a thesis asserted in the system by writing instead of a variable a significant expression, everywhere the same for the same variable. Significant expressions are defined inductively in the following way: (a) any propositional variable is a significant expression; (b) $N\alpha$ is a significant expression provided α is a

---

[1] First published in Polish: 'O znaczeniu i potrzebach logiki matematycznej' (On the Importance and Requirements of Mathematical Logic), *Nauka Polska*, vol. x, Warsaw (1929), pp. 610–12. Cf. also the German contribution quoted in p. 78, n. 2: Satz 6, p. 35.

[2] See above, section 16.

[3] Cf. my paper quoted in p. 48, n.

significant expression; (c) $C\alpha\beta$ is a significant expression provided α and β are significant expressions.

The rule of detachment is the *modus ponens* of the Stoics referred to above: if a proposition of the type $C\alpha\beta$ is asserted and its antecedent α is asserted too, it is permissible to assert its consequent β, and detach it from the implication as a new thesis.

By means of these two rules we can deduce from our set of axioms all the true theses of the C–N-system. If we want to have in the system other functors besides C and N, e.g. K, we must introduce them by definitions. This can be done in two different ways, as I shall show on the example of K. The conjunction 'p and q' means the same as 'it-is-not-true-that (if p, then not-q)'. This connexion between Kpq and $NCpNq$ may be expressed by the formula:

$$Kpq = NCpNq,$$

where the sign $=$ corresponds to the words 'means the same as'. This kind of definition requires a special rule of inference allowing us to replace the *definiens* by the *definiendum* and vice versa. Or we may express the connexion between Kpq and $NCpNq$ by an equivalence, and as equivalence is not a primitive term of our system, by two implications converse to each other:

$$CKpqNCpNq \quad \text{and} \quad CNCpNqKpq.$$

In this case a special definition-rule is not needed. I shall use definitions of the first kind.

Let us now see by an example how new theses can be derived from the axioms by the help of rules of inference. I shall deduce from T1–T3 the law of identity Cpp. The deduction requires two applications of the rule of substitution and two applications of the rule of detachment; it runs thus:

$$\text{T1. } q/CNpq \times CT3\text{–}T4$$
$$\text{T4. } CCCNpqrCpr$$
$$\text{T4. } q/p, r/p \times CT2\text{–}T5$$
$$\text{T5. } Cpp.$$

The first line is called the derivational line. It consists of two parts separated from each other by the sign $\times$. The first part, T1. $q/CNpq$, means that in T1 $CNpq$ has to be substituted for *q*. The thesis produced by this substitution is omitted in order to save space. It would be of the following form:

(I) *CCpCNpqCCCNpqrCpr*.

The second part, *C*T3–T4, shows how this omitted thesis is constructed, making it obvious that the rule of detachment may be applied to it. Thesis (I) begins with *C*, and then there follow axiom T3 as antecedent and thesis T4 as consequent. We can therefore detach T4 as a new thesis. The derivational line before T5 has a similar explanation. The stroke (/) is the sign of substitution and the short rule (–) the sign of detachment. Almost all subsequent deductions are performed in the same manner.

One must be very expert in performing such proofs if one wants to deduce from the axioms T1–T3 the law of commutation *CCpCqrCqCpr* or even the law of simplification *CpCqp*. I shall therefore explain an easy method of verifying expressions of our system without deducing them from the axioms. This method, invented by the American logician Charles S. Peirce about 1885, is based on the so-called principle of bivalence, which states that every proposition is either true or false, i.e. that it has one and only one of two possible truth-values: truth and falsity. This principle must not be mixed up with the law of the excluded middle, according to which of two contradictory propositions one must be true. It was stated as the basis of logic by the Stoics, in particular by Chrysippus.[1]

All functions of the theory of deduction are truth-functions, i.e. their truth and falsity depend only upon the truth and falsity of their arguments. Let us denote a constant false proposition by *o*, and a constant true proposition by *1*. We may define negation in the following way:

$$No = 1 \qquad \text{and} \qquad N1 = o.$$

This means: the negation of a false proposition means the same as a true proposition (or, shortly, is true) and the negation of a true proposition is false. For implication we have the following four definitions:

$$Coo = 1, \qquad Co1 = 1, \qquad C1o = o, \qquad C11 = 1.$$

---

[1] Cicero, *Acad. pr.* ii. 95 'Fundamentum dialecticae est, quidquid enuntietur (id autem appellant ἀξίωμα) aut verum esse aut falsum'; *De fato* 21 'Itaque contendit omnes nervos Chrysippus ut persuadeat omne ἀξίωμα aut verum esse aut falsum.' In the Stoic terminology ἀξίωμα means 'proposition', not 'axiom'.

This means: an implication is false only when its antecedent is true and its consequent false; in all the other cases it is true. This is the oldest definition of implication, stated by Philon of Megara and adopted by the Stoics.[1] For conjunction we have the four evident equalities:

$$Koo = o, \quad Koi = o, \quad Kio = o, \quad Kii = i.$$

A conjunction is true only when both its arguments are true; in all the other cases it is false.

Now if we want to verify a significant expression of the theory of deduction containing all or some of the functors C, N, and K we have to substitute for the variables occurring in the expression the symbols o and i in all possible permutations, and reduce the formulae thus obtained on the basis of the equalities given above. If after the reduction all the formulae give i as the final result, the expression is true or a thesis; if any one of them gives o as the final result, the expression is false. Let us take as an example of the first kind the law of transposition $CCpqCNqNp$; we get:

For p/o, q/o: $CCooCNoNo = CiCii = Cii = i$,
,, p/o, q/i: $CCoiCNiNo = CiCoi = Cii = i$,
,, p/i, q/o: $CCioCNoNi = CoCio = Coo = i$,
,, p/i, q/i: $CCiiCNiNi = CiCoo = Cii = i$.

As for all substitutions the final result is i, the law of transposition is a thesis of our system. Let us now take as an example of the second kind the expression $CKpNqq$. It suffices to try only one substitution:

p/i, q/o: $CKiNoo = CKiio = Cio = o$.

This substitution gives o as the final result, and therefore the expression $CKpNqq$ is false. In the same way we may check all the theses of the theory of deduction employed as auxiliary premises in Aristotle's syllogistic.

§ 24. *Quantifiers*

Aristotle had no clear idea of quantifiers and did not use them in his works; consequently we cannot introduce them into his syllogistic. But, as we have already seen, there are two points in his system which we can understand better if we explain them

---

[1] Sextus Empiricus, *Adv. math.* viii. 113 ὁ μὲν Φίλων ἔλεγεν ἀληθὲς γίνεσθαι τὸ συνημμένον, ὅταν μὴ ἄρχηται ἀπ' ἀληθοῦς καὶ λήγῃ ἐπὶ ψεῦδος, ὥστε τριχῶς μὲν γίνεσθαι κατ' αὐτὸν ἀληθὲς συνημμένον, καθ' ἕνα δὲ τρόπον ψεῦδος.

by employing quantifiers. Universal quantifiers are connected with the so-called 'syllogistic necessity', existential or particular quantifiers with the proofs by ecthesis. I shall now translate into symbols the proofs with existential quantifiers set down in section 19, and then the argument dependent on universal quantifiers mentioned in section 5.

I denote quantifiers by Greek capitals, the universal quantifier by Π, and the particular or existential quantifier by Σ. Π may be read 'for all', and Σ 'for some' or 'there exists'; e.g. $\Sigma cKAcbAca$ means in words: 'There exists a c such that all c is b and all c is a', or more briefly: 'For some c, all c is b and all c is a.' Every quantified expression, for instance $\Sigma cKAcbAca$, consists of three parts: part one, in our example Σ, is always a quantifier; part two, here c, is always a variable bound by the preceding quantifier; part three, here $KAcbAca$, is always a propositional expression containing the variable just bound by the quantifier as a free variable. It is by putting Σc before $KAcbAca$ that the free variable c in this last formula becomes bound. We may put it briefly: Σ (part one) binds c (part two) in $KAcbAca$ (part three).

The rules of existential quantifiers have already been set out in section 19. In derivational lines I denote by Σ_1 the rule allowing us to put Σ before the antecedent, and by Σ_2 the rule allowing us to put it before the consequent of a true implication. The following deductions will be easily understood, as they are translations of the deductions given in words in section 19, the corresponding theses bearing the same running number and having corresponding small letters as variables instead of capitals.

Proof of conversion of the I-premiss

Theses assumed as true without proof:

(1) $CIab\Sigma cKAcbAca$

(2) $C\Sigma cKAcbAcaIab$

Theses (1) and (2) can be used as a definition of the I-premiss.

(3) $CKpqKqp$ (commutative law of conjunction)

   (3) $p/Ach, q/Aca \times$ (4)
(4) $CKAcbAcaKAcaAcb$

   (4) $\Sigma 2c \times$ (5)
(5) $CKAcbAca\Sigma cKAcaAcb$

(5) $\Sigma_{I} c \times$ (6)

(6) $C\Sigma cKAcbAca\Sigma cKAcaAcb$

T1. $CCpqCCqrCpr$ (law of the hypothetical syllogism)

     T1. $p/Iab, q/\Sigma cKAcbAca, r/\Sigma cKAcaAcb \times C(1)-C(6)-(7)$

(7) $CIab\Sigma cKAcaAcb$

     (2) $b/a, a/b \times$ (8)

(8) $C\Sigma cKAcaAcbIba$

     T1. $p/Iab, q/\Sigma cKAcaAcb, r/Iba \times C(7)-C(8)-(9)$

(9) $CIabIba$

The derivational lines show that (4) and (8) result from other theses by substitution only, and (7) and (9) by substitution and two detachments. Upon this pattern the reader himself may try to construct the proof of the mood Darapti, which is easy.

Proof of the mood Bocardo

(The variables P, R, and S used in section 19 must be re-lettered, as the corresponding small letters p, r, and s are reserved to denote propositional variables: write d for P, a for R, and b for S.)

Thesis assumed without proof:

     (15) $CObd\Sigma cKAcbEcd$

Two syllogisms taken as premisses:

     (16) $CKAcbAbaAca$ (Barbara)

     (17) $CKAcaEcdOad$ (Felapton)

T6. $CCKpqrCCKrstCKKpqst$

This is the 'synthetic theorem' ascribed to Aristotle.

       T6. $p/Acb, q/Aba, r/Aca, s/Ecd, t/Oad \times C(16)-C(17)-$
       (18)

(18) $CKKAcbAbaEcdOad$

T7. $CCKKpqrsCKprCqs$ (auxiliary thesis)

     T7. $p/Acb, q/Aba, r/Ecd, s/Oad \times C(18)-(19)$

(19) $CKAcbEcdCAbaOad$

     (19) $\Sigma_{I} c \times$ (20)

(20) $C\Sigma cKAcbEcdCAbaOad$

T1. $CCpqCCqrCpr$

     T1. $p/Obd, q/\Sigma cKAcbEcd, r/CAbaOad \times C(15)-C(20)-$
     (21)

(21) $CObdCAbaOad$

This is the implicational form of the mood Bocardo. If we wish to have the usual conjunctional form of this mood, we must apply to (21) the so-called law of importation:

T8. $CCpCqrCKpqr$.

We get:

T8. $p/Obd, q/Aba, r/Oad \times C(21)-(22)$

(22) $CKObdAbaOad$ (Bocardo).

By the so-called law of exportation,

T9. $CCKpqrCpCqr$,

which is the converse of the law of importation, we can get the implicational form of the mood Bocardo back from its conjunctional form.

The rules of universal quantifiers are similar to the rules of particular quantifiers set out in section 19. The universal quantifier can be put before the antecedent of a true implication unconditionally, binding a free variable occurring in the antecedent, and before the consequent of a true implication only under the condition that the variable which is to be bound in the consequent does not occur in the antecedent as a free variable. I denote the first of these rules by $\Pi 1$, the second by $\Pi 2$.

Two derived rules result from the above primitive rules of universal quantifiers: first, it is permissible (by rule $\Pi 2$ and the law of simplification) to put universal quantifiers in front of a true expression binding free variables occurring in it; secondly, it is permissible (by rule $\Pi 1$ and the propositional law of identity) to drop universal quantifiers standing in front of a true expression. How these rules may be derived I shall explain by the example of the law of conversion of the I-premiss.

From the law of conversion

(9) $CIabIba$

there follows the quantified expression

(26) $\Pi a\Pi bCIabIba$,

and from the quantified expression (26) there follows again the unquantified law of conversion (9).

First: from (9) follows (26).

T10.   *CpCqp*   (law of simplification)

T10. $p/CIabIba \times C(9)-(23)$
(23) *CqCIabIba*

To this thesis we apply rule $\Pi2$ binding *b*, and then *a*, as neither *b* nor *a* occurs in the antecedent:

(23) $\Pi2b \times (24)$
(24) *CqΠbCIabIba*

(24) $\Pi2a \times (25)$
(25) *CqΠaΠbCIabIba*

(25) $q/CpCqp \times CT10-(26)$
(26) *ΠaΠbCIabIba*

Secondly: from (26) follows (9).

T5.   *Cpp*   (law of identity)

T5. $p/CIabIba \times (27)$
(27) *CCIabIbaCIabIba*

To this thesis we apply rule $\Pi1$ binding *b*, and then *a*:

(27) $\Pi1b \times (28)$
(28) *CΠbCIabIbaCIabIba*

(28) $\Pi1a \times (29)$
(29) *CΠaΠbCIabIbaCIabIba*

(29) $\times C(26)-(9)$
(9) *CIabIba*

Aristotle asserts: 'If some *a* is *b*, it is necessary that some *b* should be *a*.' The expression 'it is necessary that' can have, in my opinion, only this meaning: it is impossible to find such values of the variables *a* and *b* as would verify the antecedent without verifying the consequent. That means, in other words: 'For all *a*, and for all *b*, if some *a* is *b*, then some *b* is *a*.' This is our quantified thesis (26). It has been proved that this thesis is equivalent to the unquantified law of conversion 'If some *a* is *b*, then some *b* is *a*', which does not contain the sign of necessity. Since the syllogistic necessity is equivalent to a universal quantifier it may be omitted, as a universal quantifier may be omitted at the head of a true formula.

§ 25. *Fundamentals of the syllogistic*

Every axiomatized deductive system is based on three fundamental elements: primitive terms, axioms, and rules of inference.
I start from the fundamentals for asserted expressions, the fundamental elements for the rejected ones being given later.

As primitive terms I take the constants *A* and *I*, defining by
them the two other constants, *E* and *O*:

Df 1. *Eab* = *NIab*
Df 2. *Oab* = *NAab*.

In order to abbreviate the proofs I shall employ instead of the
above definitions the two following rules of inference:

Rule RE: *NI* may be everywhere replaced by *E* and conversely.
Rule RO: *NA* may be everywhere replaced by *O* and conversely.

The four theses of the system axiomatically asserted are the
two laws of identity and the moods Barbara and Datisi:

1. *Aaa*
2. *Iaa*
3. *CKAbcAabAac*   (Barbara)
4. *CKAbcIbaIac*   (Datisi).

Besides the rules RE and RO I accept the two following rules
of inference for the asserted expressions:

(*a*) Rule of substitution: If α is an asserted expression of the
system, then any expression produced from α by a valid
substitution is also an asserted expression. The only valid
substitution is to put for term-variables *a*, *b*, *c* other term-
variables, e.g. *b* for *a*.

(*b*) Rule of detachment: If *Cαβ* and α are asserted expressions
of the system, then β is an asserted expression.

As an auxiliary theory I assume the *C–N*-system of the theory
of deduction with *K* as a defined functor. For propositional
variables propositional expressions of the syllogistic may be
substituted, like *Aab*, *Iac*, *KEbcAab*, etc. In all subsequent proofs
(and also for rejected expressions) I shall employ only the
following fourteen theses denoted by roman numerals:

    I. *CpCqp*   (law of simplification)
    II. *CCqrCCpqCpr*   (law of hypothetical syllogism, 2nd form)
    III. *CCpCqrCqCpr*   (law of commutation)
    IV. *CpCNpq*   (law of Duns Scotus)
    V. *CCNppp*   (law of Clavius)
    VI. *CCpqCNqNp*   (law of transposition)
    VII. *CCKpqrCpCqr*   (law of exportation)
    VIII. *CpCCKpqrCqr*
    IX. *CCspCCKpqrCKsqr*
    X. *CCKpqrCCsqCKpsr*
    XI. *CCrsCCKpqrCKqps*
    XII. *CCKpqrCKpNrNq*
    XIII. *CCKpqrCKNrqNp*
    XIV. *CCKpNqNrCKprq*

Thesis VIII is a form of the law of exportation, theses IX–XI are compound laws of hypothetical syllogism, and XII–XIV are compound laws of transposition. All of these can be easily verified by the *o–1* method explained in section 23. Theses IV and V give together with II and III the whole *C–N*-system, but IV and V are needed only in proofs for rejected expressions.

The system of axioms 1–4 is consistent, i.e. non-contradictory. The easiest proof of non-contradiction is effected by regarding term-variables as proposition-variables, and by defining the functions *A* and *I* as always true, i.e. by putting $Aab = Iab = KCaaCbb$. The axioms 1–4 are then true as theses of the theory of deduction, and as it is known that the theory of deduction is non-contradictory, the syllogistic is non-contradictory too.

All the axioms of our system are independent of each other. The proofs of this may be given by interpretation in the field of the theory of deduction. In the subsequent interpretations the term-variables are treated as propositional variables.

Independence of axiom 1: Take *K* for *A*, and *C* for *I*. Axiom 1 is not verified, for $Aaa = Kaa$, and Kaa gives *o* for *a/o*. The other axioms are verified, as can be seen by the *o–1* method.

Independence of axiom 2: Take *C* for *A*, and *K* for *I*. Axiom 2 is not verified, for $Iaa = Kaa$. The other axioms are verified.

Independence of axiom 4: Take *C* for *A* and *I*. Axiom 4 is not verified, for $CKAbcIbaIac = CKCbcCbaCac$ gives *o* for *b/o*, *a/1*, *c/o*. The rest are verified.

Independence of axiom 3: it is impossible to prove the independence of this axiom on the ground of a theory of deduction with only two truth-values, o and 1. We must introduce a third truth-value, let us say 2, which may be regarded as another symbol for truth, i.e. for 1. To the equivalences given for C, N, and K in section 23, we have to add the following formulae:

$$Co2 = C12 = C21 = C22 = 1, \qquad C20 = o, \qquad N2 = o,$$
$$Ko2 = K20 = o, \qquad K12 = K21 = K22 = 1.$$

It can easily be shown that under these conditions all the theses of the C–N-system are verified. Let us now define Iab as a function always true, i.e. $Iab = 1$ for all values of a and b, and Aab as a function with the values

$Aaa = 1$, $Ao1 = A12 = 1$, and $Ao2 = o$ (the rest is irrelevant).

Axioms 1, 2, and 4 are verified, but from 3 we get by the substitutions $b/1$, $c/2$, a/o: $CKA12Ao1Ao2 = CK110 = C10 = o$.

It is also possible to give proofs of independence by interpretation in the field of natural numbers. If we want, for instance, to prove that axiom 3 is independent of the remaining axioms, we can define Aab as $a+1 \neq b$, and Iab as $a+b = b+a$. Iab is always true, and therefore axioms 2 and 4 are verified. Axiom 1 is also verified, for $a+1$ is always different from a. But axiom 3, i.e. 'If $b+1 \neq c$ and $a+1 \neq b$, then $a+1 \neq c$', is not verified. Take 3 for a, 2 for b, and 4 for c: the premisses will be true and the conclusion false.

It results from the above proofs of independence that there exists no single axiom or 'principle' of the syllogistic. The four axioms 1–4 may be mechanically conjoined by the word 'and' into one proposition, but they remain distinct in this inorganic conjunction without representing one single idea.

§ 26. *Deduction of syllogistic theses*

From axioms 1–4 we can derive all the theses of the Aristotelian logic by means of our rules of inference and by the help of the theory of deduction. I hope that the subsequent proofs will be quite intelligible after the explanations given in the foregoing sections. In all syllogistical moods the major term is denoted by a, the middle term by b, and the minor term by c.

The major premiss is stated first, so that it is easy to compare the formulae with the traditional names of the moods.[1]

A. The Laws of Conversion

VII. $p/Abc, q/Iba, r/Iac \times C4\text{--}5$

5. *CAbcCIbaIac*

    5. $b/a, c/a, a/b \times C1\text{--}6$

6. *CIabIba*   (law of conversion of the *I*-premiss)

III. $p/Abc, q/Iba, r/Iac \times C5\text{--}7$

7. *CIbaCAbcIac*

    7. $b/a, c/b \times C2\text{--}8$

8. *CAabIab*   (law of subordination for affirmative premisses)

II. $q/Iab, r/Iba \times C6\text{--}9$

9. *CCpIabCpIba*

    9. $p/Aab \times C8\text{--}10$

10. *CAabIba*   (law of conversion of the *A*-premiss)

    6. $a/b, b/a \times 11$

11. *CIbaIab*

VI. $p/Iba, q/Iab \times C11\text{--}12$

12. *CNIabNIba*

    12. $RE \times 13$

13. *CEabEba*   (law of conversion of the *E*-premiss)

VI. $p/Aab, q/Iab \times C8\text{--}14$

14. *CNIabNAab*

    14. RE, RO $\times 15$

15. *CEabOab*   (law of subordination for negative premisses)

B. The Affirmative Moods

X. $p/Abc, q/Iba, r/Iac \times C4\text{--}16$

16. *CCsIbaCKAbcsIac*

    16. $s/Iab \times C6\text{--}17$

17. *CKAbcIabIac*   (Darii)

---

[1] In my Polish text-book, *Elements of Mathematical Logic*, published in 1929 (see p. 46, n. 3), I showed for the first time how the known theses of the syllogistic may be formally deduced from axioms 1–4 (pp. 180–90). The method expounded in the above text-book is accepted with some modifications by I. M. Bocheński, O.P., in his contribution: *On the Categorical Syllogism*, Dominican Studies, vol. i, Oxford (1948).

16. $s/Aab \times C$10–18
18. $CKAbcAabIac$ (Barbari)

8. $a/b, b/a \times 19$
19. $CAbaIba$

16. $s/Aba \times C$19–20
20. $CKAbcAbaIac$ (Darapti)

XI. $r/Iba, s/Iab \times C$11–21
21. $CCKpqIbaCKqpIab$

4. $c/a, a/c \times 22$
22. $CKAbaIbcIca$

21. $p/Aba, q/Ibc, b/c \times C$22–23
23. $CKIbcAbaIac$ (Disamis)

17. $c/a, a/c \times 24$
24. $CKAbaIcbIca$

21. $p/Aba, q/Icb, b/c \times C$24–25
25. $CKIcbAbaIac$ (Dimaris)

18. $c/a, a/c \times 26$
26. $CKAbaAcbIca$

21. $p/Aba, q/Acb, b/c \times C$26–27
27. $CKAcbAbaIac$ (Bramantip)

C. The Negative Moods

XIII. $p/Ibc, q/Aba, r/Iac \times C$23–28
28. $CKNIacAbaNIbc$

28. $RE \times 29$
29. $CKEacAbaEbc$

29. $a/b, b/a \times 30$
30. $CKEbcAabEac$ (Celarent)

IX. $s/Eab, p/Eba \times C$13–31
31. $^{\cdot}CCKEbaqrCKEabqr$

31. $a/c, q/Aab, r/Eac \times C$30–32
32. $CKEcbAabEac$ (Cesare)

XI. $r/Eab, s/Eba \times C$13–33
33. $CCKpqEabCKqpEba$

32. $c/a, a/c \times 34$
34. $CKEabAcbEca$

33. $p/Eab, q/Acb, a/c, b/a \times C34$–35
35. $CKAcbEabEac$ (Camestres)

30. $c/a, a/c \times 36$
36. $CKEbaAcbEca$

33. $p/Eba, q/Acb, a/c, b/a \times C36$–37
37. $CKAcbEbaEac$ (Camenes)

II. $q/Eab, r/Oab \times C15$–38
38. $CCpEabCpOab$

38. $p/KEbcAab, b/c \times C30$–39
39. $CKEbcAabOac$ (Celaront)

38. $p/KEcbAab, b/c \times C32$–40
40. $CKEcbAabOac$ (Cesaro)

38. $p/KAcbEab, b/c \times C35$–41
41. $CKAcbEabOac$ (Camestrop)

38. $p/KAcbEba, b/c \times C37$–42
42. $CKAcbEbaOac$ (Camenop)

XIII. $p/Abc, q/Iba, r/Iac \times C4$–43
43. $CKNIacIbaNAbc$

43. RE, RO $\times 44$
44. $CKEacIbaObc$

44. $a/b, b/a \times 45$
45. $CKEbcIabOac$ (Ferio)

31. $a/c, q/Iab, r/Oac \times C45$–46
46. $CKEcbIabOac$ (Festino)

X. $p/Ebc, q/Iab, r/Oac \times C45$–47
47. $CCsIabCKEbcsOac$

47. $s/Iba \times C11$–48
48. $CKEbcIbaOac$ (Ferison)

31. $a/c, q/Iba, r/Oac \times C48$–49
49. $CKEcbIbaOac$ (Fresison)

10. $a/b, b/a \times 50$
50. $CAbaIab$

47. $s/Aba \times C50$–51
51. $CKEbcAbaOac$ (Felapton)

31. $a/c, q/Aba, r/Oac \times C51$–52
52. $CKEcbAbaOac$ (Fesapo)

As a result of all these deductions one remarkable fact deserves our attention: it was possible to deduce twenty syllogistic moods without employing axiom 3, the mood Barbara. Even Barbari could be proved without Barbara. Axiom 3 is the most important thesis of the syllogistic, for it is the only syllogism that yields a universal affirmative conclusion, but in the system of simple syllogisms it has an inferior rank, being necessary to prove only two syllogistic moods, Baroco and Bocardo. Here are these two proofs:

XII. p/Abc, q/Aab, $r/Aac \times C3$-53
53. $CKAbcNAacNAab$

53. RO × 54
54. $CKAbcOacOab$

54. b/c, $c/b \times 55$
55. $CKAcbOabOac$ (Baroco)

XIII. p/Abc, q/Aab, $r/Aac \times C3$-56
56. $CKNAacAabNAbc$

56. RO × 57
57. $CKOacAabObc$

57. a/b, $b/a \times 58$
58. $CKObcAbaOac$ (Bocardo)

§ 27. *Axioms and rules for rejected expressions*

Of two intellectual acts, to assert a proposition and to reject it,[1] only the first has been taken into account in modern formal logic. Gottlob Frege introduced into logic the idea of assertion, and the sign of assertion (⊢), accepted afterwards by the authors of *Principia Mathematica*. The idea of rejection, however, so far as I know, has been neglected up to the present day.

We assert true propositions and reject false ones. Only true propositions can be asserted, for it would be an error to assert a proposition that was not true. An analogous property cannot be asserted of rejection: it is not only false propositions that have to be rejected. It is true, of course, that every proposition is either true or false, but there exist propositional expressions that are neither true nor false. Of this kind are the so-called propositional functions, i.e. expressions containing free variables

---

[1] I owe this distinction to Franz Brentano, who describes the acts of believing as *anerkennen* and *verwerfen*.

and becoming true for some of their values, and false for others. Take, for instance, p, the propositional variable: it is neither true nor false, because for $p/1$ it becomes true, and for p/o it becomes false. Now, of two contradictory propositions, α and $N\alpha$, one must be true and the other false, one therefore must be asserted and the other rejected. But neither of the two contradictory propositional functions, p and Np, can be asserted, because neither of them is true: they both have to be rejected.

The syllogistic forms rejected by Aristotle are not propositions but propositional functions. Let us take an example: Aristotle says that no syllogism arises in the first figure, when the first term belongs to all the middle, but to none of the last. The syllogistic form therefore:

(i) $CKAbcEabIac$

is not asserted by him as a valid syllogism, but rejected. Aristotle himself gives concrete terms disproving the above form: take for b 'man', for c 'animal', and for a 'stone'. But there are other values for which the formula (i) can be verified: by identifying the variables a and c we get a true implication $CKAbaEabIaa$, for its antecedent is false and its consequent true. The negation of the formula (i):

(j) $NCKAbcEabIac$

must therefore be rejected too, because for c/a it is false.

By introducing quantifiers into the system we could dispense with rejection. Instead of rejecting the form (i) we could assert the thesis:

(k) $\Sigma a \Sigma b \Sigma c NCKAbcEabIac$.

This means: there exist terms a, b, and c that verify the negation of (i). The form (i), therefore, is not true for all a, b, and c, and cannot be a valid syllogism. In the same way instead of rejecting the expression (j) we might assert the thesis:

(l) $\Sigma a \Sigma b \Sigma c CKAbcEabIac$.

But Aristotle knows nothing of quantifiers; instead of adding to his system new theses with quantifiers he uses rejection. As rejection seems to be a simpler idea than quantification, let us follow in Aristotle's steps.

Aristotle rejects most invalid syllogistic forms by exemplification through concrete terms. This is the only point where we cannot follow him, because we cannot introduce into logic such concrete terms as 'man' or 'animal'. Some forms must be rejected axiomatically. I have found[1] that if we reject axiomatically the two following forms of the second figure:

$CKAcbAabIac$
$CKEcbEabIac,$

all the other invalid syllogistic forms may be rejected by means of two rules of rejection:

(c) Rule of rejection by detachment: if the implication 'If α, then β' is asserted, but the consequent β is rejected, then the antecedent α must be rejected too.

(d) Rule of rejection by substitution: if β is a substitution of α, and β is rejected, then α must be rejected too.

Both rules are perfectly evident.

The number of syllogistic forms is $4 \times 4^3 = 256$; 24 forms are valid syllogisms, 2 forms are rejected axiomatically. It would be tedious to prove that the remaining 230 invalid forms may be rejected by means of our axioms and rules. I shall only show, by the example of the forms of the first figure with premisses Abc and Eab, how our rules of rejection work on the basis of the first axiom of rejection.

Rejected expressions I denote by an asterisk put before their serial number. Thus we have:

*59. $CKAcbAabIac$ (Axiom)
*59a. $CKEcbEabIac$
     I. $p/Iac, q/KAcbAab \times 60$
  60. $CIacCKAcbAabIac$
     $60 \times C*61-*59$
*61. $Iac.$

Here for the first time is applied the rule of rejection by detachment. The asserted implication 60 has a rejected consequent, *59; therefore its antecedent, *61, must be rejected too. In this same way I get the rejected expressions *64, *67, *71, *74, and *77.

---

[1] See section 20.

      V. $p/Iac \times 62$
62. *CCNIacIacIac*

      62. RE$\times$63
63. *CCEacIacIac*

      $63 \times C$*64–*61
*64. *CEacIac*

      1. $a/c \times 65$
65. *Acc*

      VIII. p/Acc, q/Eac, $r/Iac \times C$65–66
66. *CCKAccEacIacCEacIac*

      $66 \times C$*67–*64
*67. *CKAccEacIac*

      *67$\times$*68. b/c
*68. *CKAbcEabIac*

Here the rule of rejection by substitution is applied. Expression *68 must be rejected, because by the substitution of b for c in *68 we get the rejected expression *67. The same rule is used to get* 75.

      II. q/Aab, $r/Iab \times C$8–69
69. *CCpAabCpIab*

      69. $p/KAbcEab$, $b/c \times 70$
70. *CCKAbcEabAacCKAbcEabIac*

      $70 \times C$*71–*68
*71. *CKAbcEabAac*

      XIV. p/Acb, q/Iac, $r/Aab \times 72$
72. *CCKAcbNIacNAabCKAcbAabIac*

      72. RE, RO$\times$73
73. *CCKAcbEacOabCKAcbAabIac*

      $73 \times C$*74–*59
*74. *CKAcbEacOab*

      *74$\times$*75. b/c, c/b
*75. *CKAbcEabOac*

      38. $p/KAbcEab$, $b/c \times 76$
76. *CCKAbcEabEacCKAbcEabOac*

      $76 \times C$*77–*75
*77. *CKAbcEabEac*

The rejected expressions *68, *71, *75, and *77 are the four possible forms of the first figure having as premisses *Abc* and *Eab*. From these premisses no valid conclusion can be drawn in the first figure. We can prove in the same way on the basis of the two axiomatically rejected forms that all the other invalid syllogistic forms in all the four figures must be rejected too.

§ 28. *Insufficiency of our axioms and rules*

Although it is possible to prove all the known theses of the Aristotelian logic by means of our axioms and rules of assertion, and to disprove all the invalid syllogistic forms by means of our axioms and rules of rejection, the result is far from being satisfactory. The reason is that besides the syllogistic forms there exist many other significant expressions in the Aristotelian logic, indeed an infinity of them, so that we cannot be sure whether from our system of axioms and rules all the true expressions of the syllogistic can be deduced or not, and whether all the false expressions can be rejected or not. In fact, it is easy to find false expressions that cannot be rejected by means of our axioms and rules of rejection. Such, for instance, is the expression:

(F1) *CIabCNAabAba*.

It means: 'If some *a* is *b*, then if it is not true that all *a* is *b*, all *b* is *a*.' This expression is not true in the Aristotelian logic, and cannot be proved by the axioms of assertion, but it is consistent with them and added to the axioms does not entail any invalid syllogistic form. It is worth while to consider the system of the syllogistic as thus extended.

From the laws of the Aristotelian logic:

    8. *CAabIab*   and

    50. *CAbaIab*

and the law of the theory of deduction:

    (*m*) *CCprCCqrCCNpqr*

we can derive the following new thesis 78:

        (*m*) *p*/*Aab*, *q*/*Aba*, *r*/*Iab* × *C*8–*C*50–78

    78. *CCNAabAbaIab*.

This thesis is a converse implication with regard to (F1), and together with (F1) gives an equivalence. On the ground of this equivalence we may define the functor *I* by the functor *A*:

    (F2) *Iab* = *CNAabAba*.

This definition reads: ' "Some *a* is *b*" means the same as "If it is not true that all *a* is *b*, then all *b* is *a*".' As the expression 'If not-*p*, then *q*' is equivalent to the alternation 'Either *p* or *q*', we can also say: ' "Some *a* is *b*" means the same as "Either all *a* is *b* or all *b* is *a*".' It is now easy to find an interpretation of this extended system in the so-called Eulerian circles. The terms *a*, *b*, *c* are represented by circles, as in the usual interpretation, but on the condition that no two circles shall intersect each other. Axioms 1–4 are verified, and the forms *59 *CKAcbAabIac* and *59a *CKEcbEabIac* are rejected, because it is possible to draw two circles lying outside each other and included in a third circle, which refutes the form *CKAcbAabIac*, and to draw three circles each excluding the two others, which refutes the form *CKEcbEabIac*. Consequently all the laws of the Aristotelian logic are verified, and all the invalid syllogistic forms are rejected. The system, however, is different from the Aristotelian syllogistic, because the formula (F1) is false, as we can see from the following example: it is true that 'Some even numbers are divisible by 3', but it is true neither that 'All even numbers are divisible by 3' nor that 'All numbers divisible by 3 are even'.

It results from this consideration that our system of axioms and rules is not categorical, i.e. not all interpretations of our system verify and falsify the same formulae or are isomorphic. The interpretation just expounded verifies the formula (F1) which is not verified by the Aristotelian logic. The system of our axioms and rules, therefore, is not sufficient to give a full and exact description of the Aristotelian syllogistic.

In order to remove this difficulty we could reject the expression (F1) axiomatically. But it is doubtful whether this remedy would be effective; there may be other formulae of the same kind as (F1), perhaps even an infinite number of such formulae. The problem is to find a system of axioms and rules for the Aristotelian syllogistic on which we could decide whether any given significant expression of this system has to be asserted or rejected. To this most important problem of decision the next chapter is devoted.

CHAPTER V

THE PROBLEM OF DECISION

§ 29. *The number of undecidable expressions*

I TAKE as the basis of my present investigation the following fundamental elements of the syllogistic:

(1) The four asserted axioms 1–4.

(2) The rule (*a*) of substitution and the rule (*b*) of detachment for the asserted expressions.

(3) The two rejected axioms *59 and *59*a*.

(4) The rule (*c*) of detachment and the rule (*d*) of substitution for the rejected expressions.

To this system of axioms and rules the theory of deduction must be added as the auxiliary theory. From the axioms and rules of assertion there can be derived all the known theses of the Aristotelian logic, i.e. the laws of the square of opposition, the laws of conversion, and all the valid syllogistic moods; on the basis of the axioms and rules of rejection all the invalid syllogistical forms can be rejected. But, as we have already seen, this system of axioms and rules does not suffice to describe the Aristotelian syllogistic adequately, because there exist significant expressions, for instance *CIabCNAabAba*, which can neither be proved by our axioms and rules of assertion nor disproved by our axioms and rules of rejection. I call such expressions undecidable with respect to our basis. Undecidable expressions may be either true in the Aristotelian logic or false. The expression *CIabCNAabAba* is, of course, false.

There are two questions we have to settle on this basis in order to solve the problem of decision. The first question is, Is the number of undecidable expressions finite or not? If it is finite, the problem of decision is easily solved: we may accept true expressions as new asserted axioms, and reject false expressions axiomatically. This method, however, is not practicable if the number of undecidable expressions is not finite. We cannot assert or reject an infinity of axioms. A second question arises in this case: Is it possible to complete our system of axioms and rules so that we could decide whether a given expression had to

be asserted or rejected? Both these questions were solved by
Słupecki: the first negatively by showing that the number of
undecidable expressions on our basis is not finite, the second
affirmatively by the addition of a new rule of rejection.[1]

I begin with the first question. Every student of the traditional logic is familiar with the interpretation of syllogisms
by means of Eulerian circles: according to this interpretation
the term-variables a, b, c are represented by circles, the
premiss Aab being true when and only when the circle a is
either identical with the circle b or is included in b, and the
premiss Iab being true when and only when the circles a and b
have a common area. Consequently the premiss Eab, as the
negation of Iab, is true when and only when the circles a
and b have no common area, i.e. when they exclude each
other. If, therefore, a and b are identical, Iab is true and Eab is
false.

I shall now investigate various suppositions concerning the
number of circles assumed as our 'universe of discourse', i.e.
as the field of our interpretation. It is obvious that the rules of
our basis remain valid throughout all the interpretations. If our
universe of discourse consists of three circles or more, the four
axioms of assertion are of course verified, and the axiomatically
rejected expression

*59. $CKAcbAabIac$

is rejected, as it is possible to draw two circles c and a excluding
each other and both included in the third circle b. The premisses
Acb and Aab are then true, and the conclusion Iac is false. The
expression

*59a. $CKEcbEabIac$

also is rejected, as we can draw three circles each excluding the
two others, so that the premisses Ecb and Eab are true and the
conclusion Iac is false. This interpretation therefore satisfies
the conditions of our basis, and so do all our other interpretations.

Let us now suppose that our universe of discourse consists of

---

[1] See the paper of Słupecki quoted in p. 76, n. I have tried to simplify the author's
arguments in order to make them comprehensible to readers not trained in mathematical thinking. I am, of course, alone responsible for the following exposition
of Słupecki's ideas.

only three circles, but no more, and let us consider the following expression:

(F3) *CEabCEacCEadCEbcCEbdIcd.*

This expression contains four different variables, but each of them can assume only three different values, as we can only draw three different circles. Whatever be the way to substitute these three values for the variables, two variables must always receive the same value, i.e. must be identified. But if some one of the pairs of variables, *a* and *b*, or *a* and *c*, or *a* and *d*, or *b* and *c*, or *b* and *d*, consists of identical elements, the corresponding *E*-premiss becomes false, and the whole implication, i.e. the expression (F3), is verified; and if the last pair of variables, *c* and *d*, has identical elements, the conclusion *Icd* becomes true, and the whole implication is again verified. Under the condition that only three circles can be drawn, the expression (F3) is true and cannot be disproved by our axioms and rules of rejection. If we suppose, however, that our universe of discourse consists of more than three circles, we can draw four circles, each of them excluding the three others, and (F3) becomes false. (F3) therefore cannot be proved by our axioms and rules of assertion. As (F3) can neither be proved nor disproved by the system of our axioms and rules, it is an undecidable expression.

Let us now consider an expression of the form

(F4) $C\alpha_1 C\alpha_2 C\alpha_3 ... C\alpha_n \beta$,

containing *n* different variables:

$$a_1, a_2, a_3, ..., a_n,$$

and let us suppose that: (1) every antecedent of (F4) is of the type $Ea_i a_j$, a_i differing from a_j; (2) the consequent β is of the type $Ia_k a_l$, a_k differing from a_l; (3) all the possible pairs of different variables occur in (F4). If our universe of discourse consists of only $(n-1)$ circles, (F4) is verified, because some two variables must be identified, and either one of the antecedents becomes false or the consequent is true. But if our universe of discourse consists of more than $(n-1)$ circles, (F4) is not verified, for *n* circles may be drawn each excluding the remainder, so that all the antecedents become true and the consequent is false. (F4), therefore, is an undecidable expression.

Such undecidable expressions are infinite in number, as n may be any integer whatever. It is obvious that they are all false in the Aristotelian logic, and must be rejected, for we cannot restrict the Aristotelian logic to a finite number of terms, and expressions of the form (F4) are disproved when the number of terms is infinite. This infinite number of undecidable expressions cannot be rejected otherwise than axiomatically, as results from the following consideration: (F3) cannot be disproved by the system of our axioms and rules, and therefore must be rejected axiomatically. The next undecidable expression of the form (F4) containing five different terms cannot be disproved by our system of axioms and rules together with the already rejected expression (F3), and must again be rejected axiomatically. The same argument may be repeated with respect to every other undecidable expression of the form (F4). Since it is impossible to reject axiomatically an infinity of expressions, we must look for another device if we want to solve the problem of decision affirmatively.

§ 30. *Słupecki's rule of rejection*

I start from two terminological remarks: Expressions of the type *Aab*, *Iab*, *Eab*, and *Oab* I call simple expressions; the first two are simple affirmative expressions, and the third and fourth simple negative expressions. Simple expressions as well as expressions of the type:

$$C\alpha_1 C\alpha_2 C\alpha_3...C\alpha_{n-1}\alpha_n,$$

where all the α's are simple expressions, I call elementary expressions. With the help of this terminology Słupecki's rule of rejection may be formulated as follows:

If α and β are simple negative expressions and γ is an elementary expression, then if $C\alpha\gamma$ and $C\beta\gamma$ are rejected, $C\alpha C\beta\gamma$ must be rejected too.

Słupecki's rule of rejection has a close connexion with the following metalogical principle of traditional logic: 'utraque si praemissa neget, nil inde sequetur.' This principle, however, is not general enough, as it refers only to simple syllogisms of three terms. Another formulation of the same principle, 'ex mere negativis nihil sequitur', is apparently more general, but it is false when applied not only to syllogisms but also to other expressions of the syllogistic. Such theses as *CEabEba* or *CEabOab* show clearly that something does follow from merely negative premisses. Słupecki's rule is a general rule and avoids the awkwardness of traditional formulations.

Let us explain this point more fully in order to make Słupecki's rule clear. The proposition *Aac* does not follow either from the premiss *Aab* or from the premiss *Abc*; but when we conjoin these premisses, saying '*Aab* and *Abc*', we get the conclusion *Aac* by the mood Barbara. *Eac* does not follow from *Ebc*, or from *Aab* either: but from the conjunction of these premisses '*Ebc* and *Aab*' we get the conclusion *Eac* by the mood Celarent. In both cases we obtain from the conjunction of premisses some new proposition which does not result from either of them separately. If we have, however, two negative premisses, like *Ecb* and *Eab*, we can of course obtain from the first the conclusion *Ocb* and from the second *Oab*, but from the conjunction of these premisses no new proposition can be drawn except those that follow from each of them separately. This is the meaning of Słupecki's rule of rejection: if γ does not follow either from α or from β, it cannot follow from their conjunction, as nothing can be drawn from two negative premisses that does not follow from them separately. Słupecki's rule is as plain as the corresponding principle of traditional logic.

I shall now show how this rule can be applied in the rejection of undecidable expressions. For this purpose I use the rule in a symbolic form, denoted by RS (Rule of Słupecki):

RS. *$C\alpha\gamma$, *$C\beta\gamma \rightarrow$ *$C\alpha C\beta\gamma$.

Here as everywhere I employ Greek letters to denote variable expressions satisfying certain conditions: thus, α and β must be simple negative expressions of the syllogistic, γ must be an elementary expression as explained above, and all three expressions must be such that *Cαγ* and *Cβγ* may be rejected. The arrow (→) means 'therefore'. I want to lay stress on the fact that RS is a peculiar rule, valid only for negative expressions α and β of the Aristotelian logic, and, as we have already seen, cannot be applied to affirmative expressions of the syllogistic. Nor can it be applied to the theory of deduction. This results from the following example : the expressions *CNCpqr* and *CNCqpr* are both not true and would be rejected, if rejection were introduced into this theory, but *CNCpqCNCqpr* is a thesis. Also in algebra the proposition '*a* equals *b*' does not follow either from the premiss '*a* is not less than *b*' or from the premiss '*b* is not less than *a*', but it follows from the conjunction of these premisses.

As the first application of the new rule I shall show that the expression

*59a. CKEcbEabIac,

which was rejected axiomatically, can now be disproved. This results from the following deduction:

  9. *p/Eac, a/c, b/a* × 79
 79. *CCEacIcaCEacIac*

  79 × *C**80–*64
*80. *CEacIca*

  *80 × *81. *c/a, b/c, a/c*
*81. *CEcbIac*

  *64 × *82. *b/c*
*82. *CEabIac*

  RS. α/*Ecb*, β/*Eab*, γ/*Iac* × *81, *82 → *83
*83. *CEcbCEabIac*.

The rule RS is here applied for the first time; α and β are simple negative expressions, and γ is also a simple expression. From *83 we get by the law of exportation VII the formula *59*a*:

  VII. *p/Ecb, q/Eab, r/Iac* × 84
 84. *CCKEcbEabIacCEcbCEabIac*

  84 × *C**59*a*–*83
*59a. *CKEcbEabIac*.

It follows from the above that Słupecki's rule is stronger than our axiomatically rejected expression *59*a*. Since *59*a* has to be cancelled, formula *59, i.e. *CKAcbAabIac*, remains the sole expression axiomatically rejected.

In the second place I shall apply the rule RS repeatedly to disprove the formula (F3):

  *64 × *85. *d/c, c/a*
*85. *CEadIcd*

  *85 × *86. *b/a*
*86. *CEbdIcd*

RS. α/Ead, β/Ebd, $\gamma/Icd \times$ *85, *86 → *87
*87. $CEadCEbdIcd$

*80 × *88. b/a, d/a
*88. $CEbcIcd$

RS. α/Ebc, β/Ebd, $\gamma/Icd \times$ *88, *86 → *89
*89. $CEbcCEbdIcd$

RS. α/Ead, β/Ebc, $\gamma/CEbdIcd \times$ *87, *89 → *90
*90. $CEadCEbcCEbdIcd$

*88 × *91. a/b
*91. $CEacIcd$

RS. α/Eac, β/Ebd, $\gamma/Icd \times$ *91, *86 → *92
*92. $CEacCEbdIcd$

RS. α/Eac, β/Ebc, $\gamma/CEbdIcd \times$ *92, *89 → *93
*93. $CEacCEbcCEbdIcd$

RS. α/Eac, β/Ead, $\gamma/CEbcCEbdIcd \times$ *93; *90 → *94
*94. $CEacCEadCEbcCEbdIcd$

*85 × *95. b/d
*95. $CEabIcd$

RS. α/Eab, β/Ebd, $\gamma/Icd \times$ *95, *86 → *96
*96. $CEabCEbdIcd$

RS. α/Eab, β/Ebc, $\gamma/CEbdIcd \times$ *96, *89 → *97
*97. $CEabCEbcCEbdIcd$

RS. α/Eab, β/Ead, $\gamma/CEbcCEbdIcd \times$ *97, *90 → *98
*98. $CEabCEadCEbcCEbdIcd$

RS. α/Eab, β/Eac, $\gamma/CEadCEbcCEbdIcd \times$ *98, *94 →
*99
*99. $CEabCEacCEadCEbcCEbdIcd$

The rule RS is used in this deduction ten times; α and β are always simple negative expressions, and γ is everywhere an elementary expression. In the same manner we could disprove other formulae of the form (F4), and also the formula (F1) of section 28. It is needless, however, to perform these deductions, since we can now set forth the general problem of decision.

§ 31. *Deductive equivalence*

We need for our proof of decision the concept of deductive or inferential equivalence. Since there are, in my opinion, some misunderstandings in the treatment of this concept, its meaning must be carefully defined. I shall do this on the basis of the theory of deduction.

It is usually said that two expressions, α and β, are deductively equivalent to each other when it is possible to deduce β from α if α is asserted, and conversely α from β if β is asserted. The rules of inference are always supposed as given. But they are seldom sufficient. They suffice, for instance, in the following example. From the asserted law of commutation $CCpCqrCqCpr$ we can deduce the thesis $CqCCpCqrCpr$:

(1) $CCpCqrCqCpr$

  (1) $p/CpCqr$, $r/Cpr \times C(1)-(2)$

(2) $CqCCpCqrCpr$,

and again from this thesis we can deduce the law of commutation:

  (2) $q/CqCCpCqrCpr$, p/s, $r/t \times C(2)-(3)$

(3) $CCsCCqCCpCqrCprtCst$

  (2) $q/CpCqr$, p/q, $r/Cpr \times (4)$

(4) $CCpCqrCCqCCpCqrCprCqCpr$

  (3) $s/CpCqr$, $t/CqCpr \times C(4)-(1)$

(1) $CCpCqrCqCpr$.[1]

But we cannot in this simple way deduce from the asserted expression $CNpCpq$ the law of Duns Scotus $CpCNpq$, because from the first expression we can derive new propositions only by substitution, and all the substitutions of $CNpCpq$ begin with CN, none with Cp. To deduce one of those expressions from another we must have further assistance. Speaking generally, the relation of deductive equivalence is seldom absolute, but in most cases it is relative to a certain basis of theses. In our case this basis is the law of commutation. Starting from

(5) $CNpCpq$

we get by commutation the law of Duns Scotus:

  (1) p/Np, q/p, $r/q \times C(5)-(6)$

(6) $CpCNpq$,

and starting from (6) we get again by commutation (5):

  (1) q/Np, $r/q \times C(6)-(5)$

(5) $CNpCpq$.

  [1] This neat deduction was given by A. Tarski in Warsaw.

I say therefore that $CNpCpq$ and $CpCNpq$ are deductively equivalent with respect to the law of commutation, and I write:

$$CNpCpq \sim CpCNpq \qquad \text{with respect to (1)}.$$

The sign $\sim$ denotes the relation of deductive equivalence. This relation is different from the ordinary relation of equivalence, denoted here by Q, which is defined by the conjunction of two implications each converse to the other,

$$Qpq = KCpqCqp,$$

and requires no basis. If an ordinary equivalence $Q\alpha\beta$ is asserted, and α, or a substitution of α, is asserted too, then we can assert β, or the corresponding substitution of β, and conversely. An asserted ordinary equivalence $Q\alpha\beta$ is therefore a sufficient basis for the deductive equivalence $\alpha \sim \beta$; but it is not a necessary one. This is just the point where explanation is needed.

Not only asserted or true expressions may be deductively equivalent, but also false ones. In order to solve the problem of decision for the C–N-system we have to transform an arbitrary significant expression α into the expression $CN\alpha\pi$, where π is a propositional variable not occurring in α. This can be done by means of two theses:

S1. $CpCNpq$
S2. $CCNppp$.

I say that α is deductively equivalent to $CN\alpha\pi$ with respect to S1 and S2, and I write:

I. $\alpha \sim CN\alpha\pi$ \qquad with respect to S1 and S2.

All goes easily when α is asserted. Take as example $NNCpp$. This is a thesis easily verified by the 0–1 method. I state according to formula I that

$$NNCpp \sim CNNNCppq \qquad \text{with respect to S1 and S2}.$$

Starting from

(7) $NNCpp$

we get by S1:

S1. $p/NNCpp \times C(7)-(8)$
(8) $CNNNCppq$,

and starting again from (8) we get by substitution and S2:

(8) $q/NNCpp \times (9)$
(9) $CNNNCppNNCpp$

S2. $p/NNCpp \times C(9)-(7)$

(7) $NNCpp$.

But α is an arbitrary expression; it may be false, e.g. Cpq. In this case formula I reads:

$Cpq \sim CNCpqr$ with respect to S1 and S2.

Here the difficulty begins: we can get the thesis $CCpqCNCpqr$ from S1 by the substitution p/Cpq, q/r, but we cannot derive from this thesis the consequent $CNCpqr$, for Cpq is not a thesis and cannot be asserted. Therefore $CNCpqr$ cannot be detached. A still greater difficulty arises in the other direction: we can get from S2 by the substitution p/Cpq the thesis $CCNCpqCpqCpq$, but $CNCpqCpq$ is not asserted, nor can we get $CNCpqCpq$ from $CNCpqr$ by substitution, because $CNCpqr$ is not a thesis. We cannot say: Suppose that Cpq be asserted; then $CNCpqr$ would follow. The assertion of a false expression is an error, and we cannot expect to prove anything by an error. It seems therefore that formula I is valid not for all expressions but only for those that are asserted.

There exists, in my opinion, only one way to avoid these difficulties: it is the introduction of rejection into the theory of deduction. We reject axiomatically the variable p, and accept the clear rules of rejection, (c) and (d). It can easily be shown on this basis that Cpq must be rejected. For we get from the axiom

(*10) p

and the thesis

(11) $CCCpppp$

by the rules of rejection:

$(11) \times C(*12)-(*10)$

(*12) $CCppp$

$(*12) \times (*13) \; p/Cpp, \; q/p$

(*13) Cpq.

Now we are able to prove that if Cpq is rejected, $CNCpqr$ must be rejected too; and conversely, if $CNCpqr$ is rejected, Cpq must be rejected too. Starting from

(*13) Cpq

we get by S2 and the rules of rejection:

$$\text{S2. } p/Cpq \times (14)$$
$$(14)\ CCNCpqCpqCpq$$
$$(14) \times C(*15)-(*13)$$
$$(*15)\ CNCpqCpq$$
$$(*15) \times (*16)\ r/Cpq$$
$$(*16)\ CNCpqr.$$

In the other direction we easily get Cpq from (*16) by S1:

$$\text{S1. } p/Cpq,\ q/r \times (17)$$
$$(17)\ CCpqCNCpqr$$
$$(17) \times C(*13)-(*16)$$
$$(*13)\ Cpq.$$

Formula I is now fully justified. We have, however, to correct our previous definition of deductive equivalence, saying:

> Two expressions are deductively equivalent to each other with respect to certain theses when and only when we can prove by means of these theses and of the rules of inference that if one of those expressions is asserted, the other must be asserted too, or if one of them is rejected, the other must be rejected too.

It follows from this definition that ordinary equivalence is not a necessary basis of deductive equivalence. If $Q\alpha\beta$ is a thesis, it is true that α is deductively equivalent to β with respect to $Q\alpha\beta$; but if α is deductively equivalent to β with respect to certain theses, it is not always true that $Q\alpha\beta$ is a thesis. Take as example the deductive equivalence just considered:

$$Cpq \sim CNCpqr \qquad \text{with respect to S1 and S2.}$$

The corresponding ordinary equivalence $QCpqCNCpqr$ is not a thesis, for it is false for $p/1,\ q/0,\ r/1$.

It is obvious that the relation of deductive equivalence is reflexive, symmetrical, and transitive. There are cases where α is deductively equivalent to two expressions β and γ with respect to certain theses. That means: if α is asserted, then β is asserted and γ is asserted, and consequently their conjunction 'β and γ' is asserted; and conversely, if both β and γ, or their conjunction 'β and γ', is asserted, then α is asserted too. Again, if α is rejected, then the conjunction 'β and γ' must be rejected, and in this case it is sufficient that only one of them, β or γ, should be rejected; and conversely, if only one of them is rejected, α must be rejected too.

§ 32. *Reduction to elementary expressions*

Our proof of decision is based on the following theorem:

(TA) Every significant expression of the Aristotelian syllogistic can be reduced in a deductively equivalent way, with respect to theses of the theory of deduction, to a set of elementary expressions, i.e. expressions of the form

$$C\alpha_1 C\alpha_2 C\alpha_3 ... C\alpha_{n-1}\alpha_n,$$

where all the α's are simple expressions of the syllogistic, i.e. expressions of the type *Aab*, *Iab*, *Eab*, or *Oab*.

All known theses of the syllogistic either are elementary expressions or can easily be transformed into elementary expressions. The laws of conversion, e.g. *CIabIba* or *CAabIba*, are elementary expressions. All the syllogisms are of the form $CK\alpha\beta\gamma$, and expressions of this kind are deductively equivalent to elementary expressions of the form $C\alpha C\beta\gamma$ with respect to the laws of exportation and importation. But there are other significant expressions of the syllogistic, some of them true, some false, that are not elementary. We have already met such an expression: it was thesis 78, *CCNAabAbaIab*, the antecedent of which is not a simple expression but an implication. There exists, of course, an infinity of such expressions, and they must all be taken into account in the proof of decision.

Theorem (TA) can easily be proved on the basis of an analogous theorem for the theory of deduction:

(TB) Every significant expression of the theory of deduction with C and N as primitive terms can be reduced in a deductively equivalent way with respect to a finite number of theses to a set of elementary expressions of the form

$$C\alpha_1 C\alpha_2 C\alpha_3 ... C\alpha_{n-1}\alpha_n,$$

where all the α's are simple expressions, i.e. either variables or their negations.

The proof of this theorem is not easy, but since it is essential for the problem of decision it cannot be omitted. The proof of (TB) given below is intended for readers interested in formal logic; those not trained in mathematical logic may take both theorems, (TA) and (TB), for granted.

Let α be an arbitrary significant expression of the theory of deduction other than a variable (which may, but need not, be transformed): every such expression can be transformed, as we already know, in a deductively equivalent way with respect to the theses S1 and S2:

S1. $CpCNpq$
S2. $CCNppp$

into the expression $CN\alpha\pi$, where π is a variable not occurring in α. We have therefore as transformation I:

I. $\alpha \sim CN\alpha\pi$ with respect to S1 and S2.

Transformation I allows us to reduce all significant expressions to implications that have a variable as their last term. Now we must try to transform $N\alpha$, the antecedent of $CN\alpha\pi$, into a variable or its negation. For this purpose we employ the following three transformations:

II. $CNN\alpha\beta \sim C\alpha\beta$ with respect to S3 and S4,
III. $CNC\alpha\beta\gamma \sim C\alpha CN\beta\gamma$,,   ,,   S5 and S6,
IV. $CC\alpha\beta\gamma \sim CN\alpha\gamma, C\beta\gamma$,,   .,   S7, S8, and S9.

The respective theses are: for transformation II:

S3. $CCNNpqCpq$
S4. $CCpqCNNpq$;

for transformation III:

S5. $CCNCpqrCpCNqr$
S6. $CCpCNqrCNCpqr$;

for transformation IV:

S7. $CCCpqrCNpr$
S8. $CCCpqrCqr$
S9. $CCNprCCqrCCpqr$.

Let us now explain how we can get by these transformations a variable or its negation in the antecedent of $CN\alpha\pi$. The expression α occurring in $CN\alpha\pi$ may, like every significant expression of the C–N-system, be either a variable, or a negation, or an implication. If α is a variable, no transformation is needed; if it is a negation, we get $CNN\alpha\beta$, and two negations annul each other according to transformation II; if it is an implication, we get from $CNC\alpha\beta\gamma$ the equivalent expression $C\alpha CN\beta\gamma$, the antecedent of which, α, is simpler than the initial antecedent $NC\alpha\beta$. This new α may again be a variable—no transformation is then needed—or a negation—this case has already been settled—or an implication. In this last case we get from $CC\alpha\beta\gamma$ two expressions, $CN\alpha\gamma$ and $C\beta\gamma$, with simpler antecedents than the initial antecedent $C\alpha\beta$. By repeated applications of II, III, and IV we must finally reach in the antecedent a variable or its negation.

Let us now see by examples how these transformations work.

First example: $NNCpp$.

$NNCpp \qquad \sim CNNNCppq$ by I;
$CNNNCppq \sim CNCppq \qquad$,, II;
$CNCppq \qquad \sim CpCNpq \qquad$,, III.

$NNCpp$ is thus reduced to the expression $CpCNpq$ with the variable p in the antecedent. $CpCNpq$ is an elementary expression.

Second example: $CCCpqpp$.

$CCCpqpp \qquad \sim CNCCCpqppr$ by I;
$CNCCCpqppr \sim CCCpqpCNpr \qquad$,, III;
$CCCpqpCNpr \sim CNCpqCNpr, \; CpCNpr$ by IV;
$CNCpqCNpr \sim CpCNqCNpr \quad$ by III.

$CCCpqpp$ is thus reduced to two expressions: $CpCNqCNpr$ and $CpCNpr$, both with the variable p in the antecedent; both are elementary expressions.

Third example: $CCCpqqCCqpp$.

$CCCpqqCCqpp \qquad \sim CNCCCpqqCCqppr$ by I;
$CNCCCpqqCCqppr \sim CCCpqqCNCCqppr \qquad$,, III;
$CCCpqqCNCCqppr \sim CNCpqCNCCqppr, \; CqCNCCqppr$ by IV;
$CNCpqCNCCqppr \sim CpCNqCNCCqppr \quad$ by III.

$CCCpqqCCqpp$ is reduced to two expressions $CpCNqCNCCqppr$ and $CqCNCCqppr$, both with a variable in the first antecedent. Neither of them, however, is elementary, since the first has the compound expression $NCCqpp$ as its third antecedent and the second has the same compound expression as its second antecedent.

As we can see from this last example, our task is not yet finished. By transformations I–IV we obtain implications with a variable in the first antecedent, and also expressions of the form:

$$C\alpha_1 C\alpha_2 C\alpha_3 \ldots C\alpha_{n-1}\alpha_n,$$

but not all antecedents of this form, apart from α_1, need be simple expressions. In order to get rid of such compound antecedents we need three further transformations:

V. $C\alpha C\beta\gamma \quad \sim C\beta C\alpha\gamma \quad$ with respect to S10,
VI. $C\alpha C\beta C\gamma\delta \sim C\alpha C\gamma C\beta\delta \quad$ „ „ S11,
VII. $C\alpha C\beta\gamma \quad \sim CNC\alpha N\beta\gamma \quad$ „ „ S12 and S13.

The respective theses are: for transformation V:

S10. $CCpCqrCqCpr$;

for transformation VI:

S11. $CCpCqCrsCpCrCqs$;

for transformation VII:

S12. $CCpCqrCNCpNqr$
S13. $CCNCpNqrCpCqr$.

By S10 we can move a compound antecedent from the second place to the first, and by S11 from the third place to the second. Applying these transformations to the expressions $CpCNqCNCCqppr$ and $CqCNCCqppr$ of our third example we get:

(α) $CpCNqCNCCqppr \sim CpCNCCqppCNqr$ by VI;
    $CpCNCCqppCNqr \sim CNCCqppCpCNqr$ „ V;
    $CNCCqppCpCNqr \sim CCqpCNpCpCNqr$ „ III;
    $CCqpCNpCpCNqr \sim CNqCNpCpCNqr, CpCNpCpCNqr$ by
        IV.
(β) $CqCNCCqppr \sim CNCCqppCqr$ by V;
    $CNCCqppCqr \sim CCqpCNpCqr$ „ III;
    $CCqpCNpCqr \sim CNqCNpCqr, CpCNpCqr$ by IV.

$CCCpqqCCqpp$ is thus reduced to four elementary expressions: $CNqCNpCpCNqr$, $CpCNpCpCNqr$, $CNqCNpCqr$, and $CpCNpCqr$.

Transformation VII is used in all those cases where the compound antecedent occurs in the fourth place or farther. This transformation allows us to reduce the number of antecedents;

in fact, $NCpNq$ means the same as Kpq, and S12 and S13 are other forms of the laws of importation and exportation respectively. Now $CNC\alpha N\beta\gamma$, like $CK\alpha\beta\gamma$, has only one antecedent, whereas the equivalent expression $C\alpha C\beta\gamma$ has two antecedents. If, therefore, a compound expression occurs in the fourth place, as δ in $C\alpha C\beta C\gamma C\delta\epsilon$, we can move it to the third place, applying VII and then VI:

$$C\alpha C\beta C\gamma C\delta\epsilon \quad \sim\ CNC\alpha N\beta C\gamma C\delta\epsilon \text{ by VII;}$$
$$CNC\alpha N\beta C\gamma C\delta\epsilon \sim CNC\alpha N\beta C\delta C\gamma\epsilon \text{ ,, VI.}$$

From this last expression we get by the converse application of VII the formula:

$$CNC\alpha N\beta C\delta C\gamma\epsilon \sim C\alpha C\beta C\delta C\gamma\epsilon \text{ by VII.}$$

It is now easy to bring δ to the first place by VI and V:

$$C\alpha C\beta C\delta C\gamma\epsilon \sim C\alpha C\delta C\beta C\gamma\epsilon \text{ by VI,}$$
$$C\alpha C\delta C\beta C\gamma\epsilon \sim C\delta C\alpha C\beta C\gamma\epsilon \text{ ,, V.}$$

Applying transformation VII repeatedly in both directions we can move any antecedent from the nth place to the first, and transform it, if it is compound, by II, III, and IV into a simple expression.

The proof of theorem (TB) is thus completed. It is now easy to show that this theorem entails the proof of decision for the C–N-system of the theory of deduction. If all the elementary expressions to which a given expression α has been reduced are true, i.e. if they have among their antecedents two expressions of the type p and Np, then α is a thesis and must be asserted. On the other hand, if among the elementary expressions to which α has been reduced there exists at least one expression such that no two antecedents in it are of the type p and Np, then α must be rejected. In the first case we can prove α by means of the theses S1–S13, in the second we can disprove it, adding to the above theses two new ones:

S14. $CpCCpqq$
S15. $NNCpp$,

and the axiom of rejection:

*S16. p.

Two examples will clarify this.

First example: Proof of the thesis *CpCCpqq*.

This thesis must first be reduced to elementary expressions. This is done by the following analysis (L):

$$CpCCpqq \quad \sim \quad CNCpCCpqqr \quad \text{by I};$$
$$CNCpCCpqqr \sim CpCNCCpqqr \quad \text{,, III};$$
$$CpCNCCpqqr \sim CNCCpqqCpr \quad \text{,, V};$$
$$CNCCpqqCpr \sim CCpqCNqCpr \quad \text{,, III};$$
$$CCpqCNqCpr \sim CNpCNqCpr, CqCNqCpr \text{ by IV}.$$

The elementary expressions to which *CpCCpqq* is reduced are *CNpCNqCpr* and *CqCNqCpr*. Both, like all expressions to which transformation I has been applied, have as their last term a variable not occurring in the antecedents. Such expressions can be true only on condition that they have two antecedents of the type *p* and *Np*, and any expression of this kind can be reduced by transformations V, VI, or VII to a substitution of S1 from which the proof of a thesis must always begin. Here are the required deductions:

$$S1. \ q/CNqr \times (1)$$
$$(1) \ CpCNpCNqr$$

$$S10. \ q/Np, \ r/CNqr \times C(1)-(2)$$
$$(2) \ CNpCpCNqr$$

$$S11. \ p/Np, \ q/p, \ r/Nq, \ s/r \times C(2)-(3)$$
$$(3) \ CNpCNqCpr$$

$$S1. \ p/q, \ q/Cpr \times (4)$$
$$(4) \ CqCNqCpr.$$

Having got in (3) and (4) the same elementary expressions as we reached at the end of our analysis (L), we now proceed from them to their equivalents on the left, by applying theses on which the successive transformations were based. Thus, step by step, we get our original thesis by means of S9, S6, S10, and S2:

$$S9. \ r/CNqCpr \times C(3)-C(4)-(5)$$
$$(5) \ CCpqCNqCpr$$

$$S6. \ p/Cpq, \ r/Cpr \times C(5)-(6)$$
$$(6) \ CNCCpqqCpr$$

$$S10. \ p/NCCpqq, \ q/p \times C(6)-(7)$$
$$(7) \ CpCNCCpqqr$$

S6. $q/CCpqq \times C(7)-(8)$

(8) $CNCpCCpqqr$

(8) $r/CpCCpqq \times (9)$

(9) $CNCpCCpqqCpCCpqq$

S2. $p/CpCCpqq \times C(9)-(10)$

(10) $CpCCpqq.$

Upon this model we can prove any thesis we want.

Second example: Disproof of the expression $CCNpqq$.

We first reduce this expression to elementary expressions on the basis of the following analysis:

$$CCNpqq \qquad \sim CNCCNpqqr \text{ by I};$$
$$CNCCNpqqr \sim CCNpqCNqr \text{ ,, III};$$
$$CCNpqCNqr \sim CNNpCNqr, CqCNqr \text{ by IV};$$
$$CNNpCNqr \sim CpCNqr \qquad \text{by II}.$$

The expression $CCNpqq$ is thus reduced to two elementary expressions, $CqCNqr$ and $CpCNqr$. The first of these is a thesis, but the second is not true, for it has no two antecedents of the type p and Np. The expression $CCNpqq$ therefore, which leads to this not-true consequence, must be rejected. We begin the disproof from the top, successively applying according to the given transformations the theses S1, S5, S7, and S3:

S1. $p/CCNpqq, q/r \times (11)$

(11) $CCCNpqqCNCCNpqqr$

S5. $p/CNpq \times (12)$

(12) $CCNCCNpqqrCCNpqCNqr$

S7. $p/Np, r/CNqr \times (13)$

(13) $CCCNpqCNqrCNNpCNqr$

S3. $q/CNqr \times (14)$

(14) $CCNNpCNqrCpCNqr.$

Now we must disprove the expression $CpCNqr$; we need for this purpose the new theses S14 and S15 and the axiom of rejection.

S14. $p/NNCpp, q/p \times CS15-(15)$

(15) $CCNNCpppp$

(15) $\times C(*16)-*S16$

(*16) $CNNCppp$

S14. $p/CpCNpq$, $q/CNNCppp \times CS1-(17)$

(17) $CCCpCNpqCNNCpppCNNCppp$

$(17) \times C(*18)-(*16)$

(*18) $CCpCNpqCNNCppp$

$(*18) \times (*19)$ $p/CpCNpq$, $q/NCpp$, r/p

(*19) $CpCNqr$

Having rejected $CpCNqr$, we can now successively reject its antecedents till we reach the original expression $CCNpqq$.

$(14) \times C(*20)-(*19)$

(*20) $CNNpCNqr$

$(13) \times C(*21)-(*20)$

(*21) $CCNpqCNqr$

$(12) \times C(*22)-(*21)$

(*22) $CNCCNpqqr$

$(11) \times C(*23)-(*22)$

(*23) $CCNpqq$

In this way you can disprove any not-true expression of the
$C-N$-system. All these deductions could have been made shorter,
but I was anxious to show the method implied in the proof of
decision. This method enables us to decide effectively, on the
basis of only fifteen fundamental theses, S1–S15, and the axiom
of rejection, whether a given significant expression of the $C-N$-
system should be asserted or rejected. As all the other functors
of the theory of deduction may be defined by C and N, all
significant expressions of the theory of deduction are decidable
on an axiomatic basis. A system of axioms from which the
fifteen fundamental theses can be drawn is complete in this
sense, that all true expressions of the system can be deduced in
it. Of this kind is the system of three axioms set out in section
23, and also the system of those three axioms on which transformation IV is based, viz. $CCCpqrCNpr$, $CCCpqrCqr$, and
$CCNprCCqrCCpqr$.

The proof of theorem (TA), according to which every significant expression of the Aristotelian logic can be reduced to
elementary expressions, is implicitly contained in the proof of
the analogous theorem for the theory of deduction. If we take
instead, of the Greek letters used in our transformations I–VII
(except the final variable in transformation I) propositional

expressions of the Aristotelian logic, we can apply those transformations to them in the same way as to expressions of the
theory of deduction. This can easily be seen in the example of
$CCNAabAbaIab$. We get:

$CCNAabAbaIab$ $\quad\sim CNCCNAabAbaIabp$ by I;
$CNCCNAabAbaIabp \sim CCNAabAbaCNIabp$ „ III;
$CCNAabAbaCNIabp \sim CNNAabCNIabp, CAbaCNIabp$ by IV;
$CNNAabCNIabp \quad\sim CAabCNIabp$ by II.

Instead of $NAab$ we can always write Oab, and Eab instead of
$NIab$. In what follows, however, it will be more convenient to
employ forms with N.

Both elementary expressions, $CAabCNIabp$ and $CAbaCNIabp$,
to which $CCNAabAbaIab$ has been reduced, have a propositional variable as their last term. This variable is introduced by
transformation I. We can get rid of it by the following deductively equivalent transformations where π is a propositional
variable not occurring in either α or β:

VIII. $C\alpha C\beta\pi \quad\sim C\alpha N\beta$ with respect to S17 and S18,
 IX. $C\alpha CN\beta\pi \sim C\alpha\beta$ „ „ „ S19 and S20.

Theses for transformation VIII:
 S17. $CCpCqNqCpNq$
 S18. $CCpNqCpCqr$.

Theses for transformation IX:
 S19. $CCpCNqqCpq$
 S20. $CCpqCpCNqr$.

When $C\alpha C\beta\pi$ is asserted, we get from it by substituting $N\beta$ for π
the expression $C\alpha C\beta N\beta$, and then $C\alpha N\beta$ by S17; and conversely
from $C\alpha N\beta$ the expression $C\alpha C\beta\pi$ by S18. When $C\alpha C\beta\pi$ is rejected, we get by S18 $CC\alpha N\beta C\alpha C\beta\pi$, therefore $C\alpha N\beta$ must be
rejected; and conversely, when $C\alpha N\beta$ is rejected, we get by S17
$CC\alpha C\beta N\beta C\alpha N\beta$, therefore $C\alpha C\beta N\beta$ must be rejected and consequently $C\alpha C\beta\pi$. Transformation IX can be explained in the
same way. This we can apply directly to our example. Take
Aab for α, Iab for β, and p for π; you get $CAabIab$. In the same
way from $CAbaCNIabp$ results $CAbaIab$. If we have an expression
with more antecedents than two, e.g. with n antecedents, we
must first reduce by repeated application of transformation
VII the $n-1$ antecedents to one antecedent, and then apply

transformation VIII or IX. Take, for instance, the following example:

$CNIabCAcbCAdcCIadp$ ～ $CNCNIabNAcbCAdcCIadp$
by VII;

$CNCNIabNAcbCAdcCIadp$ ～ $CNCNCNIabNAcbNAdcCIadp$
by VII;

$CNCNCNIabNAcbNAdcCIadp$ ～ $CNCNCNIabNAcbNAdcNIad$
by VIII;

$CNCNCNIabNAcbNAdcNIad$ ～ $CNCNIabNAcbCAdcNIad$
by VII;

$CNCNIabNAcbCAdcNIad$ ～ $CNIabCAcbCAdcNIad$,, VII.

Theorem (TA) is now fully proved; we can proceed therefore to our main subject, the proof of decision of the Aristotelian syllogistic.

§ 33. *Elementary expressions of the syllogistic*

According to theorem (TA), every significant expression of the Aristotelian syllogistic can be reduced in a deductively equivalent way to a set of elementary expressions, i.e. expressions of the form

$$Ca_1Ca_2Ca_3...Ca_{n-1}a_n,$$

where all the a's are simple expressions of the syllogistic, i.e. expressions of the type Aab, Iab, Eab or $NIab$, and Oab or $NAab$. Now I shall show that every elementary expression of the syllogistic is decidable, i.e. either asserted or rejected. I shall first prove that all the simple expressions, except expressions of the type Aaa and Iaa, are rejected. We have already seen (section 27, formula *61) that Iac is rejected. Here are the proofs of rejection of the other expressions:

*100 × *61. c/b
*100. Iab

8 × C*101–*100   (8. $CAabIab$)
*101. Aab

IV. $p/Aaa, q/Iab × C$1–102   (IV. $CpCNpq$)
102. $CNAaaIab$

102 × C*103–*100
*103. $NAaa$ (= Oaa)

$$*103 \times *104. \; b/a$$
$$*104. \; NAab \hspace{6cm} (= Oab)$$
$$IV. \; p/Iaa, \; q/Iab \times C2\text{--}105$$
$$105. \; CNIaaIab$$
$$105 \times C*106\text{--}*100$$
$$*106. \; NIaa \hspace{6cm} (= Eaa)$$
$$*106 \times *107. \; b/a$$
$$*107. \; NIab \hspace{6cm} (= Eab).$$

Turning now to compound elementary expressions I shall successively investigate all the possible cases, omitting the formal proofs where it is possible, and giving only hints how they could be done. Six cases have to be investigated.

First case: The consequent α_n is negative, and all the antecedents are affirmative. Such expressions are rejected.

Proof: By identifying all the variables occurring in the expression with a, all the antecedents become true, being laws of identity Aaa or Iaa, and the consequent becomes false. We see that for the solution of this case the laws of identity are essential.

Second case: The consequent is negative, and only one of the antecedents is negative. This case may be reduced to the case with only affirmative elements, and such cases, as we shall see later, are always decidable.

Proof: Expressions of the form $C\alpha CN\beta N\gamma$ are deductively equivalent to expressions of the form $C\alpha C\gamma\beta$ with respect to the theses $CCpCNrNqCpCqr$ and $CCpCqrCpCNrNq$. This is true not only for one affirmative antecedent α, but for any number of them.

Third case: The consequent is negative, and more than one antecedent is negative. Expressions of this kind can be reduced to simpler expressions, and eventually to the second case. The solution of this case requires Słupecki's rule of rejection.

Proof: Let us suppose that the original expression is of the form $CN\alpha CN\beta C\gamma...N\rho$. This supposition can always be made, as any antecedent may be moved to any place whatever. We reduce this expression to two simpler expressions $CN\alpha C\gamma...N\rho$ and $CN\beta C\gamma...N\rho$, omitting the second or the first antecedent respectively. If these expressions have more negative antecedents than one we repeat the same procedure till we get formulae with only one negative antecedent. As such formulae according to the second case are deductively equivalent to decidable affirmative expressions, they are always either asserted or rejected. If only one of them is asserted, the original expression must be asserted too, for by the law of simplification we can add to this asserted formula all the other negative antecedents which were previously omitted. If, however, all the formulae with one negative antecedent are rejected, we gather from them by repeated application of Słupecki's rule of rejection that the original expression must be rejected. Two examples will explain the matter thoroughly.

First example: *CNAabCNAbcCNIbdCIbcNAcd*, a thesis.

We reduce this expression to (1) and (2):

(1) *CNAabCNIbdCIbcNAcd*,   (2) *CNAbcCNIbdCIbcNAcd*.

In the same way we reduce (1) to (3) and (4):

(3) *CNAabCIbcNAcd*,   (4) *CNIbdCIbcNAcd*,

and (2) to (5) and (6):

(5) *CNAbcCIbcNAcd*,   (6) *CNIbdCIbcNAcd*.

Now the last expression is a thesis; it is the mood Ferison of the third figure. Putting in *CpCqp* (6) for *p*, and *NAbc* for *q*, we get (2), and applying *CpCqp* once more by putting (2) for *p*, and *NAab* for *q*, we reach the original thesis.

Second example: *CNAabCNAbcCNIcdCIbdNAad*, not a thesis.
We reduce this expression as in the foregoing example:

(1) *CNAabCNIcdCIbdNAad*,   (2) *CNAbcCNIcdCIbdNAad*;

then we reduce (1) to (3) and (4), and (2) to (5) and (6):

(3) *CNAabCIbdNAad*,   (4) *CNIcdCIbdNAad*,
(5) *CNAbcCIbdNAad*,   (6) *CNIcdCIbdNAad*.

None of the above formulae with one negative antecedent is a thesis, as can be proved by reducing them to the case with only affirmative elements. Expressions (3), (4), (5), and (6) are rejected. Applying the rule of Słupecki, we gather from the rejected expressions (5) and (6) that (2) must be rejected, and from the rejected expressions (3) and (4) that (1) must be rejected. But if (1) and (2) are rejected, then the original expression must be rejected too.

Fourth case: The consequent is affirmative, and some (or all) antecedents are negative. This case can be reduced to the third.

Proof: Expressions of the form $C\alpha CN\beta\gamma$ are deductively equivalent to expressions of the form $C\alpha CN\beta CN\gamma NAaa$ on the ground of the theses $CCpCNqrCpCNqCNrNAaa$ and $CCpCNqCNrNAaaCpCNqr$, as $NAaa$ is always false.

All the cases with negative elements are thus exhausted.

Fifth case: All the antecedents are affirmative, and the consequent is a universal affirmative proposition. Several sub-cases have to be distinguished.

(*a*) The consequent is Aaa; this expression is asserted, for its consequent is true.

(*b*) The consequent is Aab, and Aab is also one of the antecedents. The expression is of course asserted.

In what follows it is supposed that Aab does not occur as antecedent.

(*c*) The consequent is Aab, but no antecedent is of the type Aaf with f different from a (and from b, of course). Such expressions are rejected.

Proof: By identifying all variables different from a and b with b, we can only get the following antecedents:

$$Aaa, \ Aba, \ Abb, \ Iaa, \ Iab, \ Iba, \ Ibb.$$

(We cannot get Aab, for no antecedent is of the type Aaf, f being different from a.) Premisses Aaa, Abb, Iaa, Ibb can be omitted as true. (If there are no other premisses, the expression is rejected, as in the first case.) If there is Iba besides Iab, one of them may be omitted, as they are equivalent to each other. If there is Aba, both Iab and Iba may be omitted, as Aba implies them both. After these reductions only Aba or Iab can remain as antecedents. Now it can be shown that both implications,

$$CAbaAab \qquad \text{and} \qquad CIabAab,$$

are rejected on the ground of our axiom of rejection:

X. $p/Acb, \ q/Aba, \ r/Iac, \ s/Aab \times C27$–108

108. $CCAabAbaCKAcbAabIac$ (X. $CCKpqrCCsqCKpsr$;

      $108 \times C*109$–$*59$ 27. $CKAcbAbaIac$)

*109. $CAabAba$

     $*109 \times *110. \ b/a, \ a/b$

*110. $CAbaAab$.

If $CAbaAab$ is rejected, then $CIabAab$ must be rejected too, for Iab is a weaker premiss than Aba.

(*d*) The consequent is Aab, and there are antecedents of the type Aaf with f different from a. If there is a chain leading from a to b, the expression is asserted on the ground of axiom 3, the mood Barbara; if there is no such chain, the expression is rejected.

Proof: By a chain leading from a to b I understand an ordered series of universal affirmative premisses:

$$Aac_1, Ac_1c_2, ..., Ac_{n-1}c_n, Ac_nb,$$

where the first term of the series has a as its first argument, the last term b as its second argument, and the second argument of every other term is identical with the first argument of its successor. It is evident that from a series of such expressions Aab results by repeated application of the mood Barbara. If, therefore, there is a chain leading from a to b, the expression is asserted; if there is no such chain, we can get rid of antecedents of the type Aaf, identifying their second argument with a. The expression is reduced in this way to the sub-case (*c*), which was rejected.

Sixth case: All the antecedents are affirmative, and the consequent is a particular affirmative proposition. Here also we have to distinguish several sub-cases.

(*a*) The consequent is Iaa; the expression is asserted, for its consequent is true.

(*b*) The consequent is Iab, and as antecedent occurs either Aab, or Aba, or Iab, or Iba; it is obvious that in all these cases the expression must be asserted.

In what follows it is supposed that none of the above four premisses occurs as antecedent.

(*c*) The consequent is Iab, and no antecedent is of the type Afa, f different from a, or of the type Agb, g different from b. The expression is rejected.

Proof: We identify all variables different from a and b with c; then we get, besides true premisses of the type Acc or Icc, only the following antecedents:

$$Aac, Abc, Iac, Ibc.$$

Aac implies Iac, and Abc implies Ibc. The strongest combination of premisses is therefore *Aac* and *Abc*. From this combination, however, *Iab* does not result, as the formula

$$CAacCAbcIab$$

is equivalent to our axiom of rejection.

(*d*) The consequent is *Iab*, and among the antecedents there are expressions of the type *Afa* (*f* different from *a*), but not of the type *Agb* (*g* different from *b*). If there is *Abe* or *Ibe* (*Ieb*), and a chain leading from *e* to *a*:

(α) *Abe*; $Aee_1, Ae_1e_2, ..., Ae_na$,

(β) *Ibe*; $Aee_1, Ae_1e_2, ..., Ae_na$,

we get from (α) *Abe* and *Aea*, and therefore *Iab* by the mood Bramantip, and from (β) *Ibe* and *Aea*, and therefore *Iab* by the mood Dimaris. In both cases the expression is asserted. If, however, the conditions (α) and (β) are not fulfilled, we can get rid of antecedents of the type *Afa* by identifying their first arguments with *a*, and the expression must be rejected according to sub-case (*c*).

(*e*) The consequent is *Iab*, and among the antecedents there are expressions of the type *Agb* (*g* different from *b*), but not of the type *Afa* (*f* different from *a*). This case can be reduced to sub-case (*d*), as *a* and *b* are symmetrical with respect to the consequent *Iab*.

(*f*) The consequent is *Iab*, and among the antecedents there are expressions of the type *Afa* (*f* different from *a*), and expressions of the type *Agb* (*g* different from *b*). We may suppose that the conditions (α) and (β) are not fulfilled for *Afa*, or the analogous conditions for *Agb* either; otherwise, as we already know, the original expression would be asserted. Now, if there is *Aca* and a chain leading from *c* to *b*:

(γ) *Aca*; $Acc_1, Ac_1c_2, ..., Ac_nb$,

or *Adb* and a chain leading from *d* to *a*:

(δ) *Adb*; $Add_1, Ad_1d_2, ..., Ad_na$,

we get from (γ) *Aca* and *Acb*, from (δ) *Adb* and *Ada*, and therefore in both cases *Iab* by the mood Darapti. Further, if there is an antecedent *Icd* (or *Idc*) and two chains, one leading from *c* to *a*, and another from *d* to *b*:

(ε) $\begin{cases} Icd; Acc_1, Ac_1c_2, ..., Ac_na, \\ Icd; Add_1, Ad_1d_2, ..., Ad_nb, \end{cases}$

we get by the first chain the premiss Aca, by the second chain the premiss Adb, and both premisses yield together with Icd the conclusion Iab on the basis of the polysyllogism:

$$CIcdCAcaCAdbIab.$$

We prove the polysyllogism by deducing Iad from Icd and Aca by the mood Disamis, and then Iab from Iad and Adb by the mood Darii. In all these cases the original expression must be asserted. If, however, none of the conditions (γ), (δ), or (ϵ) is satisfied, we can get rid of expressions of the type Afa and Agb by identifying their first arguments with a or with b respectively, and the original expression must be rejected according to sub-case (c). All possible cases are now exhausted, and it is proved that every significant expression of the Aristotelian syllogistic is either asserted or rejected on the basis of our axioms and rules of inference.

§ 34. *An arithmetical interpretation of the syllogistic*

In 1679 Leibniz discovered an arithmetical interpretation of the Aristotelian syllogistic which deserves our attention from the historical as well as from the systematic point of view.[1] It is an isomorphic interpretation. Leibniz did not know that the Aristotelian syllogistic could be axiomatized, and he knew nothing about rejection and its rules. He only tested some laws of conversion and some syllogistic moods in order to be sure that his interpretation was not wrong. It seems, therefore, to be a mere coincidence that his interpretation satisfies our asserted axioms 1–4, the axiom of rejection *59, and the rule of Słupecki. In any case it is strange that his philosophic intuitions, which guided him in his research, yielded such a sound result.

Leibniz's arithmetical interpretation is based on a correlation of variables of the syllogistic with ordered pairs of natural numbers prime to each other. To the variable a, for instance, correspond two numbers, say a_1 and a_2, prime to each other; to the variable b correspond two other numbers, say b_1 and b_2, also prime to each other. The premiss Aab is true when and only when a_1 is divisible by b_1, and a_2 is divisible by b_2. If one of these conditions is not satisfied, Aab is false, and therefore $NAab$ is

---

[1] See L. Couturat, *Opuscules et fragments inédits de Leibniz*, Paris (1903), pp. 77 seq. Cf. also J. Łukasiewicz, 'O sylogistyce Arystotelesa' (On Aristotle's Syllogistic), *Comptes Rendus de l'Acad. des Sciences de Cracovie*, xliv, No. 6 (1939), p. 220.

true. The premiss Iab is true when and only when a_1 is prime to b_2, and a_2 is prime to b_1. If one of these conditions is not satisfied, Iab is false, and therefore $NIab$ is true.

It can easily be seen that our asserted axioms 1–4 are verified. Axiom 1, Aaa, is verified, for every number is divisible by itself. Axiom 2, Iaa, is verified, for it is supposed that the two numbers corresponding to a, a_1 and a_2, are prime to each other. Axiom 3, the mood Barbara $CKAbcAabAac$, is also verified, since the relation of divisibility is transitive. Axiom 4, the mood Datisi $CKAbcIbaIac$, is verified too; for if b_1 is divisible by c_1, b_2 is divisible by c_2, b_1 is prime to a_2, and b_2 is prime to a_1, then a_1 must be prime to c_2, and a_2 must be prime to c_1. For if a_1 and c_2 had a common factor greater than 1, a_1 and b_2 would also have the same common factor, since b_2 contains c_2. But this is against the supposition that a_1 is prime to b_2. In the same way we prove that a_2 must be prime to c_1.

It is also easy to show that the axiom *59 $CKAcbAabIac$ must be rejected. Take as examples the following numbers:

$$a_1 = 15, \; b_1 = 3, \; c_1 = 12,$$
$$a_2 = 14, \; b_2 = 7, \; c_2 = 35.$$

Acb is true, for c_1 is divisible by b_1 and c_2 is divisible by b_2; Aab is also true, for a_1 is divisible by b_1 and a_2 is divisible by b_2; but the conclusion Iac is not true, for a_1 and c_2 are not prime to each other.

The verification of Słupecki's rule of rejection is more complicated. I shall explain the matter with the help of an example. Let us take as the rejected expressions,

(*1) $CNAabCNIcdCIbdNAad$ and (*2) $CNIbcCNIcdCIbdNAad$.

From them we get, by the rule of Słupecki,

$$*CN\alpha\gamma, \; *CN\beta\gamma \rightarrow *CN\alpha CN\beta\gamma,$$

a third rejected expression,

(*3) $CNAabCNIbcCNIcdCIbdNAad$.

Expression (1) is disproved, for instance by the following set of numbers:

$$(4) \; \begin{cases} a_1 = 4, \; b_1 = 7, \; c_1 = 3, \; d_1 = 4, \\ a_2 = 9, \; b_2 = 5, \; c_2 = 8, \; d_2 = 3. \end{cases}$$

It can easily be proved that according to this interpretation Aab is false (since 4 is not divisible by 7), and therefore $NAab$ is true; Icd is false (since c_2 is not prime to d_1), and therefore $NIcd$ is true; Ibd is true (for both pairs of numbers, b_1 and d_2, b_2 and d_1, are prime to each other); but $NAad$ is false, because Aad is true (a_1 being divisible by d_1, and a_2 by d_2). All the antecedents are true, the consequent is false; therefore expression (1) is disproved.

The same set of numbers does not disprove expression (2), because Ibc is true (as both pairs of numbers, b_1 and c_2, and b_2 and c_1, are prime to each other), and therefore $NIbc$ is false. But if the antecedent of an implication is false, the implication is true. In order to disprove expression (2) we must take another set of numbers, for instance the following:

$$(5) \quad \begin{cases} a_1 = 9, \ b_1 = 3, \ c_1 = 8, \ d_1 = 3, \\ a_2 = 2, \ b_2 = 2, \ c_2 = 5, \ d_2 = 2. \end{cases}$$

According to this interpretation all the antecedents of expression (2) are true, and the consequent is false; the expression is therefore disproved. But this second set of numbers does not disprove expression (1), because Aab is true, and therefore $NAab$ is false, and a false antecedent yields a true implication. Neither, therefore, of the sets (4) and (5) disproves expression (3), which contains $NAab$ as well as $NIbc$.

There is a general method that enables us to disprove expression (3) when expressions (1) and (2) are disproved.[1] First, we write down all the prime numbers which make up the sets of numbers disproving (1) and (2). We get for (1) the series 2, 3, 5, and 7, and for (2) the series 2, 3, and 5. Secondly, we replace the numbers of the second series by new primes, all different from the primes of the first series, for instance: 2 by 11, 3 by 13, and 5 by 17. We get thus a new set of numbers:

$$(6) \quad \begin{cases} a_1 = 13 \cdot 13, \ b_1 = 13, \ c_1 = 11 \cdot 11 \cdot 11, \ d_1 = 13, \\ a_2 = 11, \qquad b_2 = 11, \ c_2 = 17, \qquad d_2 = 11. \end{cases}$$

This set also disproves (2), since the relations of divisibility and primeness remain the same as they were before the replacement.

[1] This method was discovered by Słupecki, op. cit., pp. 28–30.

Thirdly, we multiply the numbers of corresponding variables occurring in the sets (4) and (6). We thus get a new set:

$$(7) \quad \begin{cases} a_1 = 4 \cdot 13 \cdot 13, \ b_1 = 7 \cdot 13, c_1 = 3 \cdot 11 \cdot 11 \cdot 11, d_1 = 4 \cdot 13, \\ a_2 = 9 \cdot 11, \qquad b_2 = 5 \cdot 11, c_2 = 8 \cdot 17, \qquad d_2 = 3 \cdot 11. \end{cases}^{1}$$

This set disproves (3). For it is evident, first, that if to the premiss *Aef* or *Ief* there corresponds the set of numbers

$$e_1, e_2, f_1, f_2, \quad e_1 \text{ prime to } e_2, f_1 \text{ prime to } f_2,$$

and there is another set of numbers

$$e_1', e_2', f_1', f_2', \quad e_1' \text{ prime to } e_2', f_1' \text{ prime to } f_2',$$

all of them composed of different primes from the numbers of the first set, then the product of e_1 and e_1', i.e. $e_1 . e_1'$, must be prime to the product of e_2 and e_2', i.e. $e_2 . e_2'$, and $f_1 . f_1'$ prime to $f_2 . f_2'$. Secondly, if *Aef* is verified by the first set, i.e. if e_1 is divisible by f_1, and e_2 by f_2, and the same is true of the second set, so that e_1' is divisible by f_1', and e_2' by f_2', then $e_1 . e_1'$ must be divisible by $f_1 . f_1'$, and $e_2 . e_2'$ by $f_2 . f_2'$. Again, if *Ief* is verified by the first set, i.e. e_1 is prime to f_2, and e_2 is prime to f_1, and the same is true of the second set, so that e_1' is prime to f_2', and e_2' is prime to f_1', then $e_1 . e_1'$ must be prime to $f_2 . f_2'$ and $e_2 . e_2'$ prime to $f_1 . f_1'$, since all the numbers of the second set are prime to the numbers of the first set. On the contrary, if only one of the conditions for divisibility or primeness is not satisfied, the respective premisses must be false. It can be seen in our example that *Aad* and *Icd* are verified by (7), for they are verified by (4) and (6), and *Ibc* is disproved both by (4) and (6), and therefore also by (7). *Aab* is disproved only by (4) (but this suffices to disprove it by (7)), and *Ibc* is disproved only by (6) (but this also suffices to disprove it by (7)). This procedure may be applied to any case of the kind, and therefore Słupecki's rule is verified by the Leibnizian interpretation.

Leibniz once said that scientific and philosophic controversies could always be settled by a calculus. It seems to me that his famous 'calculemus' is connected with the above arithmetical interpretation of the syllogistic rather than with his ideas on mathematical logic.

---

¹ If there is a variable occurring in one of the disproved expressions but not in the other, we simply take its corresponding numbers after eventual replacement.

§ 35. *Conclusion*

The results we have reached on the basis of an historical and systematic investigation of the Aristotelian syllogistic are at more than one point different from the usual presentation. Aristotle's logic was not only misrepresented by logicians who came from philosophy, since they wrongly identified it with the traditional syllogistic, but also by logicians who came from mathematics. In text-books of mathematical logic one can read again and again that the law of conversion of the *A*-premiss and some syllogistical moods derived by this law, like Darapti or Felapton, are wrong. This criticism is based on the mistaken notion that the Aristotelian universal affirmative premiss 'All *a* is *b*' means the same as the quantified implication 'For all *c*, if *c* is *a*, then *c* is *b*', where *c* is a singular term, and that the particular affirmative premiss 'Some *a* is *b*' means the same as the quantified conjunction 'For some *c*, *c* is *a* and *c* is *b*', where *c* is again a singular term. If one accepts such an interpretation, one can say of course that the law *CAabIba* is wrong, because *a* may be an empty term, so that no *c* is *a*, and the above quantified implication becomes true (for its antecedent is false), and the above quantified conjunction becomes false (for one of its factors is false). But all this is an imprecise misunderstanding of the Aristotelian logic. There is no passage in the *Analytics* that would justify such an interpretation. Aristotle does not introduce into his logic singular or empty terms or quantifiers. He applies his logic only to universal terms, like 'man' or 'animal'. And even these terms belong only to the application of the system, not to the system itself. In the system we have only expressions with variable arguments, like *Aab* or *Iab*, and their negations, and two of these expressions are primitive terms and cannot be defined; they have only those properties that are stated by the axioms. For the same reason such a controversy as whether the Aristotelian syllogistic is a theory of classes or not is in my opinion futile. The syllogistic of Aristotle is a theory neither of classes nor of predicates; it exists apart from other deductive systems, having its own axiomatic and its own problems.

I have tried to set forth this system free from foreign elements. I do not introduce into it singular, empty, or negative terms, as Aristotle has not introduced them. I do not introduce quantifiers either; I have only tried to explain some ideas of Aristotle by the help of quantifiers. In formal proofs I employ theses of the theory of deduction, since Aristotle uses them intuitively in his proofs, and I employ rejection, because Aristotle himself rejects some formulae and even states a rule of rejection. Wherever in Aristotle's exposition there was something* not completely correct, I have been anxious to correct the flaws of his exposition, e.g. some unsatisfactory proofs by *reductio per impossibile*, or the rejection through concrete terms. It has been my intention to build up the original system of the Aristotelian syllogistic on the lines laid down by the author himself, and in accordance with the requirements of modern formal logic. The crown of the system is the solution of the problem of decision, and that was made possible by Słupecki's rule of rejection, not known to Aristotle or to any other logician.

The syllogistic of Aristotle is a system the exactness of which surpasses even the exactness of a mathematical theory, and this is its everlasting merit. But it is a narrow system and cannot be applied to all kinds of reasoning, for instance to mathematical arguments. Perhaps Aristotle himself felt that his system was not fitted for every purpose, for he added later to the theory of assertoric syllogisms a theory of modal syllogisms.[1] This was of course an extension of logic, but probably not in the right direction. The logic of the Stoics, the inventors of the ancient form of the propositional calculus, was much more important than all the syllogisms of Aristotle. We realize today that the theory of deduction and the theory of quantifiers are the most fundamental branches of logic.

Aristotle is not responsible for the fact that for many centuries his syllogistic, or rather a corrupt form of his syllogistic, was the sole logic known to philosophers. He is not responsible either for the fact that the influence of his logic on philosophy was, as it seems to me, disastrous. At the bottom of this disastrous influence there lies, in my opinion, the prejudice that every proposition has a subject and a predicate, like the premisses of Aristotelian logic. This prejudice, together with the criterion of truth known as *adaequatio rei et intellectus*, is the basis

---

[1] I take it that the theory of modal syllogisms expounded by Aristotle in Chapters 8–22 of Book I of the *Prior Analytics* was inserted later, since Chapter 23 is obviously an immediate continuation of Chapter 7.

of some famous but fantastic philosophical speculations. Kant divided all propositions (he calls them 'judgements') into analytic and synthetic according to the relation of the predicate of a proposition to its subject. His *Critique of Pure Reason* is chiefly an attempt to explain the problem how true synthetic *a priori* propositions are possible. Now some Peripatetics, for instance Alexander, were apparently already aware that there exists a large class of propositions having no subject and no predicate, such as implications, disjunctions, conjunctions, and so on.[1] All these may be called functorial propositions, since in all of them there occurs a propositional functor, like 'if—then', 'or', 'and'. These functorial propositions are the main stock of every scientific theory, and to them neither Kant's distinction of analytic and synthetic judgements nor the usual criterion of truth is applicable, for propositions without a subject or predicate cannot be immediately compared with facts. Kant's problem loses its importance and must be replaced by a much more important problem: How are true functorial propositions possible? It seems to me that here lies the starting-point for a new philosophy as well as for a new logic.

---

[1] In connexion with Aristotle's definition of the πρότασις Alexander writes, 11. 17: εἰσὶ δὲ οὗτοι οἱ ὅροι προτάσεως οὐ πάσης ἀλλὰ τῆς ἁπλῆς τε καὶ καλουμένης κατηγορικῆς· τὸ γάρ τι κατά τινος ἔχειν καὶ τὸ καθόλου ἢ ἐν μέρει ἢ ἀδιόριστον ἴδια ταύτης· ἡ γὰρ ὑποθετικὴ οὐκ ἐν τῷ τι κατά τινος λέγεσθαι ἀλλ' ἐν ἀκολουθίᾳ ἢ μάχῃ τὸ ἀληθὲς ἢ τὸ ψεῦδος ἔχει.

CHAPTER VI
ARISTOTLE'S MODAL LOGIC OF PROPOSITIONS

§ 36. *Introduction*

THERE are two reasons why Aristotle's modal logic is so little known. The first is due to the author himself: in contrast to the assertoric syllogistic which is perfectly clear and nearly free of errors, Aristotle's modal syllogistic is almost incomprehensible because of its many faults and inconsistencies. He devoted to this subject some interesting chapters of *De Interpretatione*, but the system of his modal syllogistic is expounded in Book I, chapters 3 and 8–22 of the *Prior Analytics*. Gohlke[1] suggested that these chapters were probably later insertions, because chapter 23 was obviously an immediate continuation of chapter 7. If he is right, the modal syllogistic was Aristotle's last logical work and should be regarded as a first version not finally elaborated by the author. This would explain the faults of the system as well as the corrections of Theophrastus and Eudemus, made perhaps in the light of hints given by the master himself.

The second reason is that modern logicians have not as yet been able to construct a universally acceptable system of modal logic which would yield a solid basis for the interpretation and appreciation of Aristotle's work. I have tried to construct such a system, different from those hitherto known, and built up upon Aristotle's ideas.[2] The present monograph on Aristotle's modal logic is written from the standpoint of this system.

A modal logic of terms presupposes a modal logic of propositions. This was not clearly seen by Aristotle whose modal syllogistic is a logic of terms; nevertheless it is possible to speak of an Aristotelian modal logic of propositions, as some of his theorems are general enough to comprise all kinds of proposition, and some others are expressly formulated by him with propositional variables. I shall begin with Aristotle's modal logic of propositions,

[1] Paul Gohlke, *Die Entstehung der Aristotelischen Logik*, Berlin (1936), pp. 88–94.
[2] Jan Łukasiewicz, 'A System of Modal Logic', *The Journal of Computing Systems*, vol. i, St. Paul (1953), pp. 111–49. A summary of this paper appeared under the same title in the *Proceedings of the XIth International Congress of Philosophy*, vol. xiv, Brussels (1953), pp. 82–87. A short description of the system is given below in § 49.

which is logically and philosophically far more important than
his modal syllogistic of terms.

§ 37. *Modal functions and their interrelations*

There are four modal terms used by Aristotle: ἀναγκαῖον—
'necessary', ἀδύνατον—'impossible', δυνατόν—'possible', and ἐνδεχόμενον—'contingent'. This last term is ambiguous: in the *De
Interpretatione* it means the same as δυνατόν, in the *Prior Analytics* it
has besides a more complicated meaning which I shall discuss
later.

According to Aristotle, only propositions are necessary, impossible, possible, or contingent. Instead of saying: 'The proposition "*p*" is necessary', where "*p*" is the name of the proposition
p, I shall use the expression: 'It is necessary that *p*', where *p* is a
proposition. So, for instance, instead of saying: 'The proposition
"man is an animal" is necessary', I shall say: 'It is necessary that
man should be an animal.' I shall express the other modalities in
a similar way. Expressions like: 'It is necessary that *p*', denoted
here by Lp, or 'It is possible that *p*', denoted by Mp, I call 'modal
functions'; L and M, which respectively correspond to the words
'it is necessary that' and 'it is possible that', are 'modal functors',
p is their 'argument'. As modal functions are propositions, I say
that L and M are proposition-forming functors of one propositional
argument. Propositions beginning with L or their equivalents are
called 'apodeictic', those beginning with M or their equivalents
'problematic'. Non-modal propositions are called 'assertoric'.
This modern terminology and symbolism will help us to give a
clear exposition of Aristotle's propositional modal logic.

Two of the modal terms, 'necessary' and 'possible', and their
interrelations, are of fundamental importance. In the *De Interpretatione* Aristotle mistakenly asserts that possibility implies non-
necessity, i.e. in our terminology:

(*a*) *If it is possible that p, it is not necessary that p.*[1] He later sees
that this cannot be right, because he accepts that necessity implies
possibility, i.e.:

(*b*) *If it is necessary that p, it is possible that p*, and from (*b*) and
(*a*) there would follow by the hypothetical syllogism that

---

[1] *De int.* 13, 22ᵃ15 τῷ μὲν γὰρ δυνατῷ εἶναι τὸ ἐνδέχεσθαι εἶναι (ἀκολουθεῖ), καὶ
τοῦτο ἐκείνῳ ἀντιστρέφει, καὶ τὸ μὴ ἀδύνατον εἶναι καὶ τὸ μὴ ἀναγκαῖον εἶναι.

(c) *If it is necessary that p, it is not necessary that p*, which is absurd.[1] After a further examination of the problem Aristotle rightly states that

(d) *If it is possible that p, it is not necessary that not p*,[2] but does not correct-his former mistake in the text of *De Interpretatione*. This correction is given in the *Prior Analytics* where the relation of possibility to necessity has the form of an equivalence:

(e) *It is possible that p—if and only if—it is not necessary that not p*.[3]

I gather from this that the other relation, that of necessity to possibility, which is stated in the *De Interpretatione* as an implication,[4] is also meant as an equivalence and should be given the form:

(f) *It is necessary that p—if and only if—it is not possible that not p*.

If we denote the functor 'if and only if' by Q,[5] putting it before its arguments, and 'not' by N, we can symbolically express the relations (e) and (f) thus:

1. $QMpNLNp$, i.e. *Mp—if and only if—NLNp*,
2. $QLpNMNp$, i.e. *Lp—if and only if—NMNp*.

The above formulae are fundamental to any system of modal logic.

§ 38. *Basic modal logic*

Two famous scholastic principles of modal logic: *Ab oportere ad esse valet consequentia*, and *Ab esse ad posse valet consequentia*, were known to Aristotle without being formulated by him explicitly. The first principle runs in our symbolic notation (C is the sign of the functor 'if-then'):

3. $CLpp$, i.e. *If it is necessary that p, then p*.

The second reads:

[1] Ibid. 22ᵇ11 τὸ μὲν γὰρ ἀναγκαῖον εἶναι δυνατὸν εἶναι . . . 14 ἀλλὰ μὴν τῷ γε δυνατὸν εἶναι τὸ οὐκ ἀδύνατον εἶναι ἀκολουθεῖ, τούτῳ δὲ τὸ μὴ ἀναγκαῖον εἶναι· ὥστε συμβαίνει τὸ ἀναγκαῖον εἶναι μὴ ἀναγκαῖον εἶναι, ὅπερ ἄτοπον.

[2] Ibid. 22ᵇ22 λείπεται τοίνυν τὸ οὐκ ἀναγκαῖον μὴ εἶναι ἀκολουθεῖν τῷ δυνατὸν εἶναι.

[3] *An. pr.* i. 13, 32ᵃ25 τὸ 'ἐνδέχεται ὑπάρχειν' καὶ 'οὐκ ἀδύνατον ὑπάρχειν' καὶ 'οὐκ ἀνάγκη μὴ ὑπάρχειν', ἤτοι ταὐτά ἐσται ἢ ἀκολουθοῦντα ἀλλήλοις.

[4] *De int.* 13, 22ᵃ20 τῷ δὲ μὴ δυνατῷ μὴ εἶναι καὶ μὴ ἐνδεχομένῳ μὴ εἶναι τὸ ἀναγκαῖον εἶναι καὶ τὸ ἀδύνατον μὴ εἶναι (ἀκολουθεῖ).

[5] I usually denote equivalence by *E*, but as this letter has already another meaning in the syllogistic, I have introduced (p. 108) the letter *Q* for equivalence.

4. *CpMp*, i.e. *If p, it is possible that p.*

According to a passage of the *Prior Analytics*[1] Aristotle knows that from the assertoric negative conclusion 'Not *p*', i.e. *Np*, there results the problematic consequence 'It is possible that not *p*', i.e. *MNp*. We have therefore *CNpMNp*. Alexander, commenting on this passage, states as a general rule that existence implies possibility, i.e. *CpMp*, but not conversely, i.e. *CMpp* should be rejected.[2] If we denote rejected expressions by an asterisk, we get the formula :[3]

*5. *CMpp*, i.e. *If it is possible that p, then p*—rejected.

The corresponding formulae for necessity are also stated by Alexander who says that necessity implies existence, i.e. *CLpp*, but not conversely, i.e. *CpLp* should be rejected.[4] We get thus another rejected expression :

*6. *CpLp*, i.e. *If p, it is necessary that p*—rejected.

Formulae 1–6 are accepted by the traditional logic, and so far as I know, by all the modern logicians. They are, however, insufficient to characterize *Mp* and *Lp* as modal functions, because all the above formulae are satisfied if we interpret *Mp* as always true, i.e. as '*verum* of *p*', and *Lp* as always false, i.e. as '*falsum* of *p*'. With this interpretation a system built up on the formulae 1–6 would cease to be a modal logic. We cannot therefore assert *Mp*, i.e. accept that all problematic propositions are true, or assert *NLp*, i.e. accept that all apodeictic propositions are false; both expressions should be rejected, for any expression which cannot be asserted should be rejected. We get thus two additional rejected formulae :

*7. *Mp*, i.e. *It is possible that p*—rejected, and
*8. *NLp*, i.e. *It is not necessary that p*—rejected.

Both formulae may be called Aristotelian, as they are consequences of the presumption admitted by Aristotle that there exist

---

[1] *An. pr.* i. 16, 36ᵃ15 φανερὸν δ' ὅτι καὶ τοῦ ἐνδέχεσθαι μὴ ὑπάρχειν γίγνεται συλλογισμός, εἴπερ καὶ τοῦ μὴ ὑπάρχειν. — ἐνδέχεσθαι means here the 'possible', not the 'contingent'.

[2] Alexander 209. 2 τὸ μὲν γὰρ ὑπάρχον καὶ ἐνδεχόμενον ἀληθὲς εἰπεῖν, τὸ δ' ἐνδεχόμενον οὐ πάντως καὶ ὑπάρχον.

[3] Asserted expressions are marked throughout the Chapters VI–VIII by arabic numerals without asterisks.

[4] Alexander 152. 32 τὸ γὰρ ἀναγκαῖον καὶ ὑπάρχον, οὐκέτι δὲ τὸ ὑπάρχον ἀναγκαῖον.

asserted apodeictic propositions. For, if $L\alpha$ is asserted, then $LNN\alpha$ must be asserted too, and from the principle of Duns Scotus $CpCNpq$ we get by substitution and detachment the asserted formulae $CNL\alpha p$ and $CNLNN\alpha p$. As p is rejected, $NL\alpha$ and $NLNN\alpha$ are rejected too, and consequently NLp and $NLNp$, i.e. Mp, must be rejected.

I call a system 'basic modal logic' if and only if it satisfies the formulae 1–8. I have shown that basic modal logic can be axiomatized on the basis of the classical calculus of propositions.[1] Of the two modal functors, M and L, one may be taken as the primitive term, and the other can be defined. Taking M as the primitive term and formula 2 as the definition of L, we get the following independent set of axioms of the basic modal logic:

$\quad$ 4. $CpMp$ $\quad$ *5. $CMpp$ $\quad$ *7. Mp $\quad$ 9. $QMpMNNp$,

where 9 is deductively equivalent to formula 1 on the ground of the definition 2 and the calculus of propositions. Taking L as the primitive term and formula 1 as the definition of M, we get a corresponding set of axioms:

$\quad$ 3. $CLpp$ $\quad$ *6. $CpLp$ $\quad$ *8. NLp $\quad$ 10. $QLpLNNp$,

where 10 is deductively equivalent to formula 2 on the ground of the definition 1 and the calculus of propositions. The derived formulae 9 and 10 are indispensable as axioms.

Basic modal logic is the foundation of any system of modal logic and must always be included in any such system. Formulae 1–8 agree with Aristotle's intuitions and are at the roots of our concepts of necessity and possibility; but they do not exhaust the whole stock of accepted modal laws. For instance, we believe that if a conjunction is possible, each of its factors should be possible, i.e. in symbols:

$\quad$ 11. $CMKpqMp$ $\quad$ and $\quad$ 12. $CMKpqMq$,

and if a conjunction is necessary, each of its factors should be necessary, i.e. in symbols:

$\quad$ 13. $CLKpqLp$ $\quad$ and $\quad$ 14. $CLKpqLq$.

None of these formulae can be deduced from the laws 1–8. Basic modal logic is an incomplete modal system and requires the addition of some new axioms. Let us see how it was supplemented by Aristotle himself.

[1] See pp. 114–17 of my paper on modal logic.

§ 39. *Laws of extensionality*

Aristotle's most important and—as I see it—most successful attempt to go beyond basic modal logic consisted in his accepting certain principles which may be called 'laws of extensionality for modal functors'. These principles are to be found in Book I, chapter 15 of the *Prior Analytics*, and are formulated in three passages. We read at the beginning of the chapter:

'First it has to be said that if (if α is, β must be), then (if α is possible, β must be possible too).'[1]

A few lines further Aristotle says referring to his syllogisms:

'If one should denote the premisses by α, and the conclusion by β, it would not only result that if α is necessary, then β is necessary, but also that if α is possible, then β is possible.'[2]

And at the end of the section he repeats:

'It has been proved that if (if α is, β is), then (if α is possible, then β is possible).'[3]

Let us first analyse these modal laws beginning with the second passage, which refers to syllogisms.

All Aristotelian syllogisms are implications of the form $C\alpha\beta$ where α is the conjunction of the two premisses and β the conclusion. Take as example the mood Barbara:

15. $C\underbrace{KAbaAcb}_{\alpha}\underbrace{Aca}_{\beta}.$

According to the second passage we get two modal theorems, in the form of implications taking $C\alpha\beta$ as the antecedent and $CL\alpha L\beta$ or $CM\alpha M\beta$ as the consequent, in symbols:

16. $CC\alpha\beta CL\alpha L\beta$ and   17. $CC\alpha\beta CM\alpha M\beta.$

The letters α and β stand here for the premisses and the conclusion of an Aristotelian syllogism. As in the final passage there is

---

[1] *An. pr.* i. 15, 34ᵃ5 πρῶτον δὲ λεκτέον ὅτι εἰ τοῦ A ὄντος ἀνάγκη τὸ B εἶναι, καὶ δυνατοῦ ὄντος τοῦ A δυνατὸν ἔσται καὶ τὸ B ἐξ ἀνάγκης.

[2] Ibid. 34ᵃ22 εἰ τις θείη τὸ μὲν A τὰς προτάσεις, τὸ δὲ B τὸ συμπέρασμα, συμβαίνοι ἂν οὐ μόνον ἀναγκαίου τοῦ A ὄντος ἅμα καὶ τὸ B εἶναι ἀναγκαῖον, ἀλλὰ καὶ δυνατοῦ δυνατόν.

[3] Ibid. 34ᵃ29 δέδεικται ὅτι εἰ τοῦ A ὄντος τὸ B ἔστι, καὶ δυνατοῦ ὄντος τοῦ A ἔσται τὸ B δυνατόν.

no reference to syllogisms, we may treat these theorems as special cases of general principles which we get by replacing the Greek letters by propositional variables:

18. *CCpqCLpLq*   and   19. *CCpqCMpMq*.

Both formulae may be called in a wider sense 'laws of extensionality', the first for *L*, the second for *M*. The words 'in a wider sense' require an explanation.

The general law of extensionality, taken *sensu stricto*, is a formula of the classical calculus of propositions enlarged by the introduction of variable functors, and has the form:

20. *CQpqCδpδq*.

This means roughly speaking: If *p* is equivalent to *q*, then if δ of *p*, δ of *q*, where δ is any proposition-forming functor of one propositional argument, e.g. *N*. Accordingly, the strict laws of extensionality for *L* and *M* will have the form:

21. *CQpqCLpLq*   and   22. *CQpqCMpMq*.

These two formulae have stronger antecedents than formulae 18 and 19, and are easily deducible from them, 21 from 18, and 22 from 19, by means of the thesis *CQpqCpq* and the principle of the hypothetical syllogism. It can be proved, however, on the ground of the calculus of propositions and the basic modal logic that conversely 18 is deducible from 21, and 19 from 22. I give here the full deduction of the *L*-formula:

The premisses:

23. *CCQpqrCpCCpqr*
24. *CCpqCCqrCpr*
25. *CCpCqCprCqCpr*
 3. *CLpp*.

The deduction:

      23. *r/CLpLq × C21–26*
26. *CpCCpqCLpLq*
      24. *p/Lp, q/p, r/CCpqCLpLq × C3–C26–27*
27. *CLpCCpqCLpLq*
      25. *p/Lp, q/Cpq, r/Lq × C27–18*
18. *CCpqCLpLq*.

In a similar way 19 is deducible from 22 by means of the premisses $CCQpqrCNqCCpqr$, $CCpqCCqrCpr$, $CCNpCqCrpCqCrp$, and
the transposition $CNMpNp$ of the modal thesis $CpMp$.

We see from the above that, given the calculus of propositions
and basic modal logic, formula 18 is deductively equivalent to
the strict law of extensionality 21, and formula 19 to the strict law
of extensionality 22. We are right, therefore, to call those formulae
'laws of extensionality in a wider sense'. Logically, of course, it
makes no difference whether we complete the L-system of basic
modal logic by the addition of $CCpqCLpLq$ or by the addition of
$CQpqCLpLq$; the same holds for the alternative additions to the
M-system of $CCpqCMpMq$ or $CQpqCMpMq$. Intuitively, however,
the difference is great. Formulae 18 and 19 are not so evident as
formulae 21 and 22. If p implies q but is not equivalent to it, it is
not always true that if δ of p, δ of q; e.g. $CNpNq$ does not follow
from Cpq. But if p is equivalent to q, then always if δ of p, δ of q,
i.e. if p is true, q is true, and if p is false, q is false; similarly if p is
necessary, q is necessary, and if p is possible, q is possible. This
seems to be perfectly evident, unless modal functions are regarded
as intensional functions, i.e. as functions whose truth-values do
not depend solely on the truth-values of their arguments. But
what in this case the necessary and the possible would mean, is
for me a mystery as yet.

§ 40. *Aristotle's proof of the M-law of extensionality*

In the last passage quoted above Aristotle says that he has
proved the law of extensionality for possibility. He argues in
substance thus: If α is possible and β impossible, then when α
came to be, β would not come to be, and therefore α would be
without β, which is against the premiss that if α is, β is.[1] It is
difficult to recast this argument into a logical formula, as the
term 'to come to be' has an ontological rather than a logical
meaning. The comment, however, given on this argument by
Alexander deserves a careful examination.

Aristotle defines the contingent as that which is not necessary
and the supposed existence of which implies nothing impossible.[2]

_____

[1] *An. pr.* i. 15, 34ᵃ8 εἰ οὖν τὸ μὲν δυνατόν, ὅτε δυνατὸν εἶναι, γένοιτ' ἄν, τὸ δ' ἀδύνατον,
ὅτ' ἀδύνατον, οὐκ ἂν γένοιτο, ἅμα δ' εἰ τὸ A δυνατὸν καὶ τὸ B ἀδύνατον, ἐνδέχοιτ' ἂν τὸ
A γενέσθαι ἄνευ τοῦ B, εἰ δὲ γενέσθαι, καὶ εἶναι.   [2] See below, p. 154, n. 3.

Alexander assimilates this Aristotelian definition of contingency to that of possibility by omitting the words 'which is not necessary'. He says 'that a β which is impossible cannot follow from an α which is possible may also be proved from the definition of possibility: that is possible, the supposed existence of which implies nothing impossible'.[1] The words 'impossible' and 'nothing' here require a cautious interpretation. We cannot interpret 'impossible' as 'not possible', because the definition would be circular; we must either take 'impossible' as a primitive term or, taking 'necessary' as primitive, define the expression 'impossible that *p*' by 'necessary that not *p*'. I prefer the second way and shall discuss the new definition on the ground of the *L*-basic modal logic. The word 'nothing' should be rendered by a universal quantifier, as otherwise the definition would not be correct. We get thus the equivalence:

28. *QMpΠqCCpqNLNq.*

That means in words: 'It is possible that *p*—if and only if—for all *q*, if (if *p*, then *q*), it is not necessary that not *q*.' This equivalence has to be added to the *L*-basic modal logic as the definition of *Mp* instead of the equivalence 1 which must now be proved as a theorem.

The equivalence 28 consists of two implications:

29. *CMpΠqCCpqNLNq*   and   30. *CΠqCCpqNLNqMp.*

From 29 we get by the theorem *CΠqCCpqNLNqCCpqNLNq* and the hypothetical syllogism the consequence:

31. *CMpCCpqNLNq,*

and from 31 there easily results by the substitution *q/p*, *Cpp*, commutation and detachment the implication *CMpNLNp*. The converse implication *CNLNpMp* which, when combined with the original implication, would give the equivalence 1, cannot be proved otherwise than by means of the law of extensionality for *L*: *CCpqCLpLq*. As this proof is rather complicated, I shall give it in full.

---

[1] Alexander 177. 11 δεικνύοιτο δ' ἄν, ὅτι μὴ οἷόν τε δυνατῷ ὄντι τῷ *A* ἀδύνατον ἕπεσθαι τὸ *B*, καὶ ἐκ τοῦ ὁρισμοῦ τοῦ δυνατοῦ . . . δυνατόν ἐστιν, οὗ ὑποτεθέντος εἶναι οὐδὲν ἀδύνατον συμβαίνει διὰ τοῦτο.

The premisses:

18. *CCpqCLpLq*
24. *CCpqCCqrCpr*
30. *CΠqCCpqNLNqMp*
32. *CCpqCNqNp*
33. *CCpCqrCqCpr*.

The deduction:

      18. *p/Nq, q/Np* × 34
34. *CCNqNpCLNqLNp*
      24. *p/Cpq, q/CNqNp, r/CLNqLNp* × *C*32–*C*34–35
35. *CCpqCLNqLNp*
      32. *p/LNq, q/LNp* × 36
36. *CCLNqLNpCNLNpNLNq*
      24. *p/Cpq, q/CLNqLNp, r/CNLNpNLNq* × *C*35–*C*36–37
37. *CCpqCNLNpNLNq*
      33. *p/Cpq, q/NLNp, r/NLNq* × *C*37–38
38. *CNLNpCCpqNLNq*
      38. *Π2q* × 39
39. *CNLNpΠqCCpqNLNq*
      24. *p/NLNp, q/ΠqCCpqNLNq, r/Mp* × *C*39–*C*30–40
40. *CNLNpMp*.

We can now prove the law of extensionality for *M*, which was the purpose of Alexander's argument. This law easily results from the equivalence 1 and thesis 37. We see besides that the proof by means of the definition with quantifiers is unnecessarily complicated. It suffices to retain definition 1 and to add to the *L*-system the *L*-law of extensionality in order to get the *M*-law of extensionality. In the same way we may get the *L*-law of extensionality, if we add the *M*-law of extensionality to the *M*-system and definition 2. The *L*-system is deductively equivalent to the *M*-system with the laws of extensionality as well as without them.

It is, of course, highly improbable that an ancient logician could have invented such an exact proof as that given above. But the fact that the proof is correct throws an interesting light on Aristotle's ideas of possibility. I suppose that he intuitively saw what may be shortly expressed thus: what is possible today, say a sea-fight, may become existent or actual tomorrow; but what is impossible, can never become actual. This idea seems to lie at the bottom of Aristotle's proof and of Alexander's.

§ 41. *Necessary connexions of propositions*

The *L*-law of extensionality was formulated by Aristotle only once, together with the *M*-law, in the passage where he refers to syllogisms.[1]

According to Aristotle there exists a necessary connexion between the premisses α of a valid syllogism and its conclusion β. It would seem therefore that the laws of extensionality formulated above in the form:

16. $CC\alpha\beta CL\alpha L\beta$ and   17. $CC\alpha\beta CM\alpha M\beta$,

should be expressed with necessary antecedents:

41. $CLC\alpha\beta CL\alpha L\beta$ and   42. $CLC\alpha\beta CM\alpha M\beta$,

and the corresponding general laws of extensionality should run:

43. $CLCpqCLpLq$ and   44. $CLCpqCMpMq$.

This is corroborated for the *M*-law by the first passage quoted above where we read: 'If (if α is, β must be), then (if α is possible, β is possible).'

Formulae 43 and 44 are weaker than the corresponding formulae with assertoric antecedents, 18 and 19, and can be got from them by the axiom $CLpp$ and the hypothetical syllogism 24. It is not, however, possible to derive the stronger formulae conversely from the weaker. The problem is whether we should reject the stronger formulae 18 and 19, and replace them by the weaker formulae 43 and 44. To solve this problem we have to inquire into the Aristotelian concept of necessity.

Aristotle accepts that some necessary, i.e. apodeictic, propositions are true and should be asserted. Two kinds of asserted apodeictic proposition can be found in the *Analytics*: to the one kind there belong necessary connexions of propositions, to the other necessary connexions of terms. As example of the first kind any valid syllogism may be taken, for instance the mood Barbara:

(*g*) *If every b is an a, and every c is a b, then it is necessary that every c should be an a.*

Here the 'necessary' does not mean that the conclusion is an

[1] See p. 138, n. 2.

apodeictic proposition, but denotes a necessary connexion between the premisses of the syllogism and its assertoric conclusion. This is the so called 'syllogistic necessity'. Aristotle sees very well that there is a difference between syllogistic necessity and an apodeictic conclusion when he says, discussing a syllogism with an assertoric conclusion, that this conclusion is not 'simply' (ἁπλῶς) necessary, i.e. necessary in itself, but is necessary 'on condition', i.e. with respect to its premisses (τούτων ὄντων).[1] There are passages where he puts two marks of necessity into the conclusion saying, for instance, that from the premisses: 'It is necessary that every b should be an a, and some c is a b', there follows the conclusion: 'It is necessary that some c should be necessarily an a.'[2] The first 'necessary' refers to the syllogistic connexion, the second denotes that the conclusion is an apodeictic proposition.

By the way, a curious mistake of Aristotle should be noted: he says that nothing follows necessarily from a single premiss, but only from at least two, as in the syllogism.[3] In the *Posterior Analytics* he asserts that this has been proved,[4] but not even an attempt of proof is given anywhere. On the contrary, Aristotle himself states that 'If some b is an a, it is necessary that some a should be a b', drawing thus a necessary conclusion from only one premiss.[5]

I have shown that syllogistic necessity can be reduced to universal quantifiers.[6] When we say that in a valid syllogism the conclusion necessarily follows from the premisses, we want to state that the syllogism is valid for any matter, i.e. for all values of the variables occurring in it. This explanation, as I have found afterwards, is corroborated by Alexander who asserts that: 'syllogistic combinations are those from which something necessarily follows, and such are those in which for all matter the same comes to be'.[7] Syllogistic necessity reduced to universal quantifiers can

---

[1] *An. pr.* i. 10, 30ᵇ32 τὸ συμπέρασμα οὐκ ἔστιν ἀναγκαῖον ἁπλῶς, ἀλλὰ τούτων ὄντων ἀναγκαῖον.

[2] Ibid. 9, 30ᵃ37 τὸ μὲν A παντὶ τῷ B ὑπαρχέτω ἐξ ἀνάγκης, τὸ δὲ B τινὶ τῷ Γ ὑπαρχέτω μόνον· ἀνάγκη δὴ τὸ A τινὶ τῷ Γ ὑπάρχειν ἐξ ἀνάγκης.

[3] Ibid. 15, 34ᵃ17 οὐ γὰρ ἔστιν οὐδὲν ἐξ ἀνάγκης ἑνός τινος ὄντος, ἀλλὰ δυοῖν ἐλαχίστοιν ,οἷον ὅταν αἱ προτάσεις οὕτως ἔχωσιν ὡς ἐλέχθη κατὰ τὸν συλλογισμόν.

[4] *An. post.* i. 3, 73ᵃ7 ἑνὸς μὲν οὖν κειμένου δέδεικται ὅτι οὐδέποτ᾽ ἀνάγκη τι εἶναι ἕτερον (λέγω δ᾽ ἑνός, ὅτι οὔτε ὅρου ἑνὸς οὔτε θέσεως μιᾶς τεθείσης), ἐκ δύο δὲ θέσεων πρώτων καὶ ἐλαχίστων ἐνδέχεται.

[5] *An. pr.* i. 2, 25ᵃ20 εἰ γὰρ τὸ A τινὶ τῷ B, καὶ τὸ B τινὶ τῷ A ἀνάγκη ὑπάρχειν.

[6] See § 5.

[7] Alexander 208. 16 συλλογιστικαὶ δὲ αἱ συζυγίαι αὗται αἱ ἐξ ἀνάγκης τι συνάγουσαι· τοιαῦται δέ, ἐν αἷς ἐπὶ πάσης ὕλης γίνεται τὸ αὐτό.

be eliminated from syllogistic laws, as will appear from the following consideration.

The syllogism (*g*) correctly translated into symbols would have the form:

(*h*) *LCKAbaAcbAca*,

which means in words:

(*i*) *It is necessary that (if every b is an a, and every c is a b, then every c should be an a).*

The sign of necessity in front of the syllogism shows that not the conclusion, but the connexion between the premisses and the conclusion is necessary. Aristotle would have asserted (*h*). Formula

(*j*) *CKAbaAcbLAca*,

which literally corresponds to the verbal expression (*g*), is wrong. Aristotle would have rejected it, as he rejects a formula with stronger premisses, viz.

(*k*) *CKAbaLAcbLAca*,

i.e. '*If every b is an a and it is necessary that every c should be a b, it is necessary that every c should be an a.*'[1]

By the reduction of necessity to universal quantifiers formula (*h*) can be transformed into the expression:

(*l*) *ΠaΠbΠcCKAbaAcbAca*,

i.e. 'For all *a*, for all *b*, for all *c* (if every *b* is an *a* and every *c* is a *b*, then every *c* is an *a*).' This last expression is equivalent to the mood Barbara without quantifiers:

(*m*) *CKAbaAcbAca*,

since a universal quantifier may be omitted when it stands at the head of an asserted formula.

Formulae (*h*) and (*m*) are not equivalent. It is obvious that (*m*) can be deduced from (*h*) by the principle *CLpp*, but the converse deduction is not possible without the reduction of necessity to universal quantifiers. This, however, cannot be done at all, if the above formulae are applied to concrete terms. Put, for instance,

---

[1] *An. pr.* i. 9, 30ª23 εἰ δὲ τὸ μὲν *AB* μὴ ἔστιν ἀναγκαῖον, τὸ δὲ *BΓ* ἀναγκαῖον, οὐκ ἔσται τὸ συμπέρασμα ἀναγκαῖον.

in (h) 'bird' for b, 'crow' for a, and 'animal' for c; we get the apodeictic proposition:

> (n) *It is necessary that (if every bird is a crow and every animal is a bird, then every animal should be a crow).*

From (n) results the syllogism (o):

> (o) *If every bird is a crow and every animal is a bird, then every animal is a crow,*

but from (o) we cannot get (n) by the transformation of necessity into quantifiers, as (n) does not contain variables which could be quantified.

And here we meet the first difficulty. It is easy to understand the meaning of necessity when the functor L is attached to the front of an asserted proposition containing free variables. In this case we have a general law, and we may say: this law we regard as necessary, because it is true of all objects of a certain kind, and does not allow of exception. But how should we interpret necessity, when we have a necessary proposition without free variables, and in particular, when this proposition is an implication consisting of false antecedents and of a false consequent, as in our example (n)? I see only one reasonable answer: we could say that whoever accepts the premisses of this syllogism is necessarily compelled to accept its conclusion. But this would be a kind of psychological necessity which is quite alien from logic. Besides it is extremely doubtful that anybody would accept evidently false propositions as true.

I know no better remedy for removing this difficulty than to drop everywhere the L-functor standing in front of an asserted implication. This procedure was already adopted by Aristotle who sometimes omits the sign of necessity in valid syllogistical moods.[1]

§ 42. *'Material' or 'strict' implication?*

According to Philo of Megara the implication 'If p, then q', i.e. Cpq, is true if and only if it does not begin with a true antecedent and end with a false consequent.[2] This is the so-called 'material' implication now universally accepted in the classical calculus of propositions. 'Strict' implication: 'It is necessary that

---

[1] See p. 10, n. 5. [2] See p. 83, n. 1.

if p, then q', i.e. $LCpq$, is a necessary material implication and was introduced into symbolic logic by C. I. Lewis. By means of this terminology the problem we are discussing may be stated thus: Should we interpret the antecedent of the Aristotelian laws of extensionality as material, or as strict implication? In other words, should we accept the stronger formulae 18 and 19 (I call this the 'strong interpretation'), or should we reject them accepting the weaker formulae 43 and 44 (weak interpretation)?

Aristotle was certainly not aware of the difference between these two interpretations and of their importance for modal logic. He could not know Philo's definition of the material implication. But his commentator Alexander was very well acquainted with the logic of the Stoic–Megaric school and with the heated controversies about the meaning of the implication amidst the followers of this school. Let us then see his comments on our problem.

Commenting on the Aristotelian passage 'If (if α is, β must be), then (if α is possible, β must be possible)' Alexander emphasizes the necessary character of the premiss 'If α is, β must be'. It seems therefore that he would accept the weaker interpretation $CLC\alpha\beta CM\alpha M\beta$ and the weaker M-law of extensionality $CLCpqCMpMq$. But what he means by a necessary implication is different from strict implication in the sense of Lewis. He says that in a necessary implication the consequent should always, i.e. at any time, follow from the antecedent, so that the proposition 'If Alexander is, he is so and so many years old' is not a true implication, even if Alexander were in fact so many years old at the time when this proposition is uttered.[1] We may say that this proposition is not exactly expressed, and requires the addition of a temporal qualification in order to be always true. A true material implication must be, of course, always true, and if it contains variables, must be true for all values of the variables. Alexander's comment is not incompatible with the strong interpretation; it does not throw light on our problem.

Some more light is thrown on it, if we replace in Alexander's proof of the M-law of extensionality expounded in § 40 the

[1] Alexander 176. 2 ἔστι δὲ ἀναγκαία ἀκολουθία οὐχ ἡ πρόσκαιρος, ἀλλ' ἐν ᾗ ἀεὶ τὸ εἰλημμένον ἔπεσθαι ἔστι τῷ τὸ εἰλημμένον ὡς ἡγούμενον εἶναι. οὐ γὰρ ἀληθὲς συνημμένον τὸ 'εἰ Ἀλέξανδρος ἔστιν, Ἀλέξανδρος διαλέγεται', ἢ 'εἰ Ἀλέξανδρος ἔστι, τοσῶνδε ἐτῶν ἔστι', καὶ ⟨εἰ⟩ εἴη, ὅτε λέγεται ἡ πρότασις, τοσούτων ἐτῶν.

material implication Cpq by the strict implication $LCpq$. Transforming thus the formula

31. $CMpCCpqNLNq$,

we get:

45. $CMpCLCpqNLNq$.

From 31 we can easily derive $CMpNLNp$ by the substitution q/p getting $CMpCCppNLNp$, from which our proposition results by commutation and detachment, for Cpp is an asserted implication. The same procedure, however, cannot be applied to 45. We get $CMpCLCppNLNp$, but if we want to detach $CMpNLNp$ we must assert the apodeictic implication $LCpp$. And here we encounter the same difficulty, as described in the foregoing section. What is the meaning of $LCpp$? This expression may be interpreted as a general law concerning all propositions, if we transform it into $\Pi pCpp$; but such a transformation becomes impossible, if we apply $LCpp$ to concrete terms, e.g. to the proposition 'Twice two is five'. The assertoric implication 'If twice two is five, then twice two is five' is comprehensible and true being a consequence of the law of identity Cpp; but what is the meaning of the apodeictic implication 'It is necessary that if twice two is five, then twice two should be five'? This queer expression is not a general law concerning all numbers; it may be at most a consequence of an apodeictic law, but it is not true that a consequence of an apodeictic proposition must be apodeictic too. Cpp is a consequence of $LCpp$ according to $CLCppCpp$, a substitution of $CLpp$, but is not apodeictic.

It follows from the above that it is certainly simpler to interpret Alexander's proof by taking the word συμβαίνει of his text in the sense of material rather than strict implication. Nevertheless our problem is not yet definitively solved. Let us therefore turn to the other kind of asserted apodeictic proposition accepted by Aristotle, that is to necessary connexions of terms.

§ 43. *Analytic propositions*

Aristotle asserts the proposition: 'It is necessary that man should be an animal.'[1] He states here a necessary connexion between the subject 'man' and the predicate 'animal', i.e. a

---

[1] *An. pr.* i. 9, 30ᵃ30 ζῷον μὲν γὰρ ὁ ἄνθρωπος ἐξ ἀνάγκης ἐστί.

necessary connexion between terms. He apparently regards it as obvious that the proposition 'Man is an animal', or better 'Every man is an animal', must be an apodeictic one, because he defines 'man' as an 'animal', so that the predicate 'animal' is contained in the subject 'man'. Propositions in which the predicate is contained in the subject are called 'analytic', and we shall probably be right in supposing that Aristotle would have regarded all analytic propositions based on definitions as apodeictic, since he says in the *Posterior Analytics* that essential predicates belong to things necessarily,[1] and essential predicates result from definitions.

The most conspicuous examples of analytic propositions are those in which the subject is identical with the predicate. If it is necessary that every man should be an animal, it is, *a fortiori*, necessary that every man should be a man. The law of identity 'Every *a* is an *a*' is an analytic proposition, and consequently an apodeictic one. We get thus the formula:

(*p*) $LAaa$, i.e. *It is necessary that every a should be an a.*

Aristotle does not state the law of identity Aaa as a principle of his assertoric syllogistic; there is only one passage, found by Ivo Thomas, where in passing he uses this law in a demonstration.[2] We cannot expect, therefore, that he has known the modal thesis $LAaa$.

The Aristotelian law of identity Aaa, where A means 'every–is' and *a* is a variable universal term, is different from the principle of identity Jxx, where J means 'is identical with' and x is a variable individual term. The latter principle belongs to the theory of identity which can be established on the following axioms:

(*q*) Jxx, i.e. *x is identical with x,*

(*r*) $CJxyC\phi x\phi y$, i.e. *If x is identical with y, then if x satisfies φ, y satisfies φ,*

where ϕ is a variable proposition-forming functor of one individual argument. Now, if all analytic propositions are necessary, so also is (*q*), and we get the apodeictic principle:

(*s*) $LJxx$, i.e. *It is necessary that x should be identical with x.*

---

[1] *An. post.* i. 6, 74ᵇ6 τὰ δὲ καθ᾽αὑτὰ ὑπάρχοντα ἀναγκαῖα τοῖς πράγμασιν.

[2] Ivo Thomas, O.P., 'Farrago Logica', *Dominican Studies*, vol. iv (1951), p. 71. The passage reads (*An. pr.* ii. 22, 68ᵃ19) κατηγορεῖται δὲ τὸ B καὶ αὐτὸ αὑτοῦ.

It has been observed by W. V. Quine that the principle (*s*), if asserted, leads to awkward consequences.[1] For if *LJxx* is asserted, we can derive (*t*) from (*r*) by the substitution φ/*LJx'*—*LJx* works here like a proposition-forming functor of one argument:

(*t*)   *CJxyCLJxxLJxy*,

and by commutation

(*u*)   *CLJxxCJxyLJxy*,

from which there follows the proposition:

(*v*)   *CJxyLJxy*.

That means, any two individuals are necessarily identical, if they are identical at all.

The relation of equality is usually treated by mathematicians as identity and is based on the same axioms (*q*) and (*r*). We may therefore interpret *J* as equality, *x* and *y* as individual numbers and say that equality holds necessarily if it holds at all.

Formula (*v*) is obviously false. Quine gives an example to show its falsity. Let *x* denote the number of planets, and *y* the number 9. It is a factual truth that the number of (major) planets is equal to 9, but it is not necessary that it should be equal to 9. Quine tries to meet this difficulty by raising objections to the substitution of such singular terms for the variables. In my opinion, however, his objections are without foundation.

There is another awkward consequence of the formula (*v*) not mentioned by Quine. From (*v*) we get by the definition of *L* and the law of transposition the consequence:

(*w*)   *CMNJxyNJxy*.

That means: 'If it is possible that *x* is not equal to *y*, then *x* is (actually) not equal to *y*.' The falsity of this consequence may be seen in the following example: Let us suppose that a number *x* has been thrown with a die. It is possible that the number *y* next thrown with the die will be different from *x*. But if it is possible that *x* will be different from *y*, i.e. not equal to *y*, then according to (*w*) *x* will actually be different from *y*. This consequence is obviously wrong, as it is possible to throw the same number twice.

[1] W. V. Quine, 'Three Grades of Modal Involvement', *Proceedings of the XIth International Congress of Philosophy*, vol. xiv, Brussels (1953). For the following argumentation I am alone responsible.

There is, in my opinion, only one way to solve the above difficulties: we must not allow that formula $LJxx$ should be asserted, i.e. that the principle of identity Jxx is necessary. As Jxx is a typical analytic proposition, and as there is no reason to treat this principle in a different way from other analytic propositions, we are compelled to assume that no analytic proposition is necessary.

Before dealing with this important topic let us bring to an end our investigation of Aristotle's concepts of modalities.

§ 44. *An Aristotelian paradox*

There is a principle of necessity set forth by Aristotle which is highly controversial. He says in the *De Interpretatione* that 'anything existent is necessary when it exists, and anything non-existent is impossible when it does not exist'. This does not mean, he adds, that whatever exists is necessary, and whatever does not exist is impossible: for it is not the same to say that anything existent is necessary when it does exist, and to say that it is simply necessary.[1] It should be noted that the temporal 'when' ($ὅταν$) is used in this passage instead of the conditional 'if'. A similar thesis is set forth by Theophrastus. He says, when defining the kinds of things that are necessary, that the third kind (we do not know what the first two are) is 'the existent, for when it exists, then it is impossible that it should not exist'.[2] Here again we find the temporal particles 'when' ($ὅτε$) and 'then' ($τότε$). No doubt an analogous principle occurs in medieval logic and scholars could find it there. There is a formulation quoted by Leibniz in his *Theodicee* running thus: *Unumquodque, quando est, oportet esse.*[3] Note again in this sentence the temporal *quando*.

What does this principle mean? It is, in my opinion, ambiguous. Its first meaning seems to be akin to syllogistic necessity, which is a necessary connexion not of terms, but of propositions. Alexander commenting on the Aristotelian distinction between simple and conditional necessity,[4] says that Aristotle was himself

---

[1] *De int.* 9. 19ª23 τὸ μὲν οὖν εἶναι τὸ ὄν, ὅταν ᾖ, καὶ τὸ μὴ ὂν μὴ εἶναι, ὅταν μὴ ᾖ, ἀνάγκη· οὐ μὴν οὔτε τὸ ὂν ἅπαν ἀνάγκη εἶναι οὔτε τὸ μὴ ὂν μὴ εἶναι. Οὐ γὰρ ταὐτόν ἐστι τὸ ὂν ἅπαν εἶναι ἐξ ἀνάγκης ὅτε ἔστι, καὶ τὸ ἁπλῶς εἶναι ἐξ ἀνάγκης.

[2] Alexander 156. 29 ὁ γοῦν Θεόφραστος ἐν τῷ πρώτῳ τῶν Προτέρων ἀναλυτικῶν λέγων περὶ τῶν ὑπὸ τοῦ ἀναγκαίου σημαινομένων οὕτως γράφει· 'τρίτον τὸ ὑπάρχον· ὅτε γὰρ ὑπάρχει, τότε οὐχ οἷόν τε μὴ ὑπάρχειν.'

[3] *Philosophische Schriften*, ed. Gerhardt, vol. vi, p. 131.

[4] See p. 144, n. 1.

aware of this distinction, which was explicitly made by his friends (that is, by Theophrastus and Eudemus), and quotes as a further argument the passage of the *De Interpretatione* above referred to. He is aware that this passage is formulated by Aristotle in connexion with singular propositions about future events, and calls the necessity involved 'hypothetical necessity' (ἀναγκαῖον ἐξ ὑποθέσεως).[1]

This hypothetical necessity does not differ from conditional necessity, except that it is applied not to syllogisms, but to singular propositions about events. Such propositions always contain a temporal qualification. But if we include this qualification in the content of the proposition, we can replace the temporal particle by the conditional. So, for instance, instead of saying indefinitely: 'It is necessary that a sea-fight should be, when it is', we may say: 'It is necessary that a sea-fight should be tomorrow, if it will be tomorrow.' Keeping in mind that hypothetical necessity is a necessary connexion of propositions, we may interpret this latter implication as equivalent to the proposition: 'It is necessary that if a sea-fight will be tomorrow, it should be tomorrow' which is a substitution of the formula *LCpp*.

The principle of necessity we are discussing would lead to no controversy, if it had only the meaning explained above. But it may have still another meaning: we may interpret the necessity involved in it as a necessary connexion not of propositions, but of terms. This other meaning seems to be what Aristotle himself has in mind, when he expounds the determinist argument that all future events are necessary. In this connexion a general statement given by him deserves our attention. We read in the *De Interpretatione*: 'If it is true to say that something is white or not white, it is necessary that it should be white or not white.'[2] It seems that here a necessary connexion is stated between a 'thing' as subject and 'white' as predicate. Using a propositional variable instead of the sentence 'Something is white' we get the formula: 'If it is

---

[1] Alexander 141. 1 ἅμα δὲ καὶ τὴν τοῦ ἀναγκαίου διαίρεσιν ὅτι καὶ αὐτὸς οἶδεν, ἣν οἱ ἑταῖροι αὐτοῦ πεποίηνται, δεδήλωκε διὰ τῆς προσθήκης (scil. 'τούτων' ὄντων'), ἣν φθάσας ἤδη καὶ ἐν τῷ Περὶ ἑρμηνείας δέδειχεν, ἐν οἷς περὶ τῆς εἰς τὸν μέλλοντα χρόνον λεγομένης ἀντιφάσεως περὶ τῶν καθ' ἕκαστον εἰρημένων λέγει· 'τὸ μὲν οὖν εἶναι τὸ ὄν, ὅταν ᾖ, καὶ τὸ μὴ ὂν μὴ εἶναι, ὅταν μὴ ᾖ, ἀνάγκη'. τὸ γὰρ ἐξ ὑποθέσεως ἀναγκαῖον τοιοῦτόν ἐστι.

[2] De int. 9, 18ᵃ39 εἰ γὰρ ἀληθὲς εἰπεῖν ὅτι λευκὸν ἢ ὅτι οὐ λευκόν ἐστιν, ἀνάγκη εἶναι λευκὸν ἢ οὐ λευκόν.

true that p, it is necessary that p'. I do not know whether Aristotle would have accepted this formula or not, but in any case it is interesting to draw some consequences from it.

In two-valued logic any proposition is either true or false. Hence the expression 'It is true that p' is equivalent to 'p'. Applying this equivalence to our case we see that the formula 'If it is true that p, it is necessary that p' would be equivalent to this simpler expression: 'If p, it is necessary that p' which reads in symbols: $CpLp$. We know, however, that this formula has been rejected by Alexander, and certainly by Aristotle himself. It must be rejected, for propositional modal logic would collapse, if it were asserted. Any assertoric proposition p would be equivalent to its apodeictic correspondent Lp, as both formulae, $CLpp$ and $CpLp$, would be valid, and it could be proved that any assertoric proposition p was equivalent also to its problematic correspondent Mp. Under these conditions it would be useless to construct a propositional modal logic.

But it is possible to express in symbolic form the idea implied by the formula 'If it is true that p, it is necessary that p': we need only replace the words 'It is true that p' by the expression 'α is asserted'. These two expressions do not mean the same. We can put forward for consideration not only true, but also false propositions without being in error. But it would be an error to assert a proposition which was not true. It is therefore not sufficient to say 'p is true', if we want to impart the idea that p is really true; p may be false, and 'p is true' is false with it. We must say 'α is asserted' changing 'p' into 'α', as 'p' being a substitution-variable cannot be asserted, whereas 'α' may be interpreted as a true proposition. We can now state, not indeed a theorem, but a rule:

$$(x) \quad \alpha \rightarrow L\alpha.$$

In words: 'α, therefore it is necessary that α'. The arrow means 'therefore', and the formula (x) is a rule of inference valid only when α is asserted. Such a rule restricted to 'tautologous' propositions is accepted by some modern logicians.[1]

From rule (x) and the asserted principle of identity Jxx there follows the asserted apodeictic formula $LJxx$ which leads, as we have seen, to awkward consequences. The rule seems to be doubtful, even if restricted to logical theorems or to analytic proposi-

[1] See, e.g. G. H. von Wright, *An Essay in Modal Logic*, Amsterdam (1951), pp. 14–15.

tions. Without this restriction rule (x) would yield, as appears from the example given by Aristotle, apodeictic assertions of merely factual truths, a result contrary to intuition. For this reason this Aristotelian principle fully deserves the name of a paradox.

§ 45. Contingency in Aristotle

I have already mentioned that the Aristotelian term ἐνδεχό-μενον is ambiguous. In the *De Interpretatione*, and sometimes in the *Prior Analytics*, it means the same as δυνατόν, but sometimes it has another more complicated meaning which following Sir David Ross I shall translate by 'contingent'.[1] The merit of having pointed out this ambiguity is due to A. Becker.[2]

Aristotle's definition of contingency runs thus: 'By "contingent" I mean that which is not necessary and the supposed existence of which implies nothing impossible.'[3] We can see at once that Alexander's definition of possibility results from Aristotle's definition of contingency by omission of the words 'which is not necessary'. If we add, therefore, the symbols of these words to our formula 28 and denote the new functor by 'T', we get the following definition:

$$46.\ QTpKNLpΠqCCpqNLNq.$$

This definition can be abbreviated, as $ΠqCCpqNLNq$ is equivalent to $NLNp$. The implication:

$$39.\ CNLNpΠqCCpqNLNq$$

has been already proved; the converse implication

$$47.\ CΠqCCpqNLNqNLNp$$

easily results from the thesis $CΠqCCpqNLNqCCpqNLNq$ by the substitution q/p, commutation, Cpp, and detachment. By putting in 46 the simpler expression $NLNp$ for $ΠqCCpqNLNq$ we get:

$$48.\ QTpKNLpNLNp.$$

This means in words: 'It is contingent that p—if and only if—it

---

[1] W. D. Ross, loc. cit., p. 296.

[2] See A. Becker, *Die Aristotelische Theorie der Möglichkeitsschlüsse*, Berlin (1933). I agree with Sir David Ross (loc. cit., Preface) that Becker's book is 'very acute', but I do not agree with Becker's conclusions.

[3] *An. pr.* i. 13, 32ᵃ18 λέγω δ' ἐνδέχεσθαι καὶ τὸ ἐνδεχόμενον, οὗ μὴ ὄντος ἀναγκαίου, τεθέντος δ' ὑπάρχειν, οὐδὲν ἔσται διὰ τοῦτ' ἀδύνατον.

is not necessary that p and it is not necessary that not p.' As the phrase 'not necessary that not p' means the same as 'not impossible that p', we may say roughly speaking: 'Something is contingent if and only if it is not necessary and not impossible.' Alexander shortly says: 'The contingent is neither necessary nor impossible.'[1]

We get another definition of Tp, if we transform $NLNp$ according to our definition 1 into Mp, and NLp into MNp:

49. $QTpKMNpMp$ or   50. $QTpKMpMNp$.

Formula 50 reads: 'It is contingent that p—if and only if—it is possible that p and it is possible that not p.' This defines contingency as 'ambivalent possibility', i.e. as a possibility which can indeed be the case, but can also not be the case. We shall see that the consequences of this definition, together with other of Aristotle's assertions about contingency, raise a new major difficulty.

In a famous discussion about future contingent events Aristotle tries to defend the indeterministic point of view. He assumes that things which are not always in act have likewise the possibility of being or not being. For instance, this gown may be cut into pieces, and likewise it may not be cut.[2] Similarly a sea-fight may happen tomorrow, and equally it may not happen. He says that 'Of two contradictory propositions about such things one must be true and the other false, but not this one or that one, only whichever may chance (to be fulfilled), one of them may be more true than the other, but neither of them is as yet true, or as yet false.'[3]

These arguments, though not quite clearly expressed or fully thought out, contain an important and most fruitful idea. Let us take the example of the sea-fight, and suppose that nothing is decided today about this fight. I mean that there is nothing that is real today and that would cause there to be a sea-fight tomorrow, nor yet anything that would cause there not to be one. Hence, if

---

[1] Alexander 158. 20 οὔτε γὰρ ἀναγκαῖον οὔτε ἀδύνατον τὸ ἐνδεχόμενον.

[2] *De int.* 9, 19ᵃ9 ἔστιν ἐν τοῖς μὴ ἀεὶ ἐνεργοῦσι τὸ δυνατὸν εἶναι καὶ μὴ ὁμοίως . . . 12 οἷον ὅτι τουτὶ τὸ ἱμάτιον δυνατὸν ἐστι διατμηθῆναι, . . . ὁμοίως δὲ·καὶ τὸ μὴ διατμηθῆναι δυνατόν.

[3] Ibid. 19ᵃ36 τούτων γὰρ (i.e. ἐπὶ τοῖς μὴ ἀεὶ οὖσιν ἢ μὴ ἀεὶ μὴ οὖσιν) ἀνάγκη μὲν θάτερον μόριον τῆς ἀντιφάσεως ἀληθὲς εἶναι ἢ ψεῦδος, οὐ μέντοι τόδε ἢ τόδε ἀλλ' ὁπότερ' ἔτυχε, καὶ μᾶλλον μὲν ἀληθῆ τὴν ἑτέραν, οὐ μέντοι ἤδη ἀληθῆ ἢ ψευδῆ.

truth rests on conformity of thought with reality, the proposition 'The sea-fight will happen tomorrow' is today neither true nor false. It is in this sense that I understand the words 'not yet true or false' in Aristotle. But this would lead to the conclusion that it is today neither necessary nor impossible that there will be a sea-fight tomorrow; in other words, that the propositions 'It is possible that there will be a sea-fight tomorrow' and 'It is possible that there will not be a sea-fight tomorrow' are today both true, and this future event is contingent.

It follows from the above that according to Aristotle there exist true contingent propositions, i.e. that the formula Tp and its equivalent $KMpMNp$ are true for some value of p, say α. For example, if α means 'There will be a sea-fight tomorrow', both $M\alpha$ and $MN\alpha$ would be accepted by Aristotle as true, so that he would have asserted the conjunction:

(A) $KM\alpha MN\alpha$.

There exists, however, in the classical calculus of propositions enlarged by the variable functor δ, the following thesis due to Leśniewski's protothetic:

51. $C\delta pC\delta Np\delta q$.

In words: 'If δ of p, then if δ of not p, δ of q', or roughly speaking: 'If something is true of the proposition p, and also true of the negation of p, it is true of an arbitrary proposition q.' Thesis 51 is equivalent to

52. $CK\delta p\delta Np\delta q$

on the ground of the laws of importation and exportation $CCpCqrCKpqr$ and $CCKpqrCpCqr$. From (A) and 52 we get the consequence:

52. $\delta/M,\ p/\alpha,\ q/p \times C(A)-(B)$

(B) Mp.

Thus, if there is any contingent proposition that we accept as true, we are bound to admit of any proposition whatever that it is possible. But this would cause a collapse of modal logic; Mp must be rejected, and consequently $KM\alpha MN\alpha$ cannot be asserted.

We are at the end of our analysis of Aristotle's propositional modal logic. This analysis has led us to two major difficulties: the first difficulty is connected with Aristotle's acceptance of true apodeictic propositions, the second with his acceptance of true contingent propositions. Both difficulties will reappear in Aristotle's modal syllogistic, the first in his theory of syllogisms with one assertoric and one apodeictic premiss, the second in his theory of contingent syllogisms. If we want to meet these difficulties and to explain as well as to appreciate his modal syllogistic, we must first establish a secure and consequent system of modal logic.

CHAPTER VII

THE SYSTEM OF MODAL LOGIC

§ 46. *The matrix method*

For a full understanding of the system of modal logic expounded in this chapter it is necessary to be acquainted with the matrix method. This method can be applied to all logical systems in which truth-functions occur, i.e. functions whose truth-values depend only on the truth-values of their arguments. The classical calculus of propositions is a two-valued system, i.e. it assumes two truth-values, 'truth' denoted here by 1, and 'falsity' denoted by 0. According to Philo of Megara an implication is true, unless. it begins with truth and ends with falsity. That means in symbols that $C11 = C01 = C00 = 1$, and only $C10 = 0$. Obviously the negation of a true proposition is false, i.e. $N1 = 0$, and the negation of a false proposition true, i.e. $N0 = 1$. It is usual to present these symbolic equalities by means of 'truth-tables' or 'matrices', as they are called. The two-valued matrix $M1$ of C and N may be described as follows: the truth-values of C are arranged in rows and columns forming a square, and are separated by a line from the left margin and the top. The truth-values of the first argument are put on the left, those of the second on the top, and the truth-values of C can be found in the square, where the lines which we may imagine drawn from the truth-values on the margins of the square intersect one another. The matrix of N is easily comprehensible.

$$
\begin{array}{c|cc|c}
 & \multicolumn{2}{c|}{\overbrace{}^{q}} & \\
C & 1 & 0 & N \\
\hline
p \begin{cases} 1 \\ 0 \end{cases} & \begin{matrix} 1 \\ 1 \end{matrix} & \begin{matrix} 0 \\ 1 \end{matrix} & \begin{matrix} 0 \\ 1 \end{matrix} \\
 & \multicolumn{2}{c}{M1} &
\end{array}
$$

By means of this matrix any expression of the classical calculus of propositions, i.e. of the C–N–p-calculus, can be mechanically verified, i.e. proved when asserted and disproved when rejected. It suffices for this purpose to put the values 1 and 0 in all possible combinations for the variables, and if every combination reduced according to equalities stated in the matrix gives 1 as final result, the expression is proved, but if not, it is disproved. For example, $CCpqCNpNq$ is disproved by M1, since when $p = 0$ and $q = 1$, we have: $CC01CN0N1 = C1C10 = C10 = 0$. By contrast, $CpCNpq$, one of our axioms of our C–N–p-system,[1] is proved by M1, because we have:

$$\text{For } p = 1, q = 1: C1CN11 = C1C01 = C11 = 1,$$
$$\,\,\text{,, } \quad p = 1, q = 0: C1CN10 = C1C00 = C11 = 1,$$
$$\,\,\text{,, } \quad p = 0, q = 1: C0C.N01 = C0C11 = C01 = 1,$$
$$\,\,\text{,, } \quad p = 0, q = 0: C0C.N00 = C0C10 = C00 = 1.$$

In the same way we can verify the other two axioms of the C–N–p-system, $CCpqCCqrCpr$ and $CCNppp$. As M1 is so constructed that the property of always yielding 1 is hereditary with respect to the rules of substitution and detachment for asserted expressions, all asserted formulae of the C–N–p-system can be proved by the matrix M1. And as similarly the property of not always yielding 1 is hereditary with respect to the rules of inference for rejected expressions, all rejected formulae of the C–N–p-system can be disproved by M1, if p is axiomatically rejected. A matrix which verifies all formulae of a system, i.e. proves the asserted and disproves the rejected ones, is called 'adequate' for the system. M1 is an adequate matrix of the classical calculus of propositions.

M1 is not the only adequate matrix of the C–N–p-system. We get another adequate matrix, M3, by 'multiplying' M1 by itself. The process of getting M3 can be described as follows:

First, we form ordered pairs of the values 1 and 0, viz.: $(1, 1)$, $(1, 0)$, $(0, 1)$, $(0, 0)$; these are the elements of the new matrix. Secondly, we determine the truth-values of C and N by the equalities:

(y) $C(a, b)(c, d) = (Cac, Cbd),$
(z) $N(a, b) = (Na, Nb).$

Then we build up the matrix M2 according to these equalities; and finally we transform M2 into M3 by the abbreviations: $(1, 1) = 1$, $(1, 0) = 2$, $(0, 1) = 3$, and $(0, 0) = 0$.

---

[1] See p. 80.

C	$(1,1)$	$(1,0)$	$(0,1)$	$(0,0)$	N		C	1	2	3	0	N
$(1,1)$	$(1,1)$	$(1,0)$	$(0,1)$	$(0,0)$	$(0,0)$		1	1	2	3	0	0
$(1,0)$	$(1,1)$	$(1,1)$	$(0,1)$	$(0,1)$	$(0,1)$		2	1	1	3	3	3
$(0,1)$	$(1,1)$	$(1,0)$	$(1,1)$	$(1,0)$	$(1,0)$		3	1	2	1	2	2
$(0,0)$	$(1,1)$	$(1,1)$	$(1,1)$	$(1,1)$	$(1,1)$		0	1	1	1	1	1

               M2   M3

Symbol *1* in M3 again denotes truth, and *o* falsity. The new symbols *2* and *3* may be interpreted as further signs of truth and falsity. This may be seen by identifying one of them, it does not

C	1	1	0	0	N		C	1	0	1	0	N
1	1	1	0	0	0		1	1	0	1	0	0
1	1	1	0	0	0		0	1	1	1	1	1
0	1	1	1	1	1		1	1	0	1	0	1
0	1	1	1	1	1		0	1	1	1	1	1

            M4   M5

matter which, with *1*, and the other with *o*. Look at M4, where $2 = 1$, and $3 = 0$. The second row of M4 is identical with its first row, and the fourth row with its third; similarly the second column of M4 is identical with its first column, and the fourth column with its third. Cancelling the superfluous middle rows and columns we get M1. In the same way we get M1 from M5 where $2 = 0$ and $3 = 1$.

M3 is a four-valued matrix. By multiplying M3 by M1 we get an eight-valued matrix, by further multiplication by M1 a sixteen-valued matrix, and, in general, a $2n$-valued matrix. All these matrices are adequate to the C–N–p-system, and continue to be adequate, if we extend the system by the introduction of variable functors.

§ 47. *The C–N–δ–p-system*

We have already met two theses with a variable functor δ: the principle of extensionality $CQpqC\delta p\delta q$, and the thesis $C\delta pC\delta Np\delta q$. As the latter thesis is an axiom of our system of modal logic, it is necessary to explain thoroughly the C–N–p-system extended by δ which I call, following C. A. Meredith, the C–N–δ–p-system. This is the more necessary, as systems with δ are almost unknown even to logicians.

The introduction of variable functors into propositional logic is due to the Polish logician Leśniewski. By a modification of his rule of substitution for variable functors I was able to get simple and elegant proofs.[1] First, this rule must be explained.

I denote by δ a variable functor of one propositional argument, and I accept that δP is a significant expression provided P is a significant expression. Let us see what is the meaning of the simplest significant expression with a variable functor, i.e. δp.

A variable is a single letter considered with respect to a range of values that may be substituted for it. To substitute means in practice to write instead of the variable one of its values, the same value for each occurrence of the same variable. In the C-N-p-system the range of values of propositional variables, such as p or q, consists of all propositional expressions significant in the system; besides these two constants may be introduced, 1 and 0, i.e. a constant true and a constant false proposition. What is the range of values of the functorial variable δ?

It is obvious that for δ we may substitute any value which gives together with p a significant expression of our system. Such are not only constant functors of one propositional argument, as, e.g. N, but also complex expressions working like functors of one argument, as Cq or $CCNpp$. By the substitution δ/Cq we get from δp the expression Cqp, and by $\delta/CCNpp$ the expression $CCNppp$. It is evident, however, that this kind of substitution does not cover all possible cases. We cannot get in this way either Cpq or $CpCNpq$ from δp, because by no substitution for δ can the p be removed from its final position. Nevertheless there is no doubt that the two last expressions are as good substitutions of δp, as Cqp or $CCNppp$, since δp, as I understand it, represents all significant expressions which contain p, including p and δp itself.

I was able to overcome this difficulty by the following device which I shall first explain by examples. In order to get Cpq from δp by a substitution for δ I write $\delta/C'q$, and I perform the substitution by dropping δ and filling up the blank marked by an apostrophe by the argument of δ, i.e. by p. In the same way I get from δp the expression $CpCNpq$ by the substitution $\delta/C'CN'q$. If more than one δ occurs in an expression, as in $C\delta pC\delta Np\delta q$, and I want to perform on this expression the substitution $\delta/C'r$, I must

[1] See Jan Łukasiewicz, 'On Variable Functors of Propositional Arguments', *Proceedings of the Royal Irish Academy*, Dublin (1951), 54 A 2.

everywhere drop the δ's and write in their stead *C'r* filling up the blanks by the respective arguments of δ. I get thus from δ*p*—*Cpr*, from δ*Np*—*CNpr*, from δ*q*—*Cqr*, and from the whole expression— *CCprCCNprCqr*. From the same expression *CδpCδNpδq* there follows by the substitution δ/*C''* the formula *CCppCCNpNpCqq*. The substitution δ/' means that δ should be omitted; by this substitution we get for instance from *CδpCδNpδq* the principle of Duns Scotus *CpCNpq*. The substitution δ/δ' is the 'identical' substitution and does not produce any change. Speaking generally, we get from an expression containing δ's a new expression by a substitution for δ, writing for δ a significant expression with at least one blank, and filling up the blanks by the respective arguments of the δ's. This is not a new rule of substitution, but merely a description how the substitution for a variable functor should be performed.

The *C–N–δ–p*-system can be built up on the single asserted axiom known already to us:

51. *CδpCδNpδq*,

to which the axiomatically rejected expression *p* should be added to yield all rejected expressions. C. A. Meredith has shown (in an unpublished paper) that all asserted formulae of the *C–N–p*-system may be deduced from axiom 51.[1] The rules of inference are the usual rule of detachment, and the rules of substitution for propositional and functorial variables. To give an example how these rules work I shall deduce from axiom 51 the law of identity *Cpp*. Compare this deduction with the proof of *Cpp* in the *C–N–p*-system.[2]

$$51.\ \delta/',\ q/p \times 53$$
53. *CpCNpp*
$$51.\ \delta/CpCNp',\ q/Np \times C53\text{--}54$$
54. *CCpCNpNpCpCNpNp*
$$51.\ \delta/',\ q/Np \times 55$$

---

[1] C. A. Meredith has proved in his paper 'On an Extended System of the Propositional Calculus', *Proceedings of the Royal Irish Academy*, Dublin (1951), 54 A 3, that the *C–O–δ–p*-calculus, i.e. the calculus with *C* and *O* as primitive terms and with functorial and propositional variables, may be completely built up from the axiom *CδδOδp*. His method of proving completeness can be applied to the *C–N–δ–p*-system with *CδpCδNpδq* as axiom. In my paper on modal logic quoted p. 133, n. 2, I deduce from axiom 51 the three asserted axioms of the *C–N–p*-system, i.e. *CCpqCCqrCpr*, *CCNppp*, *CpCNpq*, and some important theses in which δ occurs, among others the principle of extensionality.   [2] See p. 81.

55. *CpCNpNp*
    55. *p/CpCNpNp* × *C*55–56
56. *CNCpCNpNpNCpCNpNp*
    51. δ/C'', *p/CpCNpNp*, *q/p* × *C*54–*C*56–57
57. *Cpp*.

I should like to emphasize that the system based on axiom 51 is much richer than the C-N-p-system. Among asserted consequences containing δ there are such logical laws as *CCpqCCqpC*δ*p*δ*q*, *C*δ*CpqC*δ*p*δ*q*, *C*δ*CpqCp*δ*q*, all very important, but unknown to almost all logicians. The first law, for instance, is the principle of extensionality, being equivalent to *CQ*pq*C*δ*p*δ*q*, the second may be taken as the sole axiom of the so-called 'implicational' system, the third as an axiom of the so-called 'positive' logic. All these laws can be verified by the matrix method according to a rule given below.

In two-valued logic there exist four and only four different functors of one argument, denoted here by V, S, N, and F (see matrix M6).

p	V	S	N	F
1	*1*	*1*	*0*	*0*
0	*1*	*0*	*1*	*0*

M6

For the verification of δ-expressions the following practical rule due in substance to Leśniewski is sufficient: Write for δ successively the functors V, S, N, and F, then drop S, transform $V\alpha$ into *Cpp*, and $F\alpha$ into *NCpp*. If you get in all cases a true C-N-formula, the expression should be asserted, otherwise it should be rejected. Example: *C*δ*CpqC*δ*p*δ*q* must be asserted, because we have:

CSCpqCSpSq = *CCpqCpq*,   *CNCpqCNpNq*,
CVCpqCVpVq = *CCppCCppCpp*,   *CFCpqCFpFq* = *CNCppCNCppNCpp*.

CCpqCδ*p*δ*q* must be rejected, for *CCpqCNpNq* is not a true C-N-formula. We see thus that all expressions of the C-N-δ-p-system are easily proved or disproved by the matrix method.

§ 48. δ-*Definitions*

The functor δ may be successfully employed to express definitions. The authors of the *Principia Mathematica* express definitions by a special symbol consisting of the sign of equality '=' that connects the *definiens* with the *definiendum*, and of the letters 'Df' put after the definition. According to this method the definition of alternation would run thus:

$$CNpq = Hpq \qquad \text{Df,}$$

where *CNpq* ('If not *p*, then *q*') is the *definiens*, and *Hpq* ('either *p* or *q*') the *definiendum*.[1] The symbol '. =. Df' is associated with a special rule of inference allowing the replacement of the *definiens* by the *definiendum* and vice versa. This is the merit of this kind of definition: the result is given immediately. But it has the defect of increasing the number of primitive symbols as well as of rules of inference which should be as small as possible.

Leśniewski would write the same definition as an equivalence thereby introducing into his system no new primitive term to express definitions, because for this very purpose he chose equivalence as the primitive term of his logic of propositions enlarged by functorial variables and quantifiers, and called by him 'protothetic'. This is the merit of his standpoint. On the other hand he cannot immediately replace the *definiens* by the *definiendum* or conversely, because equivalence has its own rules which do permit such replacements.

In our *C–N–δ–p*-system equivalence is not a primitive term; hence it must be defined, but cannot be defined by an equivalence without a vicious circle. We shall see, however, that it is possible to express definitions by *C* and δ in a way which preserves the merits of both standpoints without having their defects.

The purpose of a definition is to introduce a new term which as a rule is an abbreviation of some complex expression consisting of terms already known to us. Both parts of the definition, the *definiens* as well as the *definiendum* must fulfil certain conditions in order to yield a well-formed definition. The following four conditions are necessary and sufficient for definitions of new functions introduced into our system: (*a*) The *definiens* as well as the *definiendum* should be propositional expressions. (*b*) The *definiens* should consist of primitive terms or of terms already defined by them. (*c*) The *definiendum* should contain the new term introduced by the definition. (*d*) Any free variable occurring in the *definiens*

---

[1] I usually denote alternation by *A*, but this letter has already got another meaning in my syllogistic.

should occur in the *definiendum*, and vice versa. It is easily seen that, e.g. *CNpq* as *definiens* and *Hpq* as *definiendum* comply with the four above conditions.

Let us now denote by *P* and *R* two expressions that fulfil the conditions (*a*)–(*d*), so that one of them, it does not matter which, may be taken as the *definiens*, and the other as the *definiendum*. It is supposed that neither of them contains δ. I say that the asserted expression *CδPδR* represents a definition. For instance:

58. *CδCNpqδHpq*

represents the definition of alternation. According to 58 any expression containing *CNpq* may be immediately transformed into another expression in which *CNpq* is replaced by *Hpq*. As example we may take the principle of Duns Scotus:

59. *CpCNpq*,

from which we can get the law *CpHpq*, i.e. in words: 'If *p*, then either *p* or *q*', by the following deduction:

58. δ/*Cp'* × *C*59–60
60. *CpHpq*.

If we want to apply our definition to the principle of Clavius:

61. *CCNppp*,

we must first put *p* for *q* in 58 getting thus:

58. *q*/*p* × 62
62. *CδCNppδHpp*
62. δ/*C'p* × *C*61–63
63. *CHppp*.

(Formula 63 states: 'If either *p* or *p*, then *p*', and is one of the 'primitive propositions' or axioms accepted by the authors of the *Principia Mathematica*. They rightly call this axiom the 'principle of tautology', as it states that to say the same (ταὐτὸ λέγειν) twice, '*p* or *p*', is to say simply '*p*'. The principle of Duns Scotus, for instance, is not a tautology in any reasonable sense.)

The converse implication of 58 *CδHpqδCNpq*, which enables us to replace *Hpq* by *CNpq* is given together with the first. We can prove, indeed, using only the rules of substitution and detachment the following general theorem:

(C) If P and R are any significant expressions not containing δ, and $C\delta P\delta R$ is asserted, then $C\delta R\delta P$ must be asserted too.

The proof:

(D) $C\delta P\delta R$

    (D) $\delta/C\delta'\delta P \times$ (E)

(E) $CC\delta P\delta PC\delta R\delta P$

    (D) $\delta/CC\delta P\delta'C\delta R\delta P \times$ (F)

(F) $CCC\delta P\delta PC\delta R\delta PCC\delta P\delta RC\delta R\delta P$

    (F) $\times C$(E)–C(D)–(G)

(G) $C\delta R\delta P$.

If therefore P and R do not contain δ, and one of them may be interpreted as *definiens* and the other as *definiendum*, then it is clear that any asserted expression of the form $C\delta P\delta R$ represents a definition, as P may everywhere be replaced by R, and R by P, and this is just the characteristic property of a definition.

§ 49. *The four-valued system of modal logic*

Every system of modal logic ought to include as a proper part basic modal logic, i.e. ought to have among its theses both the M-axioms $CpMp$, *$CMpp$, and *Mp, and the L-axioms $CLpp$, *$CpLp$, and *NLp. It is easily seen that both M and L are different from any of the four functors V, S, N, and F of the two-valued calculus. M cannot be V, for Mp is rejected—whereas $Vp = Cpp$ is asserted, it cannot be S, for $CMpp$ is rejected—whereas $CSpp = Cpp$ is asserted, it cannot be either N or F, for $CpMp$ is asserted—whereas $CpNp$ and $CpFp = CpNCpp$ are rejected. The same is true for L. The functors M and L have no interpretation in two-valued logic. Hence any system of modal logic must be many-valued.

There is yet another idea that leads to the same consequence. If we accept with Aristotle that some future events, e.g. a seafight, are contingent, then a proposition about such events enounced today can be neither true nor false, and therefore must have a third truth-value different from I and o. On the basis of this idea and by help of the matrix method with which I became acquainted through Peirce and Schröder I constructed in 1920 a three-valued system of modal logic developed later in a paper of 1930.[1] I see today that this system does not satisfy all our

[1] Jan Łukasiewicz, 'O logice trójwartościowej', *Ruch Filozoficzny*, vol. v, Lwów

intuitions concerning modalities and should be replaced by the system described below.

I am of the opinion that in any modal logic the classical calculus of propositions should be preserved. This calculus has hitherto manifested solidity and usefulness, and should not be set aside without weighty reasons. Fortunately enough the classical calculus of propositions has not only a two-valued matrix, but also many-valued adequate matrices. I tried to apply to modal logic the simplest many-valued matrix adequate to the C–N–δ–p-system, i.e. the four-valued matrix, and succeeded in obtaining the desired result.

As we have seen in § 46, the matrix M2 whose elements are pairs of values 1 and 0 follows for N from the equality:

(z) $N(a, b) = (Na, Nb)$.

The expression '(Na, Nb)' is a particular case of the general form $(\epsilon a, \zeta b)$ where ϵ and ζ have as values the functors V, S, N, and F of the two-valued calculus. As each of the four values of ϵ can be combined with each of the four values of ζ, we get 16 combinations, which define 16 functors of one argument of the four-valued calculus. I found among them two functors, either of which may represent M. Here I shall define one of them, the other I shall discuss later.

(α) $M(a, b) = (Sa, Vb) = (a, Cbb)$.

On the basis of (α) I got the matrix M7 for M which I transformed into the matrix M8 by the same abbreviations as in § 46, viz.: $(1, 1) = 1$, $(1, 0) = 2$, $(0, 1) = 3$, and $(0, 0) = 0$.

p	M		p	M
$(1, 1)$	$(1, 1)$		1	1
$(1, 0)$	$(1, 1)$		2	1
$(0, 1)$	$(0, 1)$		3	3
$(0, 0)$	$(0, 1)$		0	3
	M7			M8

Having thus got the matrix of M I chose C, N, and M as

(1920). Jan Łukasiewicz, 'Philosophische Bemerkungen zu mehrwertigen Systemen des Aussagenkalküls', *Comptes Rendus des Séances de la Société des Sciences et des Lettres de Varsovie*, vol. xxiii, cl. 3 (1930).

primitive terms, and based my system of modal logic on the following four axioms:

51. $C\delta pC\delta Np\delta q$ 4. $CpMp$ *5. $CMpp$ *7. Mp.

The rules of inference are the rules of substitution and detachment for asserted and rejected expressions.

Lp is introduced by a δ-definition:

64. $C\delta NMNp\delta Lp$.

That means: '$NMNp$' may be everywhere replaced by 'Lp', and conversely 'Lp' by '$NMNp$'.

The same system of modal logic can be established using C, N, and L as primitive terms with the axioms:

51. $C\delta pC\delta Np\delta q$ 3. $CLpp$ *6. $CpLp$ *8. NLp,

and the δ-definition of M:

65. $C\delta NLNp\delta Mp$.

M9 represents the full adequate matrix of the system:

C	1 2 3 0	N	M	L
1	1 2 3 0	0	1	2
2	1 1 3 3	3	1	2
3	1 2 1 2	2	3	0
0	1 1 1 1	1	3	0

M9

I hope that after the explanations given above every reader will be able to verify by this matrix any formula belonging to the system, i.e. to prove asserted formulae, and to disprove rejected ones.

It can be proved that the system is complete in the sense that every significant expression belonging to it is decidable, being either asserted or rejected. It is also consistent, i.e. non-contradictory, in the sense that no significant expression is both asserted and rejected. The set of axioms is independent.

I should like to emphasize that the axioms of the system are perfectly evident. The axiom with δ must be acknowledged by all logicians who accept the classical calculus of propositions; the axioms with M must also be accepted as true; the rules of inference are evident too. All correctly derived consequences of the system must be admitted by anyone who accepts the axioms and the rules of inference. No serious objection can be maintained against this system. We shall see that this system refutes all false inferences drawn in connexion with modal logic, explains the difficulties of the Aristotelian modal syllogistic, and reveals some unexpected logical facts which are of the greatest importance for philosophy.

§ 50. *Necessity and the four-valued system of modal logic*

Two major difficulties were stated at the end of Chapter VI: the first was connected with Aristotle's acceptance of asserted apodeictic propositions, the second with his acceptance of asserted contingent propositions. Let us solve the first difficulty.

If all analytic propositions are regarded as necessarily true, then the most typical analytic proposition, the principle of identity Jxx, must also be regarded as necessarily true. This leads, as we have seen, to the false consequence that any two individuals are necessarily identical, if they are identical at all.

This consequence cannot be derived from our system of modal logic, because it can be proved that in this system no apodeictic proposition is true. As this proof is based on the law of extensionality $CCpqCLpLq$, we must first show that this law results from our system.

A consequence of axiom 51 runs thus:

66. $C\delta CpqC\delta p\delta q$.

From 66 there follows by the substitution δ/M' the formula:

67. $CMCpqCMpMq$,

and from 67 we get by $CCpqMCpq$, a substitution of axiom 4, and by the hypothetical syllogism the stronger M-law of extensionality:

19. $CCpqCMpMq$.

The stronger L-law of extensionality $CCpqCLpLq$ is deducible from 19 by transposition. The problem left undecided in § 42, which interpretation of the Aristotelian laws of extensionality, the stronger or the weaker one, should be admitted, is thus solved in favour of the stronger interpretation. The proof that no apodeictic proposition is true will now be given with full precision.

The premisses:

*6. *CpLp*
18. *CCpqCLpLq*
33. *CCpCqrCqCpr*
68. *CCCpqrCqr*.

The deduction:

     68. *r/CLpLq* × *C*18–69
69. *CqCLpLq*
     33. *p/q, q/Lp, r/Lq* × *C*69–70
70. *CLpCqLq*
     70. *p/α, q/p* × *C**71–*6
*71. *Lα*.

The Greek variable α requires an explanation. The consequent of 70, *CqLq*, which means the same as the rejected expression *CpLp*, permits according to our rules the rejection of the antecedent *Lp*, and any substitution of *Lp*. This, however, cannot be expressed by **Lp*, because from a rejected expression nothing can be got by substitution; so, for instance, *Mp* is rejected, but *MCpp*—a substitution of *Mp*—is asserted. In order to express that the antecedent of 70 is rejected for any argument of *L*, I employ Greek letters calling them 'interpretation-variables' in opposition to the 'substitution-variables' denoted by Latin letters. As the proposition α may be given any interpretation, **Lα* represents a general law and means that any expression beginning with *L*, i.e. any apodeictic proposition, should be rejected.

This result, **Lα*, is confirmed by the matrix for *L* which is constructed from the matrices for *N* and *M* according to the definition of *L*. Anyone can recognize from a glance at M9 that *L* has only 2 and *o* as its truth-values, but never *1*.

The problem of false consequences resulting from the application of modal logic to the theory of identity is now easily solved. As *LJxx* cannot be asserted, being an apodeictic proposition, it is not possible to derive by detachment from the premiss:

    (*t*) *CJxyCLJxxLJxy*   or   *CLJxxCJxyLJxy*

the consequence: (*v*) *CJxyLJxy*. It can be matrically proved indeed that (*t*) must be asserted, giving always *1*, but (*v*) should be rejected. Since the principle of identity *Jxx* is true, i.e. *Jxx* = *1*, we get $LJxx = 2$, and $CJxyCLJxxLJxy = CJxyC_2LJxy$. Jxy may have one of the four values, 1, 2, 3, or o:

If $Jxy = 1$, then $CJxyC_2LJxy = C_1C_2L_1 = C_1C_22 = C_11 = 1$,
„ $Jxy = 2$, „ $CJxyC_2LJxy = C_2C_2L_2 = C_2C_22 = C_21 = 1$,
„ $Jxy = 3$, „ $CJxyC_2LJxy = C_3C_2L_3 = C_3C_20 = C_33 = 1$,
„ $Jxy = o$, „ $CJxyC_2LJxy = C_0C_2L_0 = C_0C_20 = C_03 = 1$.

Hence (t) is proved since the final result of its matrical reduction is always 1. On the contrary, (v) is disproved, because we have for $Jxy = 1$: $CJxyLJxy = C_1L_1 = C_12 = 2$.

A pleasing and instructive example of the above difficulty has been given by W. V. Quine who asks what is wrong with the following inference:[1]

(a) The Morning Star is necessarily identical with the Morning Star;

(b) But the Evening Star is not necessarily identical with the Morning Star (being merely identical with it in fact);

(c) But one and the same object cannot have contradictory properties (cannot both be A and not be A);

(d) Therefore the Morning Star and the Evening Star are different objects.

Given my system the solution of this difficulty is very simple. The inference is wrong, because the premisses (a) and (b) are not true and cannot be asserted, so that the conclusion (d) cannot be inferred from (a) and (b) in spite of the fact that the implication $C(a)C(b)(d)$ is correct (the third premiss may be omitted being true). The aforesaid implication can be proved in the following way:

Let x denote the Morning Star, and y the Evening Star; then (a) is $LJxx$, (b) is $NLJyx$ which is equivalent to $NLJxy$, as identity is a symmetrical relation, and (d) is $NJxy$. We get thus the formula $CLJxxCNLJxyNJxy$ which is a correct transformation of the true thesis (t).

The example given by Quine can now be verified by our four-valued matrix thus: if 'x' and 'y' have the same meaning as before, then $Jxx = Jxy = 1$; hence $LJxx = LJxy = L_1 = 2$,

---

[1] I found this example in the mimeographed *Logic Notes*, § 160, edited by the Department of Philosophy of the Canterbury University College (Christchurch, N.Z.), and sent to me by Professor A. N. Prior.

$NLJxy = N2 = 3$, and $NJxy = N1 = 0$, so that we have according to $CLJxxCNLJxyNJxy: C2C30 = C22 = 1$. The implication is true, but as not both its antecedents are true, the conclusion may be false.

We shall see in the next chapter that a similar difficulty was at the bottom of a controversy between Aristotle and his friends, Theophrastus and Eudemus. The philosophical implications of the important discovery that *No apodeictic proposition is true* will be set forth in § 62.

§ 51. *Twin possibilities*

I mentioned in § 49 that there are two functors either of which may represent possibility. One of them I denoted by M and defined by the equality:

(α) $M(a, b) = (Sa, Vb) = (a, Cbb)$,

the other I define by the equality:

(β) $W(a, b) = (Va, Sb) = (Caa, b)$,

denoting it by W which looks like an inverted M. According to this definition the matrix of W is M10, and can be abbreviated to M11. Though W is different from M it verifies axioms of the same structure as M, because $CpWp$ is proved by M11, like $CpMp$ by M8, and $*CWpp$ and $*Wp$ are disproved by M11, as $*CMpp$ and $*Mp$ are by M8. I could have denoted the matrix of W by M.

p	W	p	W
$(1, 1)$	$(1, 1)$	1	1
$(1, 0)$	$(1, 0)$	2	2
$(0, 1)$	$(1, 1)$	3	1
$(0, 0)$	$(1, 0)$	0	2
M10		M11	

It can further be shown that the difference between M and W is not a real one, but merely results from a different notation. It will be remembered that I got M3 from M2 by denoting the pair of values $(1, 0)$ by 2, and $(0, 1)$ by 3. As this notation was quite arbitrary, I could with equal justice denote $(1, 0)$ by 3, and $(0, 1)$ by 2, or choose any other figures or signs. Let us then exchange the values 2 and 3 in M9, writing everywhere 3 for 2, and *2* for *3*. We get from M9 the matrix M12, and by rearrangement of the middle rows and columns of M12, the matrix M13.

C	1 2 3 0	N	M	L
1	1 2 3 0	0	1	2
2	1 1 3 3	3	1	2
3	1 2 1 2	2	3	0
0	1 1 1 1	1	3	0

M9

C	1 3 2 0	N	–	–
1	1 3 2 0	0	1	3
3	1 1 2 2	2	1	3
2	1 3 1 3	3	2	0
0	1 1 1 1	1	2	0

M12

C	1 2 3 0	N	–	–
1	1 2 3 0	0	1	3
2	1 1 3 3	3	2	0
3	1 2 1 2	2	1	3
0	1 1 1 1	1	2	0

M13

If we compare M9 with M13, we see that the matrices for *C* and *N* remain unchanged, but the matrices corresponding to *M* and *L* become different, so that I cannot denote them by *M* and *L*. The matrix in M13 corresponding to *M* in M9 is just the matrix of *W*. Nevertheless M13 is the same matrix as M9, merely written in another notation. *W* represents the same functor as *M*, and must have the same properties as *M*. If *M* denotes possibility, then *W* does so too, and there can be no difference between these two possibilities.

In spite of their identity *M* and *W* behave differently when they both occur in the same formula. They are like identical twins who cannot be distinguished when met separately, but are instantly recognized as two when seen together. To perceive this let us consider the expressions *MWp*, *WMp*, *MMp*, and *WWp*. If *M* is identical with *W*, then those four expressions should be identical with each other too. But they are not identical. It can be proved by means of our matrices that the following formulae are asserted:

72. *MWp*   and   73. *WMp*,

for *Wp* has as its truth-values only *1* or *2*, and *M1* as well as *M2* = *1*; similarly *Mp* has as its truth-values only *1* or *3*, and both *W1* = *1* and *W3* = *1*. On the other hand it can be proved that the formulae:

74. *CMMpMp*   and   75. *CWWpWp*

are asserted, and as both *Mp* and *Wp* are rejected, *MMp* and *WWp* must be rejected too, so that we have:

*76. *MMp*   and   *77. *WWp*.

We cannot therefore, in 72 or 73, replace *M* by *W* or *W* by *M*, because we should get a rejected formula from an asserted one.

The curious logical fact of twin possibilities (and of twin necessities connected with them), which hitherto has not been observed by anybody, is another important discovery I owe to my four-valued modal system. It is too subtle and requires too great a development of formal logic to have been known to ancient logicians. The existence of these twins will both account for Aristotle's mistakes and difficulties in the theory of problematic syllogisms, and justify his intuitive notions about contingency.

§ 52. *Contingency and the four-valued system of modal logic*

We know already that the second major difficulty of Aristotle's modal logic is connected with his supposing that some contingent propositions were true. On the ground of the thesis:

52. *CKδpδNpδq*,

which is a transformation of our axiom 51, we get the following consequences:

52. *δ/M, p/α, q/p* × 78
78. *CKMαMNαMp*
78. *C*79–*7
*79. *KMαMNα*.

This means that 79 is rejected for any proposition α, as α is here an interpretation-variable. Consequently there exists no α that would verify both of the propositions: 'It is possible that α' and 'It is possible that not α', i.e. there exists no true contingent proposition *Tα*, if *Tp* is defined, with Aristotle, by the conjunction of *Mp* and *MNp*, i.e. by:

80. *CδKMpMNpδTp*.

This result is confirmed by the matrix method. Accepting the usual definition of *Kpq*:

81. *CδNCpNqδKpq*

we get for K the matrix M14, and we have:

K	1 2 3 0
1	1 2 3 0
2	2 2 0 0
3	3 0 3 0
0	0 0 0 0

M14

For $p = 1$: $KMpMNp = KM1MN1 = K1Mo = K13 = 3$

„ $p = 2$: „ $= KM2MN2 = K1M3 = K13 = 3$

„ $p = 3$: „ $= KM3MN3 = K3M2 = K31 = 3$

„ $p = 0$: „ $= KMoMNo = K3M1 = K31 = 3.$

We see that the conjunction $KMpMNp$ has the constant value 3, and is therefore never true. Hence $Tp = 3$, i.e. there exists no true contingent proposition in the sense given by definition 80.

Aristotle, however, thinks that the propositions 'It is possible that there will be a sea-fight tomorrow' and 'It is possible that there will not be a sea-fight tomorrow' may both be true today. Thus, according to his idea of contingency, there may be true contingent propositions.

There are two ways of avoiding this contradiction between Aristotle's view and our system of modal logic: we must either deny that any propositions are both contingent and true, or modify the Aristotelian definition of contingency. I choose the second way, making use of the twin types of possibility discovered above.

Tossing a coin we may throw either a head or a tail; in other words, it is possible to throw a head, and it is possible not to throw a head. We are inclined to regard both propositions as true. But they cannot be both true, if the first 'possible' is denoted by the same functor as the second. The first possibility is just the same as the second, but it does not follow that it should be denoted in the same way. The possibility of throwing a head is different from the possibility of not throwing a head. We may denote the one by M, and the other by W. The proposition with the affirmative argument 'It is possible that p' may be translated by Mp, the proposition with the negative argument 'It is possible that not p' by WNp; or the first by Wp, and the second by MNp. We get thus two functors of contingency, say X and Y, defined as follows:

82. $C\delta KMpWNp\delta Xp$ and   83. $C\delta KWpMNp\delta Yp.$

It is impossible to translate these definitions into words, as we have no names for the two kinds of possibility and contingency. Let us call them 'M-possible' and 'W-possible', 'X-contingent' and 'Y-contingent'. We may then roughly say that 'p is X-contingent' means 'p is M-possible and Np is W-possible', and 'p is Y-contingent' means 'p is W-possible and Np is M-possible'.

From definitions 82 and 83 We can derive the matrices of X and Y. We get:

For $p = 1$:
$X_1 = KM_1WN_1 = K_1Wo = K_{12} = 2$; $Y_1 = KW_1MN_1 = K_1Mo = K_{13} = 3$.
For $p = 2$:
$X_2 = KM_2WN_2 = K_1W_3 = K_{11} = 1$; $Y_2 = KW_2MN_2 = K_2M_3 = K_{23} = o$.
For $p = 3$:
$X_3 = KM_3WN_3 = K_3W_2 = K_{32} = o$; $Y_3 = KW_3MN_3 = K_1M_2 = K_{11} = 1$.
For $p = o$:
$Xo = KMoWNo = K_3W_1 = K_{31} = 3$; $Yo = KWoMNo = K_2M_1 = K_{21} = 2$.

p	X	Y
1	2	3
2	1	0
3	0	1
0	3	2

M15

Matrix M15 shows that Xp as well as Yp turns out to be true for some value of p: Xp for $p = 2$, Yp for $p = 3$. Now it has been proved that $KMpMNp$ has the constant value 3; similarly it can be shown that $KWpWNp$ has the constant value 2. We get thus two asserted formulae:

84. $XKWpWNp$ and   85. $YKMpMNp$.

This means that there exists in our system a true X-contingent and a true Y-contingent proposition. We can accommodate contingency in Aristotle's sense within our four-valued modal logic.

It also follows from M15 that the X-contingency and the Y-contingency are twins. If we replace in M15 2 by 3, and 3 by 2, X becomes Y, and Y becomes X. Nevertheless X is different from Y, and more different than M is from W, because the propositions Xp and Yp are contradictory. It can be easily seen by M15 that the following equalities hold:

(γ) $Xp = YNp = NYp$ and   (δ) $Yp = XNp = NXp$.

The laws of contradiction and of the excluded middle are true for Xp and Yp, i.e. we have:

86. $NKXpYp$ and   87. $HXpYp$.

This means: no proposition can be both X-contingent and Y-contingent, and any proposition is either X-contingent or Y-contingent. The negation of an X-contingent proposition is a Y-contingent proposition, and conversely the negation of a Y-contingent proposition is an X-contingent proposition. This sounds like a paradox, because we are accustomed to think that, what is not contingent is either-impossible or necessary, relating the impossible and the necessary to the same kind of possibility. But it is not true to say that, what is not X-contingent is either M-impossible or M-necessary; it should rather be said that, what is not X-contingent is either M-impossible or W-necessary, and that being either M-impossible or W-necessary is equivalent to being Y-contingent.

The same misunderstanding lies at the bottom of the controversy about the thesis:

88. *CKMpMqMKpq*

which is asserted in our system. C. I. Lewis in some of his modal systems accepts the formula:

89. *CMKpqKMpMq*,

but rejects its converse, i.e. 88, by the following argument:[1] 'If it is possible that p and q are both true, then p is possible and q is possible. This implication is not reversible. For example: it is possible that the reader will see this at once. It is also possible that he will not see it at once. But it is not possible that he will both see it at once and not see it at once.' The persuasiveness of this argument is illusory. What is meant by 'the reader'? If an individual reader, say R, is meant, then R either will see this at once, or R will not see this at once. In the first case the first premiss 'It is possible that R will see this at once' is true; but the second premiss is false, and how can a false proposition be possibly true? In the second case the second premiss is true, but the first is false, and a false proposition cannot be possibly true. The two premisses of the formula 88 are not both provable, and the formula cannot be refuted in this way.

If again by 'the reader' some reader is meant, then the premisses 'It is possible that some reader will see this at once' and 'It is possible that some reader will not see this at once' may be both true, but in this case the conclusion 'It is possible that some

---

[1] C. L. Lewis and C. H. Langford, *Symbolic Logic*, New York and London (1932), p. 167.

reader will see this at once and some reader will not see this at once' is obviously also true. It is, of course, not the same reader who will see this and not see this at once. The example given by Lewis does not refute formula 88; on the contrary it supports its correctness.

It seems, however, that this example has not been properly chosen. By the addition of the words 'at once' the premisses have lost the character of contingency. Saying that the reader will see this, or not, 'at once', we refer to something which is decided at the moment of seeing. The true contingent refers to undecided events. Let us take the example with the coin which is of the same sort as Aristotle's example with the sea-fight. Both examples concern events that are undecided at present, but will be decided in the future. Hence the premisses 'It is possible to throw a head' and 'It is possible not to throw a head' may at present be both true, whereas the conclusion 'It is possible to throw a head and not to throw a head' is never true. We know, however, that contingency cannot be defined by the conjunction of Mp and MNp, but either by Mp and WNp or by Wp and MNp, so that the example quoted above does not fall under the thesis 88. It cannot therefore disprove it. This was not known to Lewis and the other logicians, and on the basis of a wrong conception of contingency they have rejected the discussed thesis.

§ 53. *Some further problems*

Although the axioms and the rules of inference of our four-valued system of modal logic are perfectly evident, some consequences of the system may look paradoxical. We have already met the paradoxical thesis that the negation of a contingent proposition is also contingent; as another thesis of this kind I may quote the law of 'double contingency' according to which the following formulae are true:

90. $QpXXp$ and   91. $QpYYp$.

The problem is to find some interpretation of these formulae which will be intuitively satisfactory and will explain away their apparent oddness. When the classical calculus of propositions was only recently known there was heated opposition to some of its principles too, chiefly to $CpCqp$ and $CpCNpq$, which embody two logical laws known to medieval logicians and formulated by them in the words: *Verum sequitur ad quodlibet* and *Ad falsum sequitur quodlibet*. So far as I see, these principles are now universally acknowledged.

At any rate our modal system is not in a worse position in this respect than other systems of modal logic. Some of them contain such non-intuitive formulae, as:

*92. *QMNMpNMp*

where a problematic proposition 'It is possible that *p* is impossible' is equivalent to an apodeictic proposition 'It is impossible that *p*'. Instead of this odd formula which has to be rejected we have in our system the thesis:

93. *QMNMpMNp*   which together with
94. *QMMpMp*

enables us to reduce all combinations of modal functors consisting of *M* and *N* to four irreducible combinations known to Aristotle, viz. *M* = possible, *NM* = impossible, *MN* = non-necessary, and *NMN* = necessary.

The second problem concerns the extension of the four-valued modal logic into higher systems. The eight-valued system may serve as an example. We get the matrix M16 of this system by multiplying the matrix M9 by the matrix M1. As elements of the new matrix we form the pairs of values: $(1, 1) = 1$, $(1, 0) = 2$, $(2, 1) = 3$, $(2, 0) = 4$, $(3, 1) = 5$, $(3, 0) = 6$, $(0, 1) = 7$, $(0, 0) = 0$, and then we determine the truth-values of *C*, *N*, and *M* according to the equalities (y), (z), and (α).

C	1	2	3	4	5	6	7	0	N	M
1	1	2	3	4	5	6	7	0	0	1
2	1	1	3	3	5	5	7	7	7	1
3	1	2	1	2	5	6	5	6	6	3
4	1	1	1	1	5	5	5	5	5	3
5	1	2	3	4	1	2	3	4	4	5
6	1	1	3	3	1	1	3	3	3	5
7	1	2	1	2	1	2	1	2	2	7
0	1	1	1	1	1	1	1	1	1	7

M16

Figure *1* denotes, as usually, truth; *0* falsity; and the other figures are intermediate values between truth and falsity. If we attentively consider the matrix M16 we shall find that the second row of C is identical with the column of M. This row consequently represents the matrix of possibility. In the same way all the other rows of C, except the first and the last, represent some kinds of possibility. If we denote them by M_2 to M_7, we can state that M_i for $2 \leqslant i \leqslant 7$ satisfies all the axioms of possibility, viz.

95. CpM_ip,   *96. CM_ipp,   *97. M_ip.

Among these different kinds of possibility there are some 'stronger' and 'weaker'; because we have, for instance, CM_2pM_4p or CM_3pM_6p, but not conversely. We may say therefore that in eight-valued modal logic there exist possibilities of different degrees. I have always thought that only two modal systems are of possible philosophic and scientific importance: the simplest modal system, in which possibility is regarded as having no degrees at all, that is our four-valued modal system, and the $\aleph_0$-valued system in which there exist infinitely many degrees of possibility. It would be interesting to investigate this problem further, as we may find here a link between modal logic and the theory of probability.

CHAPTER VIII

ARISTOTLE'S MODAL SYLLOGISTIC

ARISTOTLE's modal syllogistic has, in my opinion, less importance in comparison with his assertoric syllogistic or his contributions to propositional modal logic. This system looks like a logical exercise which in spite of its seeming subtlety is full of careless mistakes and does not have any useful application to scientific problems. Nevertheless two controversial questions of this syllogistic are worth studying, chiefly for historical reasons: the question of syllogisms with one assertoric and one apodeictic premiss, and the question of syllogisms with contingent premisses.

§ 54. *Moods with two apodeictic premisses*

Aristotle deals with modal syllogisms after the pattern of his assertoric syllogistic. The syllogisms are divided into figures and moods, some moods are accepted as perfect and these need no proof as being self-evident, the imperfect moods are proved by conversion, *reductio ad absurdum*, or by 'ecthesis', as it is called. The invalid moods are rejected by interpretation through concrete terms. It is strange that with one exception Aristotle makes no use of his theorems of propositional modal logic. We shall see that this would yield in several cases better and simpler proofs than those given by him.

The laws of conversion for apodeictic propositions are analogous to those for assertoric ones. The following theses are accordingly true: 'If it is necessary that no *b* should be an *a*, it is necessary that no *a* should be a *b*', in symbols:

98. *CLEbaLEab*,

and 'If it is necessary that every *b* or some *b* should be an *a*, it is necessary that some *a* should be a *b*', in symbols:

99. *CLAbaLIab*   and   100. *CLIbaLIab*.[1]

The proofs given by Aristotle are not satisfactory.[2] He did not see

---

[1] *An. pr.* i. 3, 25ᵃ29 εἰ μὲν γὰρ ἀνάγκη τὸ Α τῷ Β μηδενὶ ὑπάρχειν, ἀνάγκη καὶ τὸ Β τῷ Α μηδενὶ ὑπάρχειν. —32 εἰ δὲ ἐξ ἀνάγκης τὸ Α παντὶ ἢ τινὶ τῷ Β ὑπάρχει, καὶ τὸ Β τινὶ τῷ Α ἀνάγκη ὑπάρχειν.

[2] Cf. A. Becker, loc. cit., p. 90.

that the laws 98–100 may be immediately deduced from the analogous laws of the assertoric syllogistic by means of the theorem:

18. *CCpqCLpLq*.

For instance, from 18, by putting *Eba* for *p* and *Eab* for *q*, we get the assertoric law of conversion in the antecedent, hence we can detach the consequent, i.e. law 98.

Syllogisms with two apodeictic premisses are, according to Aristotle, identical with assertoric syllogisms, except that the sign of necessity must be added to the premisses as well as to the conclusion.[1] The formula for the mood Barbara will accordingly run:

101. *CKLAbaLAcbLAca*.

Aristotle tacitly accepts that the moods of the first figure are perfect and need not be proved. The moods of the other figures, which are imperfect, should be proved according to the proofs of assertoric syllogisms except Baroco and Bocardo, which are proved in the assertoric syllogistic by *reductio ad absurdum*, and should here be proved by ecthesis.[2] Once again, for all these proofs it would be easier to use theorem 18, as will appear from the following example.

By means of the laws of exportation and importation, *CCKpqr-CpCqr* and *CCpCqrCKpqr*, it can be shown that 15, the assertoric mood Barbara, is equivalent to the formula :

102. *CAbaCAcbAca*.

This purely implicational form is more convenient for deriving consequences than the conjunctional form. According to the thesis 3 *CLpp* we have:

103. *CLAbaAba*,

and from 103 and 102 we get by the hypothetical syllogism:

104. *CLAbaCAcbAca*.

On the other hand we have as substitution of 18:

---

[1] *An. pr.* i. 8, 29ᵇ35 ἐπὶ μὲν οὖν τῶν ἀναγκαίων σχεδὸν ὁμοίως ἔχει καὶ ἐπὶ τῶν ὑπαρχόντων· ὡσαύτως γὰρ τιθεμένων τῶν ὅρων ἔν τε τῷ ὑπάρχειν καὶ τῷ ἐξ ἀνάγκης ὑπάρχειν ἢ μὴ ὑπάρχειν ἔσται τε καὶ οὐκ ἔσται συλλογισμός, πλὴν διοίσει τῷ προσ-κεῖσθαι τοῖς ὅροις τὸ ἐξ ἀνάγκης ὑπάρχειν ἢ μὴ ὑπάρχειν.
[2] Ibid. 30ᵃ3–14.

105. *CCAcbAcaCLAcbLAca*,

and from 104 and 105 there follows the consequence:

106. *CLAbaCLAcbLAca*,

which is equivalent to 101. All the other syllogistic moods with two apodeictic premisses can be proved in the same way without new axioms, laws of conversion, *reductio ad absurdum*, or arguments by ecthesis.

§ 55. *Moods with one apodeictic and one assertoric premiss*[1]

Syllogistic moods of the first figure with one apodeictic and one assertoric premiss are treated by Aristotle differently according to which premiss, the major or the minor, is apodeictic. He says that when the major is apodeictic and the minor assertoric we get an apodeictic conclusion, but when the minor is apodeictic and the major assertoric we can have only an assertoric conclusion.[2] This difference will be made clear by the following examples of the mood Barbara. Aristotle asserts the syllogism: 'If it is necessary that every *b* should be an *a*, then if every *c* is a *b*, it is necessary that every *c* should be an *a*.' He rejects, however, the syllogism: 'If every *b* is an *a*, then if it is necessary that every *c* should be a *b*, it is necessary that every *c* should be an *a*.' In symbols:

(ε) *CLAbaCAcbLAca*   is asserted,
(ζ) *CAbaCLAcbLAca*   is rejected.

Aristotle considers the syllogism (ε) as self-evident. He says: 'Since every *b* is necessarily an *a* or not an *a*, and *c* is one of the *b*'s, it is evident (φανερόν) that *c* too will be necessarily an *a* or not an *a*.'[3] For reasons that will be explained later it is difficult to show this by examples. But the following picture will perhaps make the syllogism (ε) more acceptable to intuition. Let us

---

[1] Cf. J. Łukasiewicz, 'On a Controversial Problem of Aristotle's Modal Syllogistic', *Dominican Studies*, vol. vii (1954), pp. 114–28.

[2] *An. pr.* i. 9, 30ª15–25 συμβαίνει δέ ποτε καὶ τῆς ἑτέρας προτάσεως ἀναγκαίας οὔσης ἀναγκαῖον γίνεσθαι τὸν συλλογισμόν, πλὴν οὐχ ὁποτέρας ἔτυχεν, ἀλλὰ τῆς πρὸς τὸ μεῖζον ἄκρον, οἷον εἰ τὸ μὲν Α τῷ Β ἐξ ἀνάγκης εἴληπται ὑπάρχον ἢ μὴ ὑπάρχον, τὸ δὲ Β τῷ Γ ὑπάρχον μόνον· οὕτως γὰρ εἰλημμένων τῶν προτάσεων ἐξ ἀνάγκης τὸ Α τῷ Γ ὑπάρξει ἢ οὐχ ὑπάρξει. (Here follows the sentence quoted in the next note.) εἰ δὲ τὸ μὲν ΑΒ μὴ ἔστιν ἀναγκαῖον, τὸ δὲ ΒΓ ἀναγκαῖον, οὐκ ἔσται τὸ συμπέρασμα ἀναγκαῖον.

[3] Ibid. 30ª21 ἐπεὶ γὰρ παντὶ τῷ Β ἐξ ἀνάγκης ὑπάρχει ἢ οὐχ ὑπάρχει τὸ Α, τὸ δὲ Γ τι τῶν Β ἐστί, φανερὸν ὅτι καὶ τῷ Γ ἐξ ἀνάγκης ἔσται θάτερον τούτων.

imagine that the expression *LAba* means: 'Every *b* is connected by a wire with an *a*.' Hence it is evident that also every *c* (since every *c* is a *b*) is connected by a wire with an *a*, i.e. *LAca*. For whatever is true in some way of every *b*, is also true in the same way of every *c*, if every *c* is a *b*. The evidence of the last proposition is beyond any doubt.

We know, however, from Alexander that the evidence of the syllogism (ε) which Aristotle asserted, was not convincing enough for his friends who were pupils of Theophrastus and Eudemus.[1] As opposed to Aristotle, they held the doctrine that if either premiss is assertoric the conclusion must be so, just as if either premiss is negative the conclusion must be so and if either premiss is particular the conclusion must be so, according to a general rule formulated later by the scholastics: *Peiorem sequitur semper conclusio partem.*

This argument can be easily refuted. The syllogism (ε) is deductively equivalent to the problematic mood Bocardo of the third figure: 'If it is possible that some *c* should not be an *a*, then if every *c* is a *b*, it is possible that some *b* should not be an *a*.' In symbols:

(η)   *CMOcaCAcbMOba.*

Syllogism (η) is as evident as (ε). Its evidence can be illustrated by examples. Let us suppose that a box contains ballots numbered from 1 to 90, and let *c* mean 'number drawn from the box', *b* 'even number drawn from the box', and *a* 'number divisible by 3'. We assume that in a certain case five even numbers have been drawn from the box, so that the premiss: 'Every number drawn from the box is an even number drawn from the box', i.e. *Acb*, is factually true. From this we can safely infer that, if it is possible in our case that some number drawn from the box should not be divisible by 3, i.e. *MOca*, it is also possible in our case that some *even* number drawn from the box should not be divisible by 3, i.e. *MOba*.

Aristotle accepts the syllogism (η) and proves it by a *reductio*

---

[1] Commenting on the passage quoted in n. 2, p. 183, Alexander says 124. 8 οὗτος μὲν οὕτως λέγει. οἱ δέ γε ἑταῖροι αὐτοῦ οἱ περὶ Εὔδημόν τε καὶ Θεόφραστον οὐχ οὕτως λέγουσι, ἀλλά φασιν ἐν πάσαις ταῖς ἐξ ἀναγκαίας τε καὶ ὑπαρχούσης συζυγίαις, ἐὰν ὦσι συγκείμεναι συλλογιστικῶς, ὑπάρχον γίνεσθαι τὸ συμπέρασμα . . . 17 τῷ ἐλάττον εἶναι τὸ ὑπάρχον τοῦ ἀναγκαίου.

ad absurdum from the syllogism (ε).[1] He does not, however, deduce
(ε) from (η), though he certainly knew that this could be done.
Alexander saw this point and explicitly proves (ε) from (η) by a
reductio ad absurdum saying that this argument should be held as
the soundest proof in favour of Aristotle's doctrine.[2] As according
to him Aristotle's friends accept the syllogism (η) which fulfils
peiorem rule, and (ε) is deducible from (η), they cannot reject (ε)
on the ground of this rule, which becomes false when applied to
modalities.

We shall see in the next Section that there was yet another
argument raised by Theophrastus and Eudemus against syllogism
(ε) which could not be refuted by Alexander, as it stands or falls
with an Aristotelian argument. In spite of Alexander's talk about
the 'soundest proof' one feels that some doubt is left in his mind,
for he finally remarks after having presented several arguments
in support of Aristotle's opinion, of which the argument quoted
above is the last, that he has shown with greater rigour in other
works which of those arguments are sound and which are not.[3]
Alexander is referring here to his work 'On the Disagreement
concerning Mixed Moods between Aristotle and his Friends',
and to his 'Logical Scholia'.[4] Unfortunately both works are lost.

Our times have seen a revival of this controversy. Sir David
Ross, commenting on syllogism (ε) and its proof from syllogism
(η), states decidedly:[5] 'Yet Aristotle's doctrine is plainly wrong.
For what he is seeking to show is that the premisses prove not only
that all C is A, but also that it is necessarily A, just as all B is

---

[1] *An. pr.* i. 21, 39ᵇ33–39 ὑπαρχέτω γὰρ τὸ μὲν B παντὶ τῷ Γ, τὸ δὲ A ἐνδεχέσθω τινὶ
τῷ Γ μὴ ὑπάρχειν· ἀνάγκη δὴ τὸ A ἐνδέχεσθαι τινὶ τῷ B μὴ ὑπάρχειν. εἰ γὰρ παντὶ τῷ
B τὸ A ὑπάρχει ἐξ ἀνάγκης, τὸ δὲ B παντὶ τῷ Γ κεῖται ὑπάρχειν, τὸ A παντὶ τῷ Γ ἐξ
ἀνάγκης ὑπάρξει· τοῦτο γὰρ δέδεικται πρότερον. ἀλλ᾽ ὑπέκειτο τινὶ ἐνδέχεσθαι μὴ
ὑπάρχειν.

[2] Alexander says, commenting on syllogism (ε), 127. 3 ἔστι δὲ πιστώσασθαι, ὅτι
τὸ λεγόμενον ὑπὸ Ἀριστοτέλους ὑγιές ἐστι, μάλιστα διὰ τῆς εἰς ἀδύνατον ἀπαγωγῆς τῆς
γινομένης ἐν τρίτῳ σχήματι . . . 12 ἐν γὰρ τῇ τοιαύτῃ συζυγίᾳ τῇ ἐν τρίτῳ σχήματι καὶ
Ἀριστοτέλει δοκεῖ καὶ τοῖς ἑταίροις αὐτοῦ ἐπὶ μέρος ἐνδεχόμενον ἀποφατικὸν γίνεσθαι
τὸ συμπέρασμα.

[3] Alexander 127. 14 τοσούτοις καὶ τοιούτοις ἄν τις χρήσαιτο παριστάμενος τῇ
περὶ τούτων Ἀριστοτέλους δόξῃ. τί δὲ τούτων ὑγιῶς ἢ μὴ ὑγιῶς λέγεσθαι δοκεῖ, ἐν
ἄλλοις ἡμῖν, ὡς ἔφην, μετὰ ἀκριβείας εἴρηται.

[4] The title of the first work reads (Alexander 125. 30): Περὶ τῆς κατὰ τὰς μίξεις
διαφορᾶς Ἀριστοτέλους τε καὶ τῶν ἑταίρων αὐτοῦ. Cf. Alexander 249. 38–250. 2, where
διαφωνίας is used instead of διαφορᾶς, and the other work is cited as Σχόλια λογικά.

[5] W. D. Ross, loc. cit., p. 43.

necessarily A, i.e. by a permanent necessity of its own nature; while what they do show is only that so long as all C is B, it is A, not by a permanent necessity of its own nature, but by a temporary necessity arising from its temporary sharing in the nature of B.'

This argument is a metaphysical one, as the terms 'nature of a thing' and 'permanent necessity of its nature' belong to metaphysics. But behind this metaphysical terminology a logical problem is hidden which can be solved by our four-valued modal logic. Let us now turn to the syllogism rejected by Aristotle.

§ 56. *Rejected moods with one apodeictic and one assertoric premiss*

Syllogism (ζ) is as evident as syllogism (ε). It is strange that Aristotle rejects the syllogism

(ζ) *CAbaCLAcbLAca*,

though it is clear that this syllogism is on the same footing as the asserted syllogism (ε). In order to show its evidence let us employ the same picture as before. If *LAcb* means that every *c* is connected by a wire with a *b*, and every *b* is an *a*, i.e. *Aba*, it is evident that every *c* is connected by a wire with an *a*, i.e. *LAca*. Speaking generally, if every *b* is an *a*, then if every *c* is connected with a *b* in any way whatever, it must be connected with an *a* in just the same way. This seems to be obvious.

The most convincing argument that syllogism (ζ) is sound results from its deductive equivalence with the problematic mood Baroco of the second figure:

(θ) *CAbaCMOcaMOcb*,   in words:

'If every *b* is an *a*, then if it is possible that some *c* should not be an *a*, it is possible that some *c* should not be a *b*.' This can be illustrated by an example. Let us turn to our box from which five numbers have been drawn, and let us suppose that every even number drawn from the box (*b*) is divisible by 3 (*a*), i.e. *Aba*. From this factual truth we can safely infer that, if it is possible that some number drawn from the box (*c*) should not be divisible by 3, i.e. *MOca*, it is also possible that some number drawn from the box should not be an *even* number, i.e. *MOcb*. This syllogism seems to be perfectly evident. In spite of its seeming so Aristotle disproves syllogism (ζ), first by a purely logical argument which will be considered later, and then by the following example: Let *c* mean 'man', *b* 'animal', and *a* 'being in movement'. He accepts that the proposition 'Every man is an animal' is necessarily true, i.e. *LAcb*; but it is not necessary that every animal should be in movement, this may be only accepted as a factual truth, i.e. *Aba*, and so it is not necessary that every man should be in movement, i.e. *LAca* is not true.[1]

Aristotle's example is not convincing enough, as we cannot admit as a factual truth that every animal is in movement. A better example is provided by our box. Let *c* mean 'number drawn from the box and divisible by 4', *b* 'even number drawn from the box', and *a* 'divisible by 3'. Aristotle would agree that the proposition 'Every number drawn from the box and divisible by 4 is an even number drawn from the box' is a necessary truth, i.e. *LAcb*, while the premiss 'Every even number drawn from the box is divisible by 3' can be only accepted as a factual truth, i.e. *Aba*, and the conclusion 'Every number drawn from the box and divisible by 4 is divisible by 3' is also only a factual truth, i.e. *Aca*, and not *LAca*. The 'nature' of a number drawn from the box and divisible by 4 does not involve any 'permanent necessity' for it to be divisible by 3.

It would seem, therefore, that Aristotle is right in rejecting syllogism (ζ). The matter, however, becomes complicated, for it can be shown that just the same argument can be raised against syllogism

(ε)   *CLAbaCAcbLAca*.

This was seen by Theophrastus and Eudemus who refute (ε) using in another order the same terms which were applied by Aristotle for disproving (ζ). Let *b* mean 'man', *a*—'animal', and *c*—'being in movement'. They agree with Aristotle that the proposition 'Every man is an animal' is necessarily true, i.e. *LAba*, and they accept as factually true that 'Everything in movement is a man', i.e. *Acb*. The premisses of (ε) are thus verified, but it is obvious that the conclusion 'Everything in movement is an animal', i.e. *Aca*, is not necessarily true.[2] This example is as

---

[1] *An. pr.* i. 9, 30ᵃ28 ἔτι καὶ ἐκ τῶν ὅρων φανερὸν ὅτι οὐκ ἔσται τὸ συμπέρασμα ἀναγκαῖον, οἷον εἰ τὸ μὲν Α εἴη κίνησις, τὸ δὲ Β ζῷον, ἐφ'ᾧ δὲ τὸ Γ ἄνθρωπος· ζῷον μὲν γὰρ ὁ ἄνθρωπος ἐξ ἀνάγκης ἐστί, κινεῖται δὲ τὸ ζῷον οὐκ ἐξ ἀνάγκης, οὐδ' ὁ ἄνθρωπος.

[2] Alexander 124.21 ἀλλὰ καὶ ἐπὶ τῆς ὕλης δεικνύουσι τοῦτο ἔχον οὕτως . . . 24 τὸ γὰρ

unconvincing as the corresponding one in Aristotle, for we cannot admit that the premiss *Acb* is factually true.

We can give a better example from our box. Let *b* mean 'number divisible by 6', *a*—'number divisible by 3', and *c*—'even number drawn from the box'. Aristotle would accept that the proposition 'Every number divisible by 6 is divisible by 3' is necessarily true, i.e. *LAba*, but it can be only factually true that 'Every even number drawn from the box is divisible by 6', i.e. *Acb*, and so it is only factually true that 'Every even number drawn from the box is divisible by 3', i.e. *Aca*. The propositions *Acb* and *Aca* are clearly equivalent to each other, and if one of them is only factually true, then the other cannot be necessarily true.

The controversy between Aristotle and Theophrastus about moods with one apodeictic and one assertoric premiss has led us to a paradoxical situation: there are apparently equally strong arguments for and against the syllogisms (ε) and (ζ). The controversy shown by the example of the mood Barbara can be extended to all other moods of this kind. This points to an error that lurks in the very foundations of modal logic, and has its source in a false conception of necessity.

§ 57. *Solution of the controversy*

The paradoxical situation expounded above is quite analogous to the difficulties we have met in the application of modal logic to the theory of identity. On the one hand, the syllogisms in question are not only self-evident, but can be demonstrated in our system of modal logic. I give here a full proof of the syllogisms (ε) and (ζ) based among others on the stronger *L*-law of extensionality known to Aristotle.

The premisses:

   3. *CLpp*
 18. *CCpqCLpLq*
 24. *CCpqCCqrCpr*
 33. *CCpCqrCqCpr*
102. *CAbaCAcbAca*.

ζῷον παντὶ ἀνθρώπῳ ἐξ ἀνάγκης, ὁ ἄνθρωπος παντὶ κινουμένῳ ὑπαρχέτω· οὐκέτι τὸ ζῷον παντὶ κινουμένῳ ἐξ ἀνάγκης.

The deduction:

       18. $p/Aba, q/Aca \times 107$
107. *CCAbaAcaCLAbaLAca*
       33. $p/Aba, q/Acb, r/Aca \times C$102–108
108. *CAcbCAbaAca*
       24. $p/Acb, q/CAbaAca, r/CLAbaLAca \times C$108–$C$107–109
109. *CAcbCLAbaLAca*
       33. $p/Acb, q/LAba, r/LAca \times C$109–110
110. *CLAbaCAcbLAca*   (ϵ)
       18. $p/Acb, q/Aca \times 111$
111. *CCAcbAcaCLAcbLAca*
       24. $p/Aba, q/CAcbAca, r/CLAcbLAca \times C$102–$C$111–112
112. *CAbaCLAcbLAca*   (ζ).

We see that the syllogisms (ϵ) and (ζ) denoted here by 110 and 112, are asserted expressions of our modal logic.

On the other hand, we get the thesis 113 from 110 by the substitution b/a, and the thesis 114 from 112 by the substitution b/c and commutation of the antecedents:

    113. *CLAaaCAcaLAca*   114. *CLAccCAcaLAca*.

Both theses have in the consequent the expression *CAcaLAca*, i.e. the proposition 'If every *c* is an *a*, then it is necessary that every *c* should be an *a*'. If this proposition were asserted, all true universally-affirmative propositions would be necessarily true which is contrary to intuition. Moreover, as *CAcaLAca* is equivalent to *CNLAcaNAca*, and *Aca* means the same as *NOca*, we should have *CNLNOcaNNOca* or *CMOcaOca*. This last proposition which means 'If it is possible that some *c* should not be an *a*, then some *c* is not an *a*' is not true, for it is certainly possible that a number drawn from the box should not be even; so that, if the proposition is true, every set of drawings would contain an odd number— a result plainly contrary to the facts.

The expression *CAcaLAca* must be therefore rejected, and we get:

  **115. *CAcaLAca*,

from which there follows according to our rules for rejected expressions the consequence:

113. $\times C^{*}$116–*115

*116. *LAaa*.

The apodeictic Aristotelian law of identity must be rejected like the apodeictic principle of identity *LJxx*. This is conformable to our general view according to which no apodeictic proposition is true. The consequent of 113, i.e. *CAcaLAca*, cannot be detached, and the incompatibility between the acceptance of true apodeictic propositions and the assertion of the stronger *L*-law of extensionality is solved in favour of the law of extensionality. I do not believe that any other system of modal logic could satisfactorily solve this ancient controversy.

I mentioned earlier that Aristotle tries to refute the syllogism (ζ) not only by examples, but also by a purely logical argument. Asserting that the premisses *Aba* and *LAcb* do not give an apodeictic conclusion he says: 'If the conclusion were necessary, there would follow from it by a syllogism of the first or the third figure that some *b* is necessarily an *a*; but this is false, because *b* may be such that possibly no *b* is an *a*.'[1] Aristotle refers here to the apodeictic moods Darii and Darapti, since from (ζ) combined with either of these moods we can derive the consequence *CAbaCLAcbLIba*. The proof from Darapti runs:

117. *CCpCqrCCrCqsCpCqs*
112. *CAbaCLAcbLAca*   (ζ)
118. *CLAcaCLAcbLIba*   (Darapti)
       117. *p*/*Aba*, *q*/*LAcb*, *r*/*LAca*, *s*/*LIba* × *C*112–*C*118–119
119. *CAbaCLAcbLIba*.

The proof from Darii gives the same consequence, but is more complicated. Aristotle seems to disregard the premiss *LAcb*, and interprets this consequence as a simple implication:

*120. *CAbaLIba*,

which is obviously false and must be rejected. Or perhaps he thought that *LAcb* could be made true by a suitable substitution for *c* and dropped. If so he was wrong and his proof is a failure. We see besides by this example how difficult it is to confirm the validity of such theses, as 119, 112, or 110, through terms yielding

---

[1] *An. pr.* i. 9, 30ᵃ25 (continuation of n. 2, p. 183) εἰ γὰρ ἔστι, συμβήσεται τὸ *A* τινὶ τῷ *B* ὑπάρχειν ἐξ ἀνάγκης διά τε τοῦ πρώτου καὶ διὰ τοῦ τρίτου σχήματος. τοῦτο δὲ ψεῦδος· ἐνδέχεται γὰρ τοιοῦτον εἶναι τὸ *B* ᾧ ἐγχωρεῖ τὸ *A* μηδενὶ ὑπάρχειν.

some would-be true apodeictic premisses. As many logicians believe that such propositions are really true, it is impossible to convince them of the validity of those syllogisms by examples.

Concluding this discussion we may say that Aristotle is right in asserting (ε), but wrong in rejecting (ζ). Theophrastus and Eudemus are wrong in both ways.

§ 58. *Moods with possible premisses*

The Aristotelian theory of problematic syllogisms displays a very strange gap: moods with possible premisses are entirely neglected in favour of moods with contingent premisses. According to Sir David Ross, 'Aristotle always takes ἐνδέχεται in a *premiss* as meaning "is neither impossible nor necessary"; where the only valid *conclusion* is one in which ἐνδέχεται means "is not impossible", he is as a rule careful to point this out'.[1] Aristotle, indeed, seems to be careful to distinguish the two meanings of ἐνδέχεσθαι when he says, expounding for instance the moods with two problematic premisses of the first figure, that ἐνδέχεσθαι in these moods should be understood according to the definition he has given, i.e. as 'contingent', and not in the sense of 'possible'. He adds, however, that this is sometimes overlooked.[2] Who may have overlooked this? Aristotle himself, of course, or some of his pupils just because of the ambiguity of the term ἐνδέχεσθαι. In the *De Interpretatione* ἐνδεχόμενον means the same as δυνατόν,[3] while in the *Prior Analytics* it has two meanings. It is always dangerous to use the same word in two meanings which may be unconsciously confused; as also to use two different words with the same meaning. Aristotle sometimes says ἐγχωρεῖ instead of ἐνδέχεται, and also uses the latter in two meanings.[4] We cannot be always sure what he means by ἐνδέχεται. The ambiguity of this term probably contributed to the controversies between himself and his friends Theophrastus and Eudemus. It is therefore a pity that he did not treat moods with possible premisses separately before introducing contingency. We shall supply this deficiency which has hitherto escaped the notice of scholars.

---

[1] W. D. Ross, loc. cit., p. 44; see also the table of the valid moods, facing p. 286.

[2] *An. pr.* i. 14, 33ᵇ21 δεῖ δὲ τὸ ἐνδέχεσθαι λαμβάνειν μὴ ἐν τοῖς ἀναγκαίοις, ἀλλὰ κατὰ τὸν εἰρημένον διορισμόν. ἐνίοτε δὲ λανθάνει τὸ τοιοῦτον.   [3] See n. 1, p. 134.

[4] Cf. for instance *An. pr.* i. 3, 25ᵇ10 (n. 1, p. 192) and i. 9, 30ª27 (n. 1, p. 190) with i. 13, 32ᵇ30 (n. 1, p. 193).

Let us first consider the laws of conversion. Aristotle begins the exposition of these laws in Book I, chapter 3 of the *Prior Analytics* with the statement that the term ἐνδέχεσθαι has several meanings. He then says, without explaining the various meanings of this term, that the laws of conversion of affirmative propositions are the same for all kinds of ἐνδέχεσθαι, but those of negative propositions differ. He states explicitly that the problematic propositions 'Every *b* may be an *a*' and 'Some *b* may be an *a*' (I use the word 'may' to cover both kinds of the problematic proposition) are convertible into the proposition 'Some *a* may be a *b*' which gives for possibility the formulae:

121. *CMAbaMIab*   and   122. *CMIbaMIab*.

The law of conversion for universally-negative propositions is explained only by examples from which we may infer the formula:

123. *CMEbaMEab*.

It is tacitly assumed that particularly-negative possible propositions are not convertible.[1] We see from this that the laws of conversion of possible propositions are somewhat negligently treated by Aristotle. He apparently does not attach any great importance to the concept of possibility.

Formulae 121–3 are correct and are easily deducible from the analogous laws of conversion for assertoric propositions by means of the theorem:

19. *CCpqCMpMq*.

The same theorem, i.e. the stronger *M*-law of extensionality, enables us to establish the whole theory of syllogisms with possible premisses. By means of the classical calculus of propositions we get from 19 the formulae:

124. *CCpCqrCMpCMqMr*   and   125. *CCpCqrCpCMqMr*.

Formula 124 yields moods with two possible premisses and a possible conclusion: we merely have to add the mark of possibility to the premisses and to the conclusion of valid assertoric

---

[1] *An. pr.* i. 3, 25ᵃ37–ᵇ14 ἐπειδὴ πολλαχῶς λέγεται τὸ ἐνδέχεσθαι, . . . ἐν μὲν τοῖς καταφατικοῖς ὁμοίως ἕξει κατὰ τὴν ἀντιστροφὴν ἐν ἅπασιν. εἰ γὰρ τὸ A παντὶ ἢ τινὶ τῷ B ἐνδέχεται, καὶ τὸ B τινὶ τῷ A ἐνδέχοιτο ἄν. . . . (ᵇ3) ἐν δὲ τοῖς ἀποφατικοῖς οὐχ ὡσαύτως, ἀλλ' ὅσα μὲν ἐνδέχεσθαι λέγεται ἢ τῷ ἐξ ἀνάγκης ὑπάρχειν ἢ τῷ μὴ ἐξ ἀνάγκης μὴ ὑπάρχειν, ὁμοίως, οἷον . . . (ᵇ9) εἰ . . . ἐνδέχεται μηδενὶ ἀνθρώπῳ ἵππον, καὶ ἄνθρωπον ἐγχωρεῖ μηδενὶ ἵππῳ, . . . (ᵇ13) ὁμοίως δὲ καὶ ἐπὶ τῆς ἐν μέρει ἀποφατικῆς.

moods. So, for instance, we get according to 124 from the assertoric mood Barbara by the substitution p/Aba, q/Acb, r/Aca the
syllogism:

126. *CMAbaCMAcbMAca*.

Formula 125 yields moods with one assertoric and one possible
premiss, it does not matter which, e.g.

127. *CAbaCMAcbMAca*   128. *CMAbaCAcbMAca*.

The system is extremely rich. Any premiss may be strengthened
by replacing the assertoric or problematic proposition by the
corresponding apodeictic proposition. Besides, there are moods
with one problematic and one apodeictic premiss which yield
apodeictic conclusions according to the formula:

129. *CCpCqrCMpCLqLr*.

Thus we have, for instance, the mood:

130. *CMAbaCLAcbLAca*

which is contrary to the *peiorem* rule accepted by Theophrastus
and Eudemus.

I think that Aristotle would have accepted—not, of course,
the last syllogistic mood—but the moods with possible premisses,
in particular 126 and 128. There is, indeed, in the *Prior Analytics*
an interesting introductory remark to the theory of problematic
syllogisms which, in my opinion, may be applied to possibility as
well as to contingency. Aristotle says that the expression 'Of anything, of which b is predicated, a may be predicated' has two
meanings the best translation of which seems to be this: 'For all c,
if every c is a b, then every c may be an a', and 'For all c, if every c
may be a b, then every c may be an a'. Then he adds that the
expression 'Of anything, of which b is predicated, a may be
predicated' means the same as 'Every b may be an a'.[1] We have
thus two equivalences: 'Every b may be an a' means either 'For
all c, if every c is a b, then every c may be an a', or 'For all c, if
every c may be a b, then every c may be an a'. If we interpret
'may' in the sense of possibility, we get the formulae:

---

[1] *An. pr.* i. 13, 32ᵇ27 τὸ γάρ, 'καθ' οὗ τὸ B, τὸ A ἐνδέχεσθαι' τούτων σημαίνει
θάτερον, ἢ 'καθ' οὗ λέγεται τὸ B' ἢ 'καθ' οὗ ἐνδέχεται λέγεσθαι'. τὸ δέ, 'καθ' οὗ τὸ B, τὸ
A ἐνδέχεσθαι' ἢ 'παντὶ τῷ B τὸ A ἐγχωρεῖν' οὐδὲν διαφέρει.

131. *QMAbaΠcCAcbMAca* and 132. *QMAbaΠcCMAcbMAca*

which are true in our system of modal logic, and from which the moods 128 and 126 are easily deducible. If, however, 'may' is interpreted in the sense of contingency which seems to be the intention of Aristotle, then the formulae given above become false.

§ 59. *Laws of conversion of contingent propositions*

Continuing his exposition of the laws of conversion of modal propositions Aristotle says at the beginning of the *Prior Analytics* that universally-negative contingent propositions are not convertible, whereas particularly-negative ones are.[1]

This curious statement demands careful examination. I shall first discuss it critically not from the point of view of my modal system, but from that of the basic modal logic accepted by Aristotle and all logicians.

According to Aristotle, contingency is that which is neither necessary nor impossible. This meaning of the contingent is clearly implicit in the somewhat clumsy definition of Aristotle, and is expressly corroborated by Alexander.[2] Let us repeat in order to ensure complete clearness: '*p* is contingent—means the same as—*p* is not necessary and *p* is not impossible', or in symbols:

48. *QTpKNLpNLNp*.

This formula is obviously equivalent to the expression:

50. *QTpKMpMNp*,

i.e. the contingent is both capable of being and capable of not being.

Formulae 48 and 50 are quite general and applicable to any proposition *p*. Let us apply them to the universally-negative proposition *Eba*. We get from 50:

133. *QTEbaKMEbaMNEba*.

As *NEba* is equivalent to *Iba*, we also have:

---

[1] *An. pr.* i. 3, 25ᵇ14 (continuation of the text quoted in n. 1, p. 192) ὅσα δὲ τῷ ὡς ἐπὶ τὸ πολὺ καὶ τῷ πεφυκέναι λέγεται ἐνδέχεσθαι, . . . οὐχ ὁμοίως ἕξει ἐν ταῖς στερητικαῖς ἀντιστροφαῖς, ἀλλ᾽ ἡ μὲν καθόλου στερητικὴ πρότασις οὐκ ἀντιστρέφει, ἡ δὲ ἐν μέρει ἀντιστρέφει.

[2] See above, § 45, in particular nn. 3, p. 154 and 1, p. 155.

134. *QTEbaKMEbaMIba.*

Now we can derive from the laws of conversion:

123. *CMEbaMEab*   and   122. *CMIbaMIab*

that *MEba* is equivalent to *MEab*, and *MIba* to *MIab*; hence we have:

135. *QKMEbaMIbaKMEabMIab.*

The first part of this formula *KMEbaMIba* is equivalent to *TEba*, the second *KMEabMIab* to *TEab*; so we get the result:

136. *QTEbaTEab.*

This means that contingent universally-negative propositions are convertible.

How was it possible for Aristotle not to see this simple proof, when he had all its premisses at his disposal? Here we touch on another infected portion of his modal logic, even more difficult to cure than the wound which his ideas about necessity inflicted on it. Let us see how he tries to disprove formula 136.

Aristotle states quite generally that contingent propositions with opposite arguments are convertible with one another in respect of their arguments. The following examples will explain this not very clear formulation. 'It is contingent that *b* should be an *a*' is convertible with 'It is contingent that *b* should not be an *a*'; 'It is contingent that every *b* should be an *a*' is convertible with 'It is contingent that not every *b* should be an *a*'; and 'It is contingent that some *b* should be an *a*' is convertible with 'It is contingent that some *b* should not be an *a*'.[1] This kind of conversion I shall call, following Sir David Ross, 'complementary conversion'.[2]

Aristotle would assert accordingly that the proposition 'It is contingent that every *b* should be an *a*' is convertible with the proposition 'It is contingent that no *b* should be an *a*', in symbols:

(ι) *QTAbaTEba*   (asserted by Aristotle).

This is the starting-point of his proof, which is performed by

[1] *An. pr.* i. 13, 32ᵃ29 συμβαίνει δὲ πάσας τὰς κατὰ τὸ ἐνδέχεσθαι προτάσεις ἀντιστρέφειν ἀλλήλαις. λέγω δὲ οὐ τὰς καταφατικὰς ταῖς ἀποφατικαῖς, ἀλλ᾽ ὅσαι καταφατικὸν ἔχουσι τὸ σχῆμα κατὰ τὴν ἀντίθεσιν, οἷον τὸ ἐνδέχεσθαι ὑπάρχειν τῷ ἐνδέχεσθαι μὴ ὑπάρχειν, καὶ τὸ παντὶ ἐνδέχεσθαι τῷ ἐνδέχεσθαι μηδενὶ καὶ μὴ παντί, καὶ τὸ τινὶ τῷ μὴ τινί.
[2] W. D. Ross, loc. cit., p. 44.

reductio ad absurdum. He argues in substance thus: If *TEba* were convertible with *TEab*, then *TAba* would be convertible with *TEab*, and as *TEab* is convertible with *TAab*, we should get the false consequence:

(κ) *QTAbaTAab*   (rejected by Aristotle).[1]

What should we say to this argument? It is quite obvious that the definition of contingency adopted by Aristotle entails the convertibility of contingent universally-negative propositions. Consequently the disproof of this convertibility must be wrong. Since it is formally correct, the error must lie in the premisses, and as there are two premisses on which the disproof is based, the asserted formula (ι), and the rejected (κ), then either it is wrong to assert (ι) or it is wrong to reject (κ). This, however, cannot be decided within basic modal logic.

Within those limits we can merely say that the truth of the asserted formula (ι) is not justified by the accepted definition of contingency. From the definition:

50. *QTpKMpMNp*

we get by the substitution *p/Np* the formula *QTNpKMNpMNNp*, and as *MNNp* is equivalent to *Mp* according to thesis 9 of basic modal logic, we have:

137. *QTNpKMpMNp.*

From 50 and 137 there results the consequence:

138. *QTpTNp,*

and applying this consequence to the premiss *Eba* we get:

139. *QTEbaTNEba*   or   140. *QTEbaTIba,*

as *NEba* means the same as *Iba.* We see that *QTEbaTIba* is justified by the definition of contingency, but that *QTEbaTAba* is not. This last formula has been accepted by Aristotle by a mistake. We shall understand this error better if we examine Aristotle's

---

[1] *An. pr.* i. 17, 36ᵇ35 πρῶτον οὖν δεικτέον ὅτι οὐκ ἀντιστρέφει τὸ ἐν τῷ ἐνδέχεσθαι στερητικόν, οἷον εἰ τὸ Α ἐνδέχεται μηδενὶ τῷ Β, οὐκ ἀνάγκη καὶ τὸ Β ἐνδέχεσθαι μηδενὶ τῷ Α. κείσθω γὰρ τοῦτο, καὶ ἐνδεχέσθω τὸ Β μηδενὶ τῷ Α ὑπάρχειν. οὐκοῦν ἐπεὶ ἀντιστρέφουσιν αἱ ἐν τῷ ἐνδέχεσθαι καταφάσεις ταῖς ἀποφάσεσι, καὶ αἱ ἐναντίαι καὶ αἱ ἀντικείμεναι, τὸ δὲ Β τῷ Α ἐνδέχεται μηδενὶ ὑπάρχειν, φανερὸν ὅτι καὶ παντὶ ἂν ἐνδέχοιτο τῷ Α ὑπάρχειν. τοῦτο δὲ ψεῦδος· οὐ γὰρ εἰ τόδε τῷδε παντὶ ἐνδέχεται, καὶ τόδε τῷδε ἀναγκαῖον· ὥστ' οὐκ ἀντιστρέφει τὸ στερητικόν.

refutation of an attempt to prove the law of conversion for *TEba* by *reductio ad absurdum*. This attempt reads: if we suppose that it is contingent that no *b* should be an *a*, then it is contingent that no *a* should be a *b*. For if the latter proposition were false, then it would be necessary that some *a* should be a *b*, and hence it would be necessary that some *b* should be an *a* which is contrary to our supposition.[1] In symbols: If *TEba* is supposed to be true, then *TEab* also must be true. For from *NTEab* would result *LIab*, and consequently *LIba*, which is incompatible with the supposition *TEba*.

Refuting this argument Aristotle rightly points out that *LIab* does not follow from *NTEab*.[2] We have, indeed, according to 48 the equivalence:

141. *QTEabKNLEabNLNEab*   or
142. *QTEabKNLEabNLIab*.

Thus for *NTEab*, applying *QNKNpNqHpq*, i.e. one of the so-called 'De Morgan's laws',[3] we have the formula:

143. *QNTEabHLEabLIab*.

It can be seen that by means of 143 and the thesis *CCHpqrCqr* we can derive *NTEab* from *LIab*, but the converse implication does not hold, since from *NTEab* we can derive only the alternation *HLEabLIab* from which, of course, *LIab* does not follow. The attempted proof is wrong, but it does not follow that the conclusion which was to be proved is false.

One point in this reduction deserves our attention: it is apparent that instead of 143 Aristotle accepts the formula:

(λ) *QNTEabHLOabLIab*

which is not justified by definition 48. Similarly for the case of *NTAab* he adopts the formula:[4]

---

[1] *An. pr.* i. 17, 37ᵃ9 ἀλλὰ μὴν οὐδ' ἐκ τοῦ ἀδυνάτου δειχθήσεται ἀντιστρέφον, οἷον εἴ τις ἀξιώσειεν, ἐπεὶ ψεῦδος τὸ ἐνδέχεσθαι τὸ Β τῷ Α μηδενὶ ὑπάρχειν, ἀληθὲς τὸ μὴ ἐνδέχεσθαι μηδενί (φάσις γὰρ καὶ ἀπόφασις), εἰ δὲ τοῦτ', ἀληθὲς ἐξ ἀνάγκης τινὶ τῷ Α ὑπάρχειν· ὥστε καὶ τὸ Α τινὶ τῷ Β· τοῦτο δ' ἀδύνατον.

[2] Ibid. 37ᵃ14 (continuation of the foregoing note) οὐ γὰρ εἰ μὴ ἐνδέχεται μηδενὶ τὸ Β τῷ Α, ἀνάγκη τινὶ ὑπάρχειν. τὸ γὰρ μὴ ἐνδέχεσθαι μηδενὶ διχῶς λέγεται, τὸ μὲν εἰ ἐξ ἀνάγκης τινὶ ὑπάρχει, τὸ δ' εἰ ἐξ ἀνάγκης τινὶ μὴ ὑπάρχει.

[3] These should properly be called Ockham's Laws, for so far as we know, Ockham was the first to state them. See Ph. Boehner, 'Bemerkungen zur Geschichte der De Morganschen Gesetze in der Scholastik', *Archiv für Philosophie* (September 1951), p. 115, n.

[4] *An. pr.* i. 17, 37ᵃ24 τῷ ἐνδέχεσθαι παντὶ ὑπάρχειν τό τ' ἐξ ἀνάγκης τινὶ ὑπάρχειν ἀντίκειται καὶ τὸ ἐξ ἀνάγκης τινὶ μὴ ὑπάρχειν.

(μ) *QNTAabHLOabLIab*

which, again, is not justified by 48, whereas the correct formula runs:

144. *QNTAabHLOabLAab.*

From (λ) and (μ) Aristotle may have deduced the equivalence *QNTAabNTEab*, and then (ι), which is not justified by his definition of contingency.

§ 60. *Rectification of Aristotle's mistakes*

Aristotle's theory of contingent syllogisms is full of grave mistakes. He does not draw the right consequences from his definition of contingency, and denies the convertibility of universally-negative contingent propositions, though it is obviously admissible. Nevertheless his authority is still so strong that very able logicians have in the past failed to see these mistakes. It is obvious that if somebody, Albrecht Becker for example, accepts the definition

48. *QTpKNLpNLNp*

with *p* as propositional variable, then he must also accept the formula:

141. *QTEabKNLEabNLNEab*

which is derived from 48 by the substitution *p/Eab*. And since by valid logical transformations formula 141 yields the thesis

143. *QNTEabHLEabLIab,*

he must also accept 143. Yet Becker rejects this thesis in favour of 'structural formulae'—a product of his imagination.[1]

The remarks of the foregoing section were written from the standpoint of basic modal logic which is an incomplete system. Let us now discuss our problem from the point of view of four-valued modal logic.

From the Aristotelian definition of contingency we obtained the consequence 138, *QTpTNp*, from which we may deduce the implication:

---

[1] See A. Becker, loc. cit., p. 14, where formula T11 = 48 written in another symbolism, but with the propositional variable *p*, is accepted, and p. 27 where formula 143 is rejected.

145. *CTpTNp*.

Now we get from the premisses:

  51. *CδpCδNpδq*   (axiom of the *C–N–δ–p*-system)
  146. *CCpCqrCCpqCpr*   (principle of Frege)

the consequences:

        51. δ/*T'*×147
  147. *CTpCTNpTq*
        146. *p/Tp, q/TNp, r/Tq*×*C*147–*C*145–148
  148. *CTpTq*,

and as the converse implication *CTqTp* is also true, as may be proved by the substitutions *p/q* and *q/p* in 148, we have the equivalence:

  149. *QTpTq*.

From 149 we get by substitution first the law of conversion 136 *QTEbaTEab*, then formula (*ι*) *QTAbaTEba* which Aristotle asserts, and formula (*κ*) *QTAbaTAab* which he rejects. We can now determine where the flaw in Aristotle's disproof of the law of conversion is: Aristotle is wrong in rejecting (*κ*).

Formula *QTpTq* shows that the truth-value of the function *Tp* is independent of the argument *p*, which means that *Tp* is a constant. We know, in fact, from § 52 that *KMpMNp* which is the *definiens* of *Tp* has the constant value *3*, and therefore *Tp* also has the constant value *3* and is never true. For this reason *Tp* is not suitable to denote a contingent proposition in Aristotle's sense, since he believes that some contingent propositions are true. *Tp* must be replaced by *Xp* or *Yp*, i.e. by the function '*p* is *X*-contingent' or its twin '*p* is *Y*-contingent'. I shall take into consideration merely *X*-contingency, as what is true of *X*-contingency will also be true of *Y*-contingency.

First, I should like to state that the convertibility of universally-negative contingent propositions is independent of any definition of contingency. As *Eba* is equivalent to *Eab*, we must accept the formula

  150. *CδEbaδEab*

according to the principle of extensionality *CQpqCδpδq*, which results from our axiom 51. From 150 we get a true statement for any value of δ, hence also for δ/*X'*:

151. *CXEbaXEab.*

Alexander reports that Theophrastus and Eudemus, unlike Aristotle, accepted the convertibility of universally-negative contingent propositions,[1] but says in another passage that in proving this law they used *reductio ad absurdum*.[2] This seems doubtful, for the only correct thing Aristotle had done in this matter was to refute the proof of convertibility by *reductio*, a refutation which cannot have been unknown to his pupils. *Reductio* can be used to prove, from *CLIbaLIab*, the convertibility of universally-negative propositions when they are possible (that is, to prove *CMEbaMEab*), but not when they are contingent. Another proof is given by Alexander, continuing the former passage, but he scarcely formulates it clearly enough. We know that Theophrastus and Eudemus interpreted universally-negative premisses, *Eba* as well as *Eab*, as denoting a symmetric relation of disconnexion between *b* and *a*,[3] and they may have argued accordingly that if it is contingent for *b* to be disconnected from *a*, it is also contingent for *a* to be disconnected from *b*.[4] This proof would conform with the principle of extensionality. At any rate, Theophrastus and Eudemus have corrected the gravest mistake in Aristotle's theory of contingency.

Secondly, it follows from the definition of *X*-contingency:

82. *CδKMpWNpδXp*

that the so-called 'complementary conversion' cannot be admitted. *QTpTNp* is true, but *QXpXNp* must be rejected, because its negation, i.e.:

152. *NQXpXNp*

is asserted in our system as can be verified by the matrix method. It is therefore not right in our system to convert the proposition

---

[1] Alexander 220. 9 Θεόφραστος μέντοι καὶ Εὔδημος . . . ἀντιστρέφειν φασὶ καὶ τὴν καθόλου ἀποφατικὴν (scil. ἐνδεχομένην) αὐτῇ, ὥσπερ ἀντέστρεφε καὶ ἡ ὑπάρχουσα καθόλου ἀποφατικὴ καὶ ἡ ἀναγκαία.

[2] Ibid. 223. 3 δόξει τισὶ διά γε τῆς εἰς ἀδύνατον ἀπαγωγῆς δύνασθαι δείκνυσθαι ἡ καθόλου ἀποφατικὴ ἐνδεχομένη ἀντιστρέφουσα. τῇ αὐτῇ δείξει καὶ οἱ ἑταῖροι αὐτοῦ κέχρηνται.

[3] See ibid. 31. 4–10.

[4] Ibid. 220. 12 ὅτι δὲ ἀντιστρέφει, δεικνύουσιν οὕτως· εἰ τὸ *Α* τῷ *Β* ἐνδέχεται μηδενί, καὶ τὸ *Β* τῷ *Α* ἐνδέχεται μηδενί. ἐπεὶ γὰρ ἐνδέχεται τὸ *Α* τῷ *Β* μηδενί, ὅτε ἐνδέχεται μηδενί, τότε ἐνδέχεται ἀπεζεῦχθαι τὸ *Α* πάντων τῶν τοῦ *Β*· εἰ δὲ τοῦτ', ἔσται τότε καὶ τὸ *Β* τοῦ *Α* ἀπεζευγμένον· εἰ δὲ τοῦτο, καὶ τὸ *Β* τῷ *Α* ἐνδέχεται μηδενί.

'It is contingent that every *b* should be an *a*' into the proposition
'It is contingent that some *b* should not be an *a*', or into the
proposition 'It is contingent that no *b* should be an *a*', conver-
sions which Aristotle accepts without any justification.[1] I think
that Aristotle was led to a wrong conception of 'complementary
conversion' by the ambiguity of the term 'contingent' (ἐνδεχόμενον). He uses this term in the *De Interpretatione* as a synonym of
the term 'possible' (δυνατόν),[2] and continues to use it thus in the
Prior Analytics, although the phrase 'It is contingent that *p*' has
there got another meaning, viz. 'It is possible that *p* and it is
possible that not *p*'. If we replace in the last phrase the term
'possible' by the term 'contingent', as Aristotle apparently does,
we get the nonsense that 'It is contingent that *p*' means the same
as 'It is contingent that *p* and it is contingent that not *p*'. So far
as I know, this nonsense has hitherto not been observed by anybody.

Thirdly, it follows from definition 82 that *Xp* is stronger than
Mp, because we have the thesis:

153. *CXpMp*,

but not conversely. This thesis is important, because it enables us
to retain, with a little correction, a large number of syllogisms
with contingent premisses, in spite of the serious mistakes made by
Aristotle.

§ 61. *Moods with contingent premisses*

There is no need to enter into a detailed description of the
syllogistic moods with contingent premisses, as Aristotle's definition of contingency is wrong and his syllogistic should be rebuilt
according to the correct definition. This, however, does not seem
to be worth while, for it is very doubtful whether a syllogistic with
contingent premisses will ever find a useful application. I think
that the following general remarks will be sufficient.

First, it may be shown that all the Aristotelian moods with a
contingent conclusion are wrong. Let us take as an example the
mood Barbara with contingent premisses and conclusion, i.e.
the mood

*154. *CXAbaCXAcbXAca*.

---

[1] See n. 1, p. 195.   [2] See n. 1, p. 134.

This mood though accepted by Aristotle[1] must be rejected. Take *Aba* and *Acb* as false, and *Aca* as true. These conditions fulfil the assertoric mood Barbara, but from 154, applying the matrices M9 and M15, we get the following equations: $CXoCXoX_1 = C_3C_{32} = C_{32} = 2$. Similarly mood

*155. *CXAbaCAcbXAca*

also accepted by Aristotle[2] must be rejected, since, for *Aba* = 0, and *Acb* = *Aca* = *1*, we have: $CXoC_1X_1 = C_3C_{12} = C_{32} = 2$. It was just these two moods that I was referring to when I said at the end of § 58 that formulae 131 and 132, which Aristotle asserts, became false, if we interpreted ἐνδέχεσθαι as 'contingent'. It may be said too that formulae 154 and 155 become true, if for *X* is put *T*, but *T*-contingency is a useless concept.

Secondly, all the moods got by complementary conversion should be rejected. I shall show by an example how Aristotle deals with this sort of mood. He applies to 154 the formula

*156. *QXAbaXEba*

which should be rejected (take *Aba* = *1*, and *Eba* = 0), and gets the following moods:

*157. *CXAbaCXEcbXAca*
*158. *CXEbaCXEcbXAca*

which must be rejected too.[3] To show this, it suffices to choose the terms *a*, *b*, and *c* of 157 in such a way that *Aba* = *Ecb* = 0, and *Aca* = *1*, and those of 158 in such a way that *Eba* = *Ecb* = 0, and *Aca* = *1*. We then have in both cases: $CXoCXoX_1 = C_3C_{32} = C_{32} = 2$.

It seems that Aristotle does not put much trust in these moods,

---

[1] *An. pr.* i. 14, 32ᵇ38 ὅταν οὖν τὸ Α παντὶ τῷ Β ἐνδέχηται καὶ τὸ Β παντὶ τῷ Γ, συλλογισμὸς ἔσται τέλειος ὅτι τὸ Α παντὶ τῷ Γ ἐνδέχεται ὑπάρχειν. τοῦτο δὲ φανερὸν ἐκ τοῦ ὁρισμοῦ· τὸ γὰρ ἐνδέχεσθαι παντὶ ὑπάρχειν οὕτως ἐλέγομεν.

[2] Ibid. 15, 33ᵇ25 ἐὰν δ' ἡ μὲν ὑπάρχειν ἡ δ' ἐνδέχεσθαι λαμβάνηται τῶν προτάσεων, ὅταν μὲν ἡ πρὸς τὸ μεῖζον ἄκρον ἐνδέχεσθαι σημαίνῃ, τέλειοί τ' ἔσονται πάντες οἱ συλλογισμοὶ καὶ τοῦ ἐνδέχεσθαι κατὰ τὸν εἰρημένον διορισμόν.

[3] Ibid. 14, 33ᵃ5 ὅταν δὲ τὸ Α παντὶ τῷ Β ἐνδέχηται, τὸ δὲ Β ἐνδέχηται μηδενὶ τῷ Γ, διὰ μὲν τῶν εἰλημμένων προτάσεων οὐδεὶς γίνεται συλλογισμός, ἀντιστραφείσης δὲ τῆς ΒΓ κατὰ τὸ ἐνδέχεσθαι γίνεται ὁ αὐτὸς ὅσπερ πρότερον. —33ᵃ12 ὁμοίως δὲ καὶ εἰ πρὸς ἀμφοτέρας τὰς προτάσεις ἡ ἀπόφασις τεθείη μετὰ τοῦ ἐνδέχεσθαι. λέγω δ' οἷον εἰ τὸ Α ἐνδέχεται μηδενὶ τῷ Β καὶ τὸ Β μηδενὶ τῷ Γ· διὰ μὲν γὰρ τῶν εἰλημμένων προτάσεων οὐδεὶς γίνεται συλλογισμός, ἀντιστρεφομένων δὲ πάλιν ὁ αὐτὸς ἔσται ὅσπερ καὶ πρότερον.

because he does not call them syllogisms at all. He merely says that they can be reduced to syllogisms by means of complementary conversion. But moods reduced by the ordinary conversion are called by him syllogisms; why does he make a difference between ordinary and complementary conversion, if both kinds of conversion are equally valid?

Light upon this question is thrown by Alexander who, commenting on this passage, refers to a very important remark of his master on two ontological meanings of contingency: 'In one sense "contingent" means "usual (ἐπὶ τὸ πολύ) but not necessary" or "natural", e.g. it is contingent that men should go grey; in another sense it is used of the indefinite, which is capable of being thus and of not being thus, or in general of that which is by chance. In either sense contingent propositions are convertible with respect to their contradictory arguments, but not for the same reason: "natural" propositions because they do not express something necessary, "indefinite" propositions because there is not, in their case, a greater tendency to be more thus than not thus. About the indefinite there is no science or syllogistic demonstration, because the middle term is only accidentally connected with the extremes; only about the "natural" are there such things, and most arguments and inquiries are concerned with what is contingent in this sense.'[1]

Alexander discusses this passage: his idea seems to be that, if we take any scientifically useful syllogism the premisses of which are contingent in the sense of 'usual' (ἐπὶ τὸ πολύ) or even 'most usual' (ἐπὶ τὸ πλεῖστον), then we get premisses and a conclusion which are indeed contingent but are very seldom (ἐπ' ἔλαττον) realized: such a syllogism is useless (ἄχρηστος). Perhaps this is why Aristotle refuses to call what is so obtained a syllogism.[2]

---

[1] An. pr. i. 13, 32ᵇ4–21 τὸ ἐνδέχεσθαι κατὰ δύο λέγεται τρόπους, ἕνα μὲν τὸ ὡς ἐπὶ τὸ πολὺ γίνεσθαι καὶ διαλείπειν τὸ ἀναγκαῖον, οἷον τὸ πολιοῦσθαι ἄνθρωπον . . ., ἢ ὅλως τὸ πεφυκὸς ὑπάρχειν . . ., ἄλλον δὲ τὸ ἀόριστον, ὃ καὶ οὕτως καὶ μὴ οὕτως δυνατόν, . . . ἢ ὅλως τὸ ἀπὸ τύχης γινόμενον. —(ᵇ13) ἀντιστρέφει μὲν οὖν καὶ κατὰ τὰς ἀντικειμένας προτάσεις ἑκάτερον τῶν ἐνδεχομένων, οὐ μὴν τὸν αὐτόν γε τρόπον, ἀλλὰ τὸ μὲν πεφυκὸς εἶναι τῷ μὴ ἐξ ἀνάγκης ὑπάρχειν . . ., τὸ δ' ἀόριστον τῷ μηδὲν μᾶλλον οὕτως ἢ ἐκείνως. ἐπιστήμη δὲ καὶ συλλογισμὸς ἀποδεικτικὸς τῶν μὲν ἀορίστων οὐκ ἔστι διὰ τὸ ἄτακτον εἶναι τὸ μέσον, τῶν δὲ πεφυκότων ἔστι, καὶ σχεδὸν οἱ λόγοι καὶ αἱ σκέψεις γίνονται περὶ τῶν οὕτως ἐνδεχομένων.

[2] Alexander 169. 1 τῷ γὰρ ὡς ἐπὶ τὸ πλεῖστον ἀποφατικῷ ἐνδεχομένῳ τὸ ἐπ' ἔλαττον καταφατικὸν ἀντιστρέφει. —5 τούτου δὲ κειμένου συλλογισμὸς μὲν ἔσται, οὐ μὴν χρήσιμόν τι ἔχων, ὡς αὐτὸς προεῖπε. διὸ καὶ ἐροῦμεν ταύτας τὰς συζυγίας . . .

This point, more than any other, reveals a capital error in Aristotle's syllogistic, viz. his disregard of singular propositions. It is possible that an individual, Z, should be going grey while growing older, indeed this is probable, though not necessary, since it is the natural tendency to do so. It is also possible, though rather improbable, that Z should not be going grey. What Alexander says about the different degrees of possibility is true when applied to singular propositions but becomes false when applied to universal or particular propositions. If there is no general law that every old man should go grey, because this is merely 'usual' and some old men do not go grey, then, of course, the latter proposition is true and therefore possible, but the former is simply false, and from our point of view a false proposition is neither possibly nor contingently true.

Thirdly, from a valid mood with possible premisses we can get other valid moods by replacing a possible premiss by the corresponding contingent one. This rule is based on formula 153 which states that Xp is stronger than Mp, and it is obvious that any implication will remain true, if one or more of its antecedents is replaced by a stronger antecedent. So we get, for instance, from

126. $CMAbaCMAcbMAca$ the mood   159. $CXAbaCXAcbMAca$

and from

128. $CMAbaCAcbMAca$ the mood   160. $CXAbaCAcbMAca$.

Comparing the rejected moods 154 and 155 with the asserted moods 159 and 160, we see that they differ only by the substitution of M for X in the conclusion. If we examine the table of Aristotelian syllogistic moods with problematic premisses, given by Sir David Ross,[1] we shall find it a useful rule that by this small correction, M in the conclusion, instead of X, all those moods become valid. Only the moods obtained by complementary conversion cannot be corrected, and must be definitively rejected.

ἀχρήστους τε καὶ ἀσυλλογίστους εἶναι. —10 ἴσως δὲ καὶ αὐτὸς τοῦτο ὑφορώμενος εἶπε τὸ 'ἢ οὐ γίνεται συλλογισμός'. Cf. W. D. Ross's paraphrase of this passage, loc. cit., p. 326.

[1] W. D. Ross, loc. cit., facing p. 286; in the conclusion the index c should everywhere be replaced by p.

§ 62. *Philosophical implications of modal logic*

It may seem that the Aristotelian modal syllogistic, even when corrected, has no useful application to scientific or philosophic problems. But in reality, Aristotle's propositional modal logic is historically and systematically of the greatest importance for philosophy. All elements required for a complete system of modal logic are to be found in his works: basic modal logic and the theorems of extensionality. But Aristotle was not able to combine those elements in the right way. He did not know the logic of propositions which was created after him by the Stoics; he tacitly accepted the logical principle of bivalence, i.e. the principle that every proposition is either true or false, whereas modal logic cannot be a two-valued system. Discussing the contingency of a future sea-fight he comes very near to the conception of a many-valued logic, but he lays no stress on this great idea, and for many centuries his suggestion remained fruitless. Owing to Aristotle I was able to discover this idea in 1920 and to construct the first many-valued system of logic in opposition to the logic, hitherto known, which I called 'two-valued logic' thus introducing a term now commonly accepted by logicians.[1]

Under the influence of Plato's theory of ideas Aristotle developed a logic of universal terms and set forth views on necessity which were, in my opinion, disastrous for philosophy. Propositions which ascribe essential properties to objects are according to him not only factually, but also necessarily true. This erroneous distinction was the beginning of a long evolution which led to the division of sciences into two groups: the *a priori* sciences consisting of apodeictic theorems, such as logic and mathematics, and the *a posteriori* or empirical sciences consisting chiefly of assertoric statements based on experience. This distinction is, in my opinion, false. There are no true apodeictic propositions, and from the standpoint of logic there is no difference between a mathematical and an empirical truth. Modal logic can be described as an extension of the customary logic by the introduction of a 'stronger'

---

[1] See J. Łukasiewicz, 'Logika dwuwartościowa' (Two-valued Logic), *Przegląd Filozoficzny*, 23, Warszawa (1921). A passage of this paper concerning the principle of bivalence was translated into French by W. Sierpiński, 'Algèbre des ensembles', *Monografie Matematyczne*, 23, p. 2, Warszawa-Wrocław (1951). An appendix of my German paper quoted in n. 1, p. 166, is devoted to the history of this principle in antiquity.

and a 'weaker' affirmation; the apodeictic affirmation Lp is stronger, and the problematic Mp weaker than the assertoric affirmation p. If we use the non-committal expressions 'stronger' and 'weaker' instead of 'necessary' and 'contingent', we get rid of some dangerous associations connected with modal terms. Necessity implies compulsion, contingency implies chance. We assert the necessary, for we feel compelled to do so. But if $L\alpha$ is merely a stronger affirmation than α, and α is true, why should we assert $L\alpha$? Truth is strong enough, there is no need to have a 'supertruth' stronger than truth.

The Aristotelian *a priori* is analytic, based on definitions, and definitions may occur in any science. Aristotle's example 'Man is necessarily an animal', based on the definition of 'man' as a 'two-footed animal', belongs to an empirical science. Every science, of course, must have at its disposal an exactly constructed language and for this purpose well-formed definitions are indispensable, as they explain the meaning of words, but they cannot replace experience. The analytic statement 'I am an animal' made by a man—analytic because 'animal' belongs to the essence of man—conveys no useful information, and can be seen to be silly by comparison with the empirical statement 'I was born the 21st December 1878'. If we want to know what the 'essence' of man is—if there is such a thing as 'essence' at all—we cannot rely on the meanings of words but must investigate human individuals themselves, their anatomy, histology, physiology, psychology, and so on, and this is an endless task. It is not a paradox to say even today that man is an unknown being.

The same is true for the deductive sciences. No deductive system can be based on definitions as its ultimate fundamentals. Every definition supposes some primitive terms, by which other terms may be defined, but the meaning of primitive terms must be explained by examples, axioms or rules, based on experience. The true *a priori* is always synthetic. It does not arise, however, from some mysterious faculty of the mind, but from very simple experiments which can be repeated at any time. If I know by inspection that a certain ballot box contains only white balls, I can say *a priori* that only a white ball will be drawn from it. And if the box contains white and black balls, and two drawings are made, I can foretell *a priori* that only four combinations can possibly occur: white-white, white-black, black-white, and black-

black. On such experiments the axioms of logic and mathematics are based; there is no fundamental difference between *a priori* and *a posteriori* sciences.

While Aristotle's treatment of necessity is in my opinion a failure, his concept of ambivalent possibility or contingency is an important and fruitful idea. I think that it may be successfully applied to refute determinism.

By determinism I understand a theory which states that if an event E happens at the moment t, then it is true at any moment earlier than t that E happens at the moment t. The strongest argument in defence of this theory is based on the law of causality which states that every event has a cause in some earlier event. If so, it seems to be evident that all future events have causes which exist today, and existed from eternity, and therefore all are predetermined.

The law of causality, however, understood in its full generality should be regarded as merely a hypothesis. It is true, of course, that astronomers, relying on some laws known to govern the universe, are able to predict for years in advance the positions and motions of heavenly bodies with considerable accuracy. Just at the moment I finished writing the previous sentence a bee flew humming past my ear. Am I to believe that this event too has been predetermined from all eternity and by some unknown laws governing the universe? To accept this would look more like indulging in whimsical speculation than relying on scientifically verifiable assertions.

But even if we accept the law of causality as generally true, the argument given above is not conclusive. We may assume that every event has a cause, and nothing happens by chance, yet the chain of causes producing a future event, though infinite, does not reach the present moment. This can be explained by a mathematical analogy. Let us denote the present moment by o, the moment of the future event by 1, and the moments of its causes by fractions greater than $\frac{1}{2}$. As there exists no smallest fraction greater than $\frac{1}{2}$, every event has a cause in an earlier event, but the whole chain of these causes and effects has a limit at the moment $\frac{1}{2}$, later than o.

We may therefore assume that the Aristotelian sea-fight of tomorrow, though it will have a cause which itself will have cause and so on, does not have a cause today. Similarly we may assume that nothing exists today which would prevent there being a sea-fight tomorrow. If truth consists in the conformity of thought to reality, we may say that those propositions are true today which conform with today's reality or with future reality in so far as that is predetermined by causes existing today. As the sea-fight of tomorrow is not real today, and its future existence or non-existence has no real cause today, the proposition 'There will be a sea-fight tomorrow' is today neither true nor false. We can only say: 'There may be a sea-fight tomorrow' and 'There may not be a sea-fight tomorrow'. Tomorrow's sea-fight is a contingent event, and if there are such events, determinism is refuted.

INDEX

A, constant functor, means 'all—is' or 'belongs to all', pp. 14, 77.

Aaa, axiom, p. 88; syllogistic law of identity independent of other theses, p. 45; compared with the propositional law of identity, p. 48; used by Aristotle in a demonstration but not stated explicitly, p. 149, n. 1.

Aab, means 'all *a* is *b*' or '*b* belongs to all *a*', p. 77.

ab esse ad posse valet consequentia, known to Aristotle but not formulated explicitly, pp. 135–6, n. 1.

ab oportere ad esse valet consequentia, known to Aristotle but not formulated explicitly, p. 135.

ad falsum sequitur quodlibet, p. 179.

ἀδύνατον, impossible, p. 134.

Aenesidemus, pp. 58, 59, n. 1.

affirmation, 'stronger' and 'weaker', pp. 205–6.

Alexander, on definition of the premiss, p. 4, n. 4; on indefinite premisses, p. 5, n. 2; on variables, p. 8, n. 2; validity of moods not dependent on the shape of variables, p. 9, n. 2; his proof of conversion of the *E*-premiss, p. 10, n. 1; on non-methodically conclusive arguments of the Stoics, p. 15 n.; on formulations of the syllogisms with 'to belong' and 'to be', p. 17, n. 3; on the formalism of the Stoics, p. 19 n.; knows the law of identity *Aaa*, p. 20, n. 1; quotes syllogisms as rules of inference, p. 21 n.; on Theophrastus' addition of five moods to the first figure, p. 27, n. 2; his definition of the first figure different from the Aristotelian, p. 27, n. 4; does there exist in the second figure a major and a minor term φύσει?, p. 31, nn. 1–2; his polemic against Herminus' definition of the major term, p. 31, n. 3; his own definition of the major term, p. 32, n. 1; θέσις of terms in the three figures, p. 33, nn. 3–5; calls perfect syllogisms ἀναπόδεικτοι, p. 43, n. 2; on equivalence of *Oab* and *NAab*, p. 46, n. 2; explains proof by ecthesis of the conversion of the *I*-premiss, p. 60, n. 2; ascribes perceptual character to proofs by ecthesis, p. 60, n. 3; his criticism of the proof of Darapti by ecthesis, p. 63, nn. 2–3; on the proof of Bocardo by ecthesis, p. 66 n.; ascribes the 'synthetic theorem' to Aristotle, p. 65 n.; misunderstands rejection, p. 68, n. 1; his polemic against Herminus on rejection, p. 70, n. 1; on the difference of the categorical and hypothetical premisses, p. 132 n.; states a general rule that existence implies possibility but not conversely, p. 136, n. 2; says that necessity implies existence but not conversely, p. 136, n. 4; assimilates Aristotelian definition of contingency to that of possibility, p. 141 n.; his definition of possibility discussed on the ground of the *L*-basic modal logic, p. 141; on syllogistic necessity, p. 144, n. 7; acquainted with the logic of the Stoic–Megaric school, p. 147; his interpretation of the necessary implication, p. 147 n.; quotes Theophrastus on the meaning of necessity, p. 151, n. 2; on the Aristotelian distinction between simple and conditional necessity, pp. 151, 152, n. 1; his definition of contingency, p. 155, n. 1, 194; on the controversy concerning moods with mixed premisses, pp. 184 n., 185, nn. 2–4, 187, n. 2; his lost writings, p. 185, n. 4; on Theophrastus' doctrine concerning the convertibility of universally-negative contingent propositions, p. 200, nn. 1–4; on Aristotle's doctrine concerning two ontological meanings of contingency, p. 203, n. 2.

ἄμεσος πρότασις, *see* immediate premiss.

Ammonius, on relation of logic to philosophy, p. 13 n.; scholium preserved with his fragments, p. 39.

p. 132 n.; functorial propositions have no subjects or predicates, p. 132; apodeictic, p. 134; problematic, p. 134; assertoric, p. 134; analytic, definition and examples of, p. 149.
propositional function, pp. 94–95.

Q, sign of equivalence, p. 108; means 'if and only if', is employed instead of the usual '*E*', p. 135, n. 5.
quantified expressions, explained, p. 84.
quantifiers, universal denoted by *Π*, existential or particular denoted by *Σ*, p. 84; rules of existential quantifiers, p. 62; rules of universal quantifiers, p. 86; universal quantifiers correspond to the syllogistic necessity, pp. 11, 87; existential quantifiers may explain proofs by ecthesis, pp. 61–66; universal quantifiers may be omitted at the head of an asserted formula, p. 145.
Quine, W. V., on consequences of the apodeictic principle of identity, p. 150 n., his example of the difficulty resulting from the application of modal logic to the theory of identity, p. 171; solution of the difficulty, pp. 171–2.

RE, rule allowing to replace *NI* by *E* and conversely, p. 88.
reductio ad absurdum, see *reductio ad impossibile*.
reductio ad impossibile, characterized by Aristotle, p. 55 n.; proofs by, pp. 54–59; unsatisfactory for Baroco and Bocardo, pp. 54–55, 182.
reduction of axioms to a minimum, has a predecessor in Aristotle, p. 45.
reduction of syllogistical moods to the first figure, means proof, p. 44; Keynes's opinion criticized, p. 44.
reduction to elementary expressions, in the theory of deduction, pp. 111–15; in the syllogistic, pp. 118–20.
rejected expressions, denoted by an asterisk, pp. 96, 136.
rejection, used by Aristotle by exemplification through concrete terms, p. 67, n. 2; a rule of rejection stated by him, p. 70, n. 2; its meaning explained, p. 96; its rules, pp. 71–72, 96; how these rules work, pp. 96–97; reasons for its introduction into the theory of deduction, p. 109.
RO, rule allowing to replace *NA* by *O* and conversely, p. 88.
Ross, Sir David, pp. vii, viii, 8, n. 1, 24 n., 46, n. 1, 47, n. 2, 154, nn. 1–2, 185, n. 5, 191, n. 1, 195, n. 2, 203, n. 2, 204 n.
RS, Słupecki's rule of rejection, p. 104.
rule, '*α*, therefore it is necessary that *α*', accepted by some modern logicians, p. 153.
rule for the verification of δ-expressions, p. 163.
rule of detachment—*modus ponens* of the Stoics, pp. 16, 19, 81.
rule of Słupecki, formulated, pp. 75, 103; explained, p. 104; employed, pp. 105–6.
rule of substitution for variable functors, explained, pp. 161–2.
rules of inference, different from propositions, p. 21; for asserted expressions: by substitution, pp. 80, 88; by detachment, pp. 81, 88; for rejected expressions: by substitution, pp. 72, 96; by detachment, pp. 71, 96.
Russell, B., p. 1, n. 1; wrongly criticizes Aristotle, p. 1, n. 3; see also *Principia Mathematica*.

Scholz, H., p. ix; on Galen's authorship of the fourth figure, p. 39.
Schröder, E., p. 166.
sea-fight, pp. 152, 155, 175, 178, 207–8.
Sextus Empiricus, quotes a Peripatetic syllogism, p. 1, n. 2; gives the Stoic proof of the compound law of transposition, p. 59, n. 1; quotes Philo's definition of implication, p. 83 n.
Sierpiński, W., p. 205.

OTHER TITLES IN THIS HARDBACK REPRINT PROGRAMME FROM SANDPIPER BOOKS LTD (LONDON) AND POWELLS BOOKS (CHICAGO)

ISBN 0–19–	Author	Title
8143567	ALFÖLDI A.	The Conversion of Constantine and Pagan Rome
6286409	ANDERSON George K.	The Literature of the Anglo-Saxons
8228813	BARTLETT & MacKAY	Medieval Frontier Societies
8111010	BETHURUM Dorothy	Homilies of Wulfstan
8114222	BROOKS Kenneth R.	Andreas and the Fates of the Apostles
8203543	BULL Marcus	Knightly Piety & Lay Response to the First Crusade
8216785	BUTLER Alfred J.	Arab Conquest of Egypt
8148348	CAMPBELL J.B.	The Emperor and the Roman Army 31 BC to 235 AD
826643X	CHADWICK Henry	Priscillian of Avila
826447X	CHADWICK Henry	Boethius
8219393	COWDREY H.E.J.	The Age of Abbot Desiderius
8148992	DAVIES M.	Sophocles: Trachiniae
825301X	DOWNER L.	Leges Henrici Primi
8154372	FAULKNER R.O.	The Ancient Egyptian Pyramid Texts
8221541	FLANAGAN Marie Therese	Irish Society, Anglo-Norman Settlers, Angevin Kingship
8143109	FRAENKEL Edward	Horace
8201540	GOLDBERG P.J.P.	Women, Work and Life Cycle in a Medieval Economy
8140215	GOTTSCHALK H.B.	Heraclides of Pontus
8266162	HANSON R.P.C.	Saint Patrick
8224354	HARRISS G.L.	King, Parliament and Public Finance in Medieval England to 1369
8581114	HEATH Sir Thomas	Aristarchus of Samos
8140444	HOLLIS A.S.	Callimachus: Hecale
8212968	HOLLISTER C. Warren	Anglo-Saxon Military Institutions
8223129	HURNARD Naomi	The King's Pardon for Homicide – before AD 1307
8140401	HUTCHINSON G.O.	Hellenistic Poetry
8142560	JONES A.H.M.	The Greek City
8218354	JONES Michael	Ducal Brittany 1364–1399
8271484	KNOX & PELCZYNSKI	Hegel's Political Writings
8225253	LE PATOUREL John	The Norman Empire
8212720	LENNARD Reginald	Rural England 1086–1135
8212321	LEVISON W.	England and the Continent in the 8th century
8148224	LIEBESCHUETZ J.H.W.G.	Continuity and Change in Roman Religion
8141378	LOBEL Edgar & PAGE Sir Denys	Poetarum Lesbiorum Fragmenta
8241445	LUKASIEWICZ, Jan	Aristotle's Syllogistic
8152442	MAAS P. & TRYPANIS C.A .	Sancti Romani Melodi Cantica
8148178	MATTHEWS John	Western Aristocracies and Imperial Court AD 364–425
8223447	McFARLANE K.B.	Lancastrian Kings and Lollard Knights
8226578	McFARLANE K.B.	The Nobility of Later Medieval England
8148100	MEIGGS Russell	Roman Ostia
8148402	MEIGGS Russell	Trees and Timber in the Ancient Mediterranean World
8142641	MILLER J. Innes	The Spice Trade of the Roman Empire
8147813	MOORHEAD John	Theoderic in Italy
8264259	MOORMAN John	A History of the Franciscan Order
8116020	OWEN A.L.	The Famous Druids
8131445	PALMER, L.R.	The Interpretation of Mycenaean Greek Texts
8143427	PFEIFFER R.	History of Classical Scholarship (vol 1)
8111649	PHEIFER J.D.	Old English Glosses in the Epinal-Erfurt Glossary
8142277	PICKARD–CAMBRIDGE A.W.	Dithyramb Tragedy and Comedy
8269765	PLATER & WHITE	Grammar of the Vulgate
8213891	PLUMMER Charles	Lives of Irish Saints (2 vols)
820695X	POWICKE Michael	Military Obligation in Medieval England
8269684	POWICKE Sir Maurice	Stephen Langton
821460X	POWICKE Sir Maurice	The Christian Life in the Middle Ages
8225369	PRAWER Joshua	Crusader Institutions
8225571	PRAWER Joshua	The History of The Jews in the Latin Kingdom of Jerusalem
8143249	RABY F.J.E.	A History of Christian Latin Poetry
8143257	RABY F.J.E.	A History of Secular Latin Poetry in the Middle Ages (2 vols)
8214316	RASHDALL & POWICKE	The Universities of Europe in the Middle Ages (3 vols)
8148380	RICKMAN Geoffrey	The Corn Supply of Ancient Rome
8141076	ROSS Sir David	Aristotle: Metaphysics (2 vols)
8141092	ROSS Sir David	Aristotle: Physics
8264178	RUNCIMAN Sir Steven	The Eastern Schism
814833X	SALMON J.B.	Wealthy Corinth
8171587	SALZMAN L.F.	Building in England Down to 1540
8218362	SAYERS Jane E.	Papal Judges Delegate in the Province of Canterbury 1198–1254
8221657	SCHEIN Sylvia	Fideles Crucis

8148135	SHERWIN WHITE A.N.	The Roman Citizenship
8113927	SISAM, Kenneth	Studies in the History of Old English Literature
8642040	SOUTER Alexander	A Glossary of Later Latin to 600 AD
8222254	SOUTHERN R.W.	Eadmer: Life of St. Anselm
8251408	SQUIBB G.	The High Court of Chivalry
8212011	STEVENSON & WHITELOCK	Asser's Life of King Alfred
8212011	SWEET Henry	A Second Anglo-Saxon Reader—Archaic and Dialectical
8148259	SYME Sir Ronald	History in Ovid
8143273	SYME Sir Ronald	Tacitus (2 vols)
8200951	THOMPSON Sally	Women Religious
8201745	WALKER Simon	The Lancastrian Affinity 1361–1399
8161115	WELLESZ Egon	A History of Byzantine Music and Hymnography
8140185	WEST M.L.	Greek Metre
8141696	WEST M.L.	Hesiod: Theogony
8148542	WEST M.L.	The Orphic Poems
8140053	WEST M.L.	Hesiod: Works & Days
8152663	WEST M.L.	Iambi et Elegi Graeci
822799X	WHITBY M. & M.	The History of Theophylact Simocatta
8206186	WILLIAMSON, E.W.	Letters of Osbert of Clare
8114877	WOOLF Rosemary	The English Religious Lyric in the Middle Ages
8119224	WRIGHT Joseph	Grammar of the Gothic Language